WALKING HOME GROUND

WALKING
HOME
GROUND

*In the Footsteps
of Muir, Leopold,
and Derleth*

Robert Root

WISCONSIN HISTORICAL SOCIETY PRESS

Published by the Wisconsin Historical Society Press
Publishers since 1855

The Wisconsin Historical Society helps people connect to the past by
collecting, preserving, and sharing stories. Founded in 1846,
the Society is one of the nation's finest historical institutions.
Order books by phone toll free: (888) 999-1669
Order books online: shop.wisconsinhistory.org
Join the Wisconsin Historical Society: wisconsinhistory.org/membership

wisconsinhistory.org

Cover photograph © Jamie Heiden
All interior photographs courtesy of Robert Root

Printed in the United States of America
Designed by Sara DeHaan

21 20 19 18 17   1 2 3 4

Library of Congress Cataloging-in-Publication Data
applied for.

∞ The paper used in this publication meets the minimum requirements of
the American National Standard for Information Sciences—Permanence
of Paper for Printed Library Materials, ANSI Z39.48-1992.

For Sue,
the center of my home ground

And for Becky, Paul, Tom, Caroline,
Tim, Zola, Ezra, Louie, Lilly, and Eliza,
the principal points of my compass

The discipline of a writer is to learn to be still and listen to what his subject has to tell him. —RACHEL CARSON

We tend to think of landscapes as affecting us most strongly when we are in them or on them, when they offer us the primary sensations of touch and sight. But there are also the landscapes we bear with us in absentia, those places that live in memory long after they have withdrawn in actuality, and such places—retreated to most often when we are remote from them—are among the most important landscapes we possess. —ROBERT MACFARLANE

Contents

Acknowledgments

IF I LOOK BACK at almost any of the books I've written, I find they usually begin in my reading, in the inspiration that other writers provide and the curiosity they prompt, which leads me to explore not only their writing but also the world in which I live. Wisconsin has been very fruitful for me in that regard, and I'm not done reading all the past and present authors who will bring me closer to my home ground. I'm also grateful to the members of the Waukesha/ Milwaukee Chapter of the Ice Age Trail Alliance (IATA), the people with whom I share stewardship for the Ice Age Trail (IAT) in Waukesha County and from whom I've learned so much about where I live. I've been lucky to have Marlin Johnson as a teacher and friend. My contacts with the Aldo Leopold Foundation, the August Derleth Society, the Waukesha Preservation Alliance, and the Waukesha 1834 Club have enhanced my knowledge of the subjects they are so passionate about, and I appreciate their efforts at education and preservation. I value highly the editorial diligence, encouragement, and conscientious attention Carrie Kilman gave this book.

For more than thirty years my wife, Sue, has walked with me on most of the trails I've walked, and she's walked most of the trails in this book as well. I'm grateful for her presence on and off the trail and hope we have many more miles to walk together in the years to come.

Prologue

THE MIDDLE OF MARCH—NOT yet officially spring, but closing in on it. A few weeks of warmer weather has melted the snow that four months of winter mounded across the view from my study window. The river behind us has been open for weeks, and the rising waters from the snowmelt have defrosted its banks and submerged the shoreline exposed below the ragged, bending mop of autumn grass. The current runs more quickly, more purposefully.

A paved bike path leads from our street back around our complex, edges close to the river, and circles through and around a park of woods and fields. In winter, the parks department keeps it plowed. I barely turn the corner of my building before my view is filled with the open wetlands of the river's floodplain. The long sedges the snow has matted down for a third of a year are clumped and flattened, a shag carpet of dry beige and pale brown interrupted only by the blue glint of the river meandering through it.

People seldom venture onto the wetlands, mostly avid fishermen with more optimism than skill. The bikers and hikers and joggers and dog walkers in the neighborhood stick to the bike path and quickly find their sight of the river disrupted by the trees lining the wetlands and by the rise that separates the bike path from the lowlands farther on. To the east of the path a substantial forest flourishes, and where the river wanders away from it, the forest spreads toward the riverbank. A wooden overlook deck stands at the point where river and path nudge one another, a place where several times a year the path is made impassable by high water. The overlook is a pleasant spot, right at the bend in the river, open across the floodplain in one direction and shadowed by forest in the other.

The forest is well canopied in verdant seasons, the path more dappled than illuminated, but in winter, when the ground is white with snow and the bare trees are stark shapes of brown and gray competing for attention with their shadows on the snow, the forest is a monochromatic still life shapeshifting with every step the walker takes. The faster you go the more you feel like a figure in the center of a zoetrope.

Snow will linger longest here, on the north-facing slopes and in the deep kettles between high ridges. The path circles the forest, affording views from every angle, and in a mere couple of miles the land rises and falls and rises again. Off the paved path a network of trails cuts through the forest, fit for winter snowshoeing and summer hiking. The trees are mostly red oak, bur oak, shagbark hickory, and other species that do well in hilly glacial soil; red pine and white oak grow here too, more sparsely. The trees are tall and the forest floor is mostly open.

It's not a very big forest and it's not a very long stretch of river. I can see houses in the distance across the wetlands and often glimpse the neighborhood in which I live on the borders of the park. It takes an hour to walk the circuit, and if we stay on the pavement, we cross broad open spaces, always aware of what surrounds the park. But when we take the forest trails, I'm calmed by the sense of enclosure and isolation curling around me. I take comfort in the constancy of the river, in the persistence of the forest, and find some momentary sense of renewal here, but it's taken me a while to realize that these woods and wetlands have been urging me to reconnect to the land.

❧

I came to Wisconsin a few years ago almost without anticipation. I am after all, I told myself, a Great Lakes boy. My youth was spent in an escarpment town in western New York, overlooking the lake plain of Lake Ontario. For nearly three decades I lived in the center of Michigan, a state bounded by Lakes Superior, Michigan, Huron, and Erie. My wife, Sue, grew up on the Lake Michigan coastline, and we returned often to her parents' house above nearby dunes and beach. I felt the Great Lakes states so deeply in my bones that Wisconsin inspired no need for expectations.

After leaving Michigan, we lived for four years in Colorado, close to the Front Range where the atmosphere, the altitude, the terrain were so alien it took all my energy and intellect to understand where I was. By going often to the mountains I eventually began to feel a connection to the land, a growing sense of belonging there. It was a lesson in how to adapt to new ground.

When we decided to leave Colorado, for reasons of employment and to live near one of our three children scattered on three coasts, we had no sense of venturing forth but rather of settling in. The turmoil of finding what would likely be our final dwelling, of moving in and determining the course of our days, preoccupied me. We settled in Wisconsin twenty miles inland from Lake Michigan, about the same distance I'd lived from Lake Ontario growing up. I felt like a Great Lakes boy back on home turf; I thought I didn't need to develop a sense of place here because I was back in the place I'd been most of my life.

I was wrong.

～

The seasons have cycled through several times since we came here, and we have repeated our circuit along the river and through the park in every one of them. We've hiked or snowshoed most of the woodland trails. I look for the trees I've become familiar with: the stand of red pines at the northern entrance to the park, the straight bare trunks lifting a crown so high as to almost go unnoticed; the gnarly, sprawling white oak sometimes shielded by low bushes just outside the entrance; the solitary white cedar standing almost demurely just within; the shagbark hickory near the observation deck. I look for the small marsh at the bottom of the kettle near the northern border of the woods. I glance at the red pine we heard something scuffling up as we passed in the dusk one evening. I gaze out across the wetlands to a bend in the river where we saw sandhill cranes standing on dry riverbed in a summer when the water was low. I peer above me whenever I hear Canada geese flying to or from the river, sometimes a few at a time, sometimes in squadrons. We hear the geese in every season, as they fly above our neighborhood on their way to and from nearby farmlands.

The bottomlands along the river and the ridges and hollows of the forest have made me alert to similar terrain wherever we drive in Wisconsin. In the middle of an unfamiliar subdivision, a dip in the road will open up into a long patch of wetlands; a sharp rise will make the steep slope of a moraine apparent; oaks will loom above the shoulders. These brief echoes of my local terrain remind me that, for all my walking in the park, I haven't left the path enough, reached the river across the wetlands, descended slopes into kettles where no trails lead, climbed pathless slopes where the summit is obscured by trees. I haven't paid enough attention; I haven't applied what I've learned about adapting and connecting to the land.

It's time to immerse myself more deeply where I am.

Whether I really knew this time would come, I've been circumspectly preparing for it by reading Wisconsin writers who have centered on place. A few, like Frederika Bremer and Reuben Gold Thwaites, date back to the nineteenth century; others, like Michael Perry and Laurie Lawlor, are alive and kicking and still writing at the beginning of the twenty-first. But as I more and more feel the urge to walk my new home ground more conscientiously, I realize that three writers in particular attract me as literary walking companions: John Muir, Aldo Leopold, and August Derleth. Two of them transplanted themselves into the terrain they wrote about, and only one was native to his; but for all three, the connection to home ground was vital, integral to who they were, essential. I've been walking their home grounds with them through their writing. Now I want to walk their landscapes on my own to see what remains of what they witnessed. I think I might learn where we are in Wisconsin by learning where we were.

I've also been walking the Ice Age Trail through the county where my wife and I transplanted ourselves; I've been walking along my own stretch of river and through my own patch of woods. "When humans make themselves at home in a new landscape," Robert Moor writes in *On Trails,* like deer they learn the lay of the land, its resources and routes, and "over time that field acquires an additional layer of significance . . . not just resources, but stories, spirits, sacred nodes. . . . Over time, more thoughts accrete, like footprints, and new layers of significance form." With the examples of Muir, Leopold, and Derleth to inspire me, I'll hope to discover layers of significance forming on my own home ground. By this roundabout journey across time and place, I might be able to end up certain of where I am now.

PART ONE

Interlude

THURSDAY, JANUARY 8, 2009. Wind chill seems to be a constant factor of every day. The temperature means very little when the wind can make it feel twenty degrees colder than you expect when you step outside, and even on a sunny day the sunshine brings no warmth. By the time we attempt a short walk on the Fox River Pathway, the wind has picked up, the air is bright with snow flurries, and the sky is the dirty white of winter. We don't get far before Sue's cell phone rings and she returns to the condo to take a business call; I keep on a little farther. The path has been plowed and in places a thin sheet of ice coats the pavement. I watch my footing, while I try to observe my surroundings.

The path immediately behind our condo gives an open view of the floodplain. In winter, with the foliage gone and the sedges pressed down from the snow, the wetlands have a vast uneven surface, like a thick, lumpy white bed quilt; we gain only a hint of the river's meandering course midway across, remembering its presence rather than seeing it. In the distance, where the terrain rises again, is a jumbled cluster of houses and the campus of West High School. On nights in autumn, the lights of the football field glare across the horizon.

By the time I reach the edge of our complex, low trees along the sides of the path obscure the view and tall trees begin to tower before me. A single bird, likely a chickadee, makes a quick looping flight across the path from one set of trees to another. The path weaves through the western edge of the woods, and the forest rises thickly up a slope to the east. I push on toward a point where meandering river and meandering path meet up near the wooden overlook above a sweeping bend of the river. In the sharp wind I bundle up and hope the destination is not too far.

The Fox River that flows near my home in southeast Wisconsin is not the Fox River of history and literature, the one farther north that flows near John Muir's boyhood home, the one that explorers and voyageurs portaged from to reach the Wisconsin River. My Fox River flows south from around Menomonee Falls, in the northeast corner of Waukesha County, through Waukesha, which treats it like a big deal, down through Racine and Kenosha Counties, and finally across the border with Illinois. It wanders west of Chicago, meets a branch flowing entirely within Illinois, and empties into the Illinois River at Ottawa. From there the Illinois River carries its waters into the Mississippi.

I'm attracted to my Fox River because it's so immediately accessible to me and because the forest that makes up much of the Fox River Park we so often walk in (or did before winter set in), though small, is so dense and isolating. Trails wander through it, short but engaging, and though the paved path is quickly plowed after a snowfall, the trails stay snow covered and are good prospects for snowshoeing.

This morning, as I walk on well-cleared asphalt among leafless trees and snow-covered ground, I become aware that I've entered a study in grayscale. Color has drained from the world: gray sky, gray-brown trees, white ground, gray-black path. My sleeves and gloves and the fringes of my parka hood are faded brown. I blend in with the landscape I'm passing through, and I like the thought. The forest canopy is high and dense enough in the warmer months to discourage much undergrowth. The thick layers of fallen oak leaves keep the ground shades of moldering brown before the snows come, and only thin young shade-resistant saplings rise among the older trees. Against the backdrop of white the upright shafts of brown and gray make an abstract landscape painting of the open forest floor. The curves in the path lead you through and toward continually changing studies in vertical stark shapes.

The overlook and a few yards of riverbank beyond it are the only places where the forest gives way to the floodplain. The planks of the overlook are icy, snow-packed, and uncleared, and I step carefully out to the end, to make a slow, sweeping survey of the river and its banks. Flurries dance and swirl lightly before my eyes, too light to obscure my vision.

With gray sky for a backdrop and the unblemished snow of the banks lining its course, the Fox River here swings east from the center of the wetlands and flows toward the overlook, then bends south to flow away from it. In the distance I see four small shapes on the water, mallards drifting with the current. The river seems to be barely moving, only occasionally disturbed, looking like gleaming smoked glass, shades and tints of black and gray, its surface impenetrable to the eye.

I listen and hear nothing but the insistent wind, and after a few moments' gazing, to lock the landscape in memory, I turn back. Near the edge of the forest I hear the honking of geese and through the trees discern in the distance a wedge of twenty or so hurling themselves across the gray sky. They too are studies in black, white, and gray, but at this moment they are only dark silhouettes against a sky filling with snow.

Nature Streaming into Us:
Walking with John Muir

1

AT EIGHT O'CLOCK THIS May morning, Ennis Lake (or Muir's Lake, as the neighbors once called it, or Fountain Lake, as the Muirs themselves called it in the mid-nineteenth century) is calm and still. Above the eastern shore the sun glares across the tree-tops. Squinting and blinking, I survey that shoreline, first with the naked eye, then with binoculars. I'm alone at the lake, anticipating a solitary walk around it, but I make myself stand quietly for a few minutes longer, inhaling the calmness, listening to birdsong around the shoreline and in the surrounding woodlands. The morning invites me to go slowly, attentively.

The rewards of quiet attention are confirmed at once. The first bird of the morning appears a few yards away, an ovenbird, his white breast black-speckled, his eye fixed on me. Near the water's edge a yellow warbler flits through the undergrowth, and a boreal chickadee lands on a limb above him. A tree swallow crosses my peripheral vision to light and hop into a nest hole at the top of a nearby tree. A white-throated sparrow calls in the distance, "Oh, Peabody, Peabody, Peabody," like reassurance from an old friend. I smile back at the day.

At the trailhead, on the hill above the lake, a mown path leads down a gentle slope toward an open field, past a widespread stand of tall, bare oaks standing apart from one another. I've read the Wisconsin Department of Natural Resources (DNR) write-up of the upland and wetland communities found in this state natural area and have maps in my backpack to help me distinguish among them. In early spring, after a long, unrelenting winter, most of the easily identifiable flora won't have established themselves, but a stand of oaks doesn't challenge my knowledge of botany.

Heavy rains have fallen in the past few weeks, and rivers are flooding all along the Mississippi watershed, which is to say most of the United States. A subcontinental divide separates the Wisconsin River—the swollen tributary of the Mississippi that I drove across earlier today—from the Fox River, which meanders just across the road. This Fox River (Muir's, not mine) is the one that runs through Lake Winnebago to Green Bay and the Great Lakes, the one explorers, voyageurs, and traders traveled up, before portaging across to the Wisconsin River to reach the Mississippi.

A small stream connects Ennis Lake and the Fox River. The lake bottom is marl, not a porous soil, and the lake itself is a kettle lake, formed by glacial ice and surrounded by glacial uplands.

From all that rain and runoff from the uplands, the fens and sedge meadows along the lakeshore should be well saturated.

Past the oak opening the path descends, circles the northern end of the lake, and crosses the edge of a wet-mesic prairie. The grasses here are tall, five feet or more, big bluestem and Indian grass. They are high enough, and my vantage point is low enough, that I can barely see the lake at the bottom of the gentle slope, only the eastern shoreline and the tree-covered uplands above it. I walk through a willow thicket, which is just beginning to bud, higher and denser than the grasses, and when I emerge, two sandhill cranes rise out of the grass and wing away from me. I'm so chagrined at startling them that I barely hear the whoomp of their beating wings as they disappear beyond the woods. Red-winged blackbirds nearby ignore me and continue their shrill song at the lake edge and throughout the meadow.

The path arches through another stand of trees. Across the field I see a stone house, the one that the ecologist and Muir scholar Erik Brynildson restored and lives in, on the site of the house the Muirs built on Fountain Lake Farm. Seeing it, I gain at once a sense of the space between the homestead and the lake.

A ridge rises above the eastern shoreline of the lake, topped with a sprawling stand of oaks. In *The Story of My Boyhood and Youth*, Muir includes a picture of the lake he drew as a boy, sitting on the roof of the bur oak shanty his family first inhabited on the site. I clamber up among the oaks to the top of the ridge, hoping to find the angle at which he sketched the lake. Muir's drawing takes in what he identified as the garden meadow and seems to be a view from a higher angle than possible anywhere nearby—the bur oak shanty was nearer to the site of the house—but this ridge, much closer to the lake, is the best angle I'm likely to have. From here I can see the clear brightness of the sky and the outline of the western shore mirrored in the placid waters of the lake.

Layers of leaves keep the ground open below the oaks,

and the bare trees cast stark shadows in the morning sun. A yellow-rumped warbler darts among the trees, and a downy woodpecker works along a high branch farther into the woods. When I stop scuffling through the leaves, his pecking is the only sound breaking the silence. Only when I turn back to the lake do I realize that a woman and her dog are standing near a bench down on the trail, the dog clearly aware that I'm up on the ridge. He watches me while I descend as amiably as I can.

The woman is fit, mature, and comfortably dressed for an early May outing. We chat for a few minutes. I learn that she is a retired biologist with ties to the DNR. She lives nearby and walks this trail often, usually collecting whatever trash she spots along the way. This is a good time to stroll the park, she tells me—it's too early in the season for picnickers and too early for mosquitoes and deerflies. She mentions I was lucky the man in the stone house didn't see me on the ridge; he's been known to yell at people who get off the trail, herself included. A vibrant goldfinch in the fen shrubs between the trail and the lake captures our attention. It reminds her of her recent, rare sighting of a redheaded woodpecker. She also tells me that she spotted the first blossom of spring, a pasque flower, by the side of the path just beyond the trailhead. As a man supposedly intent on close observation of the terrain, I'm embarrassed to have missed it.

After we part, I take my time jotting down a few notes, giving her time before I follow so we both can get back into our solitudes. The trail moves away from the lake and through a stand of trees, and I let myself be delayed a little more by first an eastern towhee in a slender tree and shortly after, as I cross a boardwalk, a rose-breasted grosbeak in the shrubbery. I haven't come for the birding, but after spotting these two I feel a little better about overlooking the pasque flower.

A short bridge crosses a meandering stream in the middle of a sedge meadow thick with hummock sedge and more shrubs at the outskirts. The water runs shallow, the streambed clearly visible. When I look upstream I again notice the stone house in the distance and understand more certainly where Muir was when he drew his picture of the lake and the garden meadow. I appreciate how the scholar in the house gets to see the lake from Muir's perspective every day.

The forest is thicker on this side of the lake. Several trees seem very old. A stand of evergreens dominates the highest ground, and more grow intermittently on distant hills around the south shore. On the lake side of the trail the sedge meadow opens up again across a wide stretch of exposed space. In the middle of the lake two fishermen drift quietly in their boat. Just a little way up the hill, near a very old, very gnarly bur oak at the southeast corner of the trail, I spot a gate leading to an old field and remind myself that the Fountain Lake Farm was more extensive than the area the county park and the state natural area now enclose. Around the bottom of the lake the trail enters oak woodland along and upon the hills that go up the west side, follows the shoreline of the lake a short distance, then veers away from it. All the while I am under towering oaks with an open, leaf-littered forest floor and yellow-rumped warblers plentiful and preoccupied along the way.

I start up the west side of the lake anticipating the arc that the trail makes around a large fen. For a while shrubbery mostly obscures the spring-fed pool at its center. I hear abundant birdsong in the thickets but see nary a bird. The pool comes into clear view when I reach the fen's north side. By now I'm out of the state natural area and back in the county's Muir Park. After passing through a swath of dandelions spread across a mown lawn, I'm able to stand on the shoreline and see the marl of the lake bottom close up, a hard gray mud visible through clear water.

From the dock I gaze again across the lake, a deeper blue now that the sun is higher. The fishermen have drifted out of sight, the woman and her dog have left the park, and I'm alone again, trying to store deep in my memory the panorama of vibrant blue lake and vibrant blue sky and the mirror image of green hills on the opposite shore dividing them.

One hundred sixty-two years earlier, in spring, young John Muir first took sight of Fountain Lake and the terrain around it and found it glorious. Now I understand—to some degree—his attachment to the place. I feel a touch of envy for the woman walking her dog and the Muir scholar living close by, and their chance to walk around this lake whenever they wish.

Before I leave, I return to the trailhead and move slowly down the trail until I spot them. Three pale lavender cups low to the ground in a wilderness of grasses. The first pasque flowers. They convince me spring is here.

⌒

Back roads take me to Observatory Hill. Three trucks are parked in the old field, up in the grass beyond the gravel parking area. The men standing by them tell me they've been spraying garlic mustard, an invasive plant, along the roadside and in the field; they say that, unless I want my shoes to turn blue, I should watch where I step until I get into the woods.

The trail starts where the woods do, near a brass marker commemorating the Carey family, who donated this natural area to the state; it's also where a tiny bright blue butterfly dances around a large stone. I'll be passing through a forest of red oaks, white oaks, shagbark hickory, and basswood and making a steep, rocky climb three hundred feet up to the summit. At eleven hundred feet, this is the highest point in Marquette County. (In comparison, Muir Park's elevation is around eight hundred feet.) The hill is said to be a monadnock, and I confess the word itself inspires me; entirely on Thoreau's recommendation, I've gone up Mount Monadnock in New Hampshire, a true mountain. Observatory Hill really is a hill by comparison, but each is, by definition, an

erosion-resistant remnant of a loftier mountain range. The core of
Observatory Hill is igneous rock estimated to be 1.75 billion years
old. It bears witness to glaciation with 12,000-year-old grooves
and striations on exposed surfaces.

The higher up I climb away from the farmland below, the more
exposed rock I see. Soon a region of red cedars takes over. Midway
to the summit, a long rock wall appears, topped with cedars anchored in its cracks and crevices. The trail veers around it, growing rockier and rougher as the woods grow thicker and darker
and the undergrowth disappears. For a moment I'm uncertain
how much farther I have to go, but then the cedars open up and
I wander out onto exposed spaces open to the sky.

I've reached the heights that offer a sweeping view of the landscape off to the south, and I realize I don't know what I'm looking
at. The two large, connected lakes below may be Madden Lakes,
a name I remember from a Marquette County map, and the ring
of hills on the far horizon may be the Baraboo Hills, but I'm uncertain of the other landmarks I can see. I scour the southwest
for any sign of Ennis Lake or the stone house overlooking it; but
even on Observatory Hill, I'm not high enough to see past the
woodlands that abound in every direction. Farms and pastures
interrupt them, of course, but leafless trees dominate the view,
making a nearly uniform gray panorama. I wonder how much
of what I'm seeing varies from what John Muir would have seen
when he and his companions would climb to the summit and
lay out watching the stars. Surely the landscape would have been
more open, with wide stretches of prairie and oak savanna. I seem
to have the habit of setting out to visit the past without remembering that only the present lives there now.

The sky is still clear, cloudless, a pale and uniform blue. Occasionally shadows pass across my face and the rock where I sit,
and when I look up, I see two vultures lazily circling overhead.

They seem to be keeping an eye on me. I sit for a while and make notes and wonder, if I stayed until dark, whether the sky would be clear enough for me to stargaze for a while. The night sky would surely still be the one John Muir saw, wouldn't it?

As I head back down the trail, steeling myself for the long drive home, I know that I've spent the morning in places that mattered most to young John Muir, but I'm newly aware that I don't fully understand where I've been.

2

Fen, sedge meadow, wet-mesic prairie, oak opening. The terms keep repeating in my brain like some childhood chant, or like a fragment of an old-time tune for which I've forgotten all the lyrics except for those words. In my circuit around Muir Park, these habitats are what I passed, according to what I've read and maps I've consulted, like the multicolored one on the information board at the trailhead. Fen, sedge meadow, wet-mesic prairie, oak opening. My habitat litany here.

But I'm no more certain of what I'm seeing than young John Muir would have been when he saw the lake for the first time. I've seen such features of the Wisconsin landscape before, but I haven't been diligent enough to be able to name them. The books I turn to offer good prospects for sorting things out. They range from sweeping overviews of the region to detailed catalogs of habitats, from a collection of cursory capsulations of locales to a thorough exploration of a single site. Like a conscientious student I accurately copy all their explanations and write a long quotation-rich passage that covers all their bases. Eventually I recognize that I'm entirely dependent on those quotations, can't talk about these things without using their words verbatim, don't yet own this information. So I tear my pages apart and sort through the pieces and try to find a way to explain it all to myself, as if *I* knew what I was talking about.

My approach is almost like zooming in on a satellite map, starting from a long way above the landscape and incrementally enlarging smaller and smaller patches of terrain. It's the best way to understand the context of what you're examining and to keep yourself from misreading the uniqueness of the site you're focusing on. Wisconsin has a lot in common with Minnesota and with Michigan, as states that weathered the same glacial epochs. Looking at such features as climate and vegetation helps to separate some sections of the landscape from other sections in ways that transcend the artificial limits suggested by state borders.

Biologists identify the northern parts of Wisconsin and Minnesota as the Northern Forest Floristic Province, essentially what we usually think of as the North Woods, and the southern parts as the Prairie-Forest Floristic Province. Between the two is a meandering vegetation tension zone, where the floras of both provinces mingle.

Zoom in more closely and you can see the details that divide these provinces and zones into certain eco-regions—areas determined by their distinctive ecologies—and then subdivide those eco-regions into even more specific areas. Within the Prairie-Forest Floristic Province, a single eco-region encompasses Muir's Fountain Lake Farm, Aldo Leopold's shack, and August Derleth's Sac Prairie, as well as Waukesha County, where I live. However, the Muir and Leopold sites can be found in the same smaller subregion, called the Central Wisconsin Sand Plain, while my home is in another, the Southeastern Wisconsin Till Plain, and Derleth's site is on the border between both subregions. I'll settle for sharing the same eco-region with the three of them and ponder the consequences of having different subregions another time. For now I feel more firmly located on an ecological map of the Midwest.

Returning to Muir Park, I'm aware that its 150 acres contain various wetland and upland communities. Its wetlands include small fens, a tamarack bog, sedge meadow, and wet-mesic prairie; its uplands include oak woodland and oak savanna. This is the point where I need to dig into specifics. I can tell a wetland from an upland, but learning that the fens contain such plants as grass of Parnassus, Kalm's lobelia, and false asphodel, or that the bog contains pitcher plant, bog birch, and poison sumac isn't much help, since I can't distinguish among them and it's too soon in the season for most of these to be flowering. For now I need simply to clarify the distinctions among the wetlands communities. Fen, bog, sedge meadow, wet-mesic prairie.

The standard distinction between bogs and fens seems to rest most definitively on how the pools at their center acquire water. A bog has the same origin as a kettle lake—a block of ice deposited by a glacier that melts and leaves a water-filled depression. For the bog, whatever water remains can only be replenished by precipitation, rain or melted snow; it has no source of inflow or outflow, no spring or stream emptying into it or flowing away from it. Lacking the nutrients for its plant life that wetlands supplied by ground-water and continuous internal flow have, bogs develop acidic soils and foster the growth of sphagnum moss, which contributes the decomposed vegetation that forms peat on the bog bottom. The sphagnum moss creates a bog mat that encourages the growth of acidity- and low-nutrient-tolerant plants like various "ericaceous" shrubs (belonging to the heath family) and evergreens like black spruce and tamarack. Over time, a bog can fill in and close up and become forest floor.

A fen is fed by groundwater, by springs that provide an internal flow of water. It supports plant life that thrives in calcareous (chalky, calcium carbonate laden), alkaline (rather than acidic) waters. These plants, too, decay into peat, but among peatlands, fens can range from near-bogs to near-marshes or near–wet meadows, depending on the level of mineral enrichment the groundwater provides. The shrubs of a fen, like shrubby cinquefoil, will be deciduous rather than evergreen, and its plants will have a high tolerance for calcium. In a calcareous fen, sphagnum moss is absent.

So far so good. Bog: acidic, fed by rain, evergreen and heathy with sphagnum moss, eventually closed up. Fen: alkaline, fed by groundwater, deciduous and calcareous without sphagnum moss, generally longer lived.

With sedge meadows and wet-mesic prairies, I am, figuratively at least, on more solid ground, though there seems to be something of a gradient here as well. Some authors feel the need to distinguish between a sedge meadow and a fen and between a sedge meadow and a marsh. The distinction that a marsh is an aquatic community and the sedge meadow a saturated land community is helpful. A sedge meadow will have emergent plants, dominated by sedge (primarily carex), growing on saturated areas or soils covered by standing water up to six inches deep during the growing season. A wet-mesic prairie—I learn that "mesic" means "intermediate between wet and dry conditions; moderately moist"; "wet-mesic" is more wet than dry—occurs where the water source is variable rather than consistent and where soils may be saturated or inundated during the growing season. In a wet-mesic prairie the dominant plants are prairie grasses, such as big bluestem and prairie cordgrass, and some prairie forbs (broad-leafed flowering plants). The wet-mesic prairie is less saturated than a sedge meadow. In talking about wetlands, the degree of saturation or inundation, as well as water source and plant life, determine the kind of habitat I'm likely to encounter.

Fen, bog, sedge meadow, wet-mesic prairie. It's all well and good to sort these terms out on the page. It's more of a challenge to sort these wetland communities out on the ground. I'll need to walk in John Muir's footsteps one more time, without consulting the maps that may already be firmly locked in memory, to identify what I see. Even more challenging, I'll need to be able to identify them in places other than where I know they already are, especially if they happen to be on my own home ground.

3

John Muir thought Fountain Lake was beautiful. He described it as "one of the many small glacier lakes that adorn the Wisconsin landscapes. It is fed by twenty or thirty meadow springs, is about half a mile long, half as wide, and surrounded by low finely-modeled hills dotted with oak and hickory, and meadows full of grasses and sedges and many beautiful orchids and ferns." He was particularly enthusiastic about the lake itself, with its "zone of green, shining rushes, and just beyond the rushes a zone of white and orange water-lilies fifty or sixty feet wide." He recalled, "On bright days, when the lake was rippled by a breeze, the lilies and sun-spangles danced together in radiant beauty, and it became difficult to discriminate between them."

Muir was born in Dunbar, Scotland, April 21, 1838, and his childhood was spent close to the sea. In *The Story of My Boyhood and Youth*, he claimed that as "a boy in Scotland I was fond of everything that was wild" and "with red-blooded playmates, wild as myself, I loved to wander in the fields to hear the birds sing, and along the seashore to gaze and wonder at the shells and seaweeds, eels and crabs in the pools among the rocks when the tide was low." He and his brothers and his friends often ran off "to hear the birds sing and hunt their nests, glorying in the number we had discovered and called our own." His memory of the song and flight of the skylark is so vivid he devotes two pages to describing it. He also mentions "a few natural-history sketches that . . . left a deep impression," one about the fish hawk (the osprey) and the bald eagle by Alexander Wilson, the Scotch ornithologist who wrote the nine-volume *American Ornithology*, and one about the passenger pigeon by John James Audubon, the artist of *Birds of America*. With both accounts lodged in his memory, he became an indefatigable observer of the natural world at an early age and one inclined to record his observations.

In Scotland, when his father told him one night that "we're gan to America the morn," John Muir was exhilarated by the images that opened up in his imagination: "boundless woods full of mysterious good things; trees full of sugar, growing in ground full of gold; hawks, eagles, pigeons, filling the sky; millions of birds' nests, and no gamekeepers to stop us in all the wild, happy land. We were utterly, blindly glorious." Muir's fascination with the natural world was deep-seated and thorough, and his excitement held throughout a sea voyage of six and a half weeks, followed by weeks more of overland travel from New York to central Wisconsin.

Muir arrived in Wisconsin in 1849, the year after it became a state and at the beginning of decades of settlement and development that essentially changed the nature of the country. His father, Daniel Muir, brought three of his children—John, almost eleven, Sarah, thirteen, and David, nine—to the New World to establish a home to which his wife and the rest of his seven children would later emigrate.

Originally they were bound for Canada, but conversations along the way convinced Daniel Muir that Wisconsin had greater opportunities for profitable farming. In short order, he found property near the Fox River, north of Portage, at a site he described as "fine land for a farm in sunny open woods on the side of a lake." The children waited at the home of Alexander Gray, another Scots immigrant who had befriended Daniel, while their father, with the help of new neighbors, built a bur oak shanty for immediate shelter. Gray's team of oxen hauled them and all their possessions to the site. Muir writes of their arrival: "To this charming hut, in the sunny woods, overlooking a flowery glacier meadow and a lake rimmed with white water-lilies, we were hauled by an ox-team across trackless carex swamps and low rolling hills sparsely dotted with round-headed oaks." Daniel named the lake Fountain Lake, because of the springs that fed it. Fountain Lake Farm would be the center of John Muir's world for the next decade and more.

Much in *The Story of My Boyhood and Youth* chronicles the clash between Daniel Muir's harsh, parsimonious approach to life and his oldest son's energetic and spirited approach—the boys were often thrashed for misbehavior or the hint of misbehavior or the prospect of misbehavior, meals were small, workdays on the farm were long, joy was discouraged—yet the book is not so much a memoir of a tough childhood and adolescence as it is an exuberant celebration of the natural world that opened up to the boy in Wisconsin. Muir writes of his brother David and himself, at the very moment the ox team approaches the shanty, leaping from the wagon to race to a tree where they had spotted a blue jay's nest, climbing the tree, and "[feasting] our eyes on the beautiful green eggs and beautiful birds,—our first memorable discovery." Dropping out of the tree, they "ran along the brow of the hill that the shanty stood on, and down to the meadow, searching the trees and grass tufts and bushes, and soon discovered a bluebird's and a woodpecker's nest, and began an acquaintance with the frogs and snakes and turtles in the creeks and springs."

At this point Muir bursts into an unrestrained paean to the new world opening up to him.

This sudden plash into pure wildness—baptism in Nature's warm heart—how utterly happy it made us! Nature streaming into us, wooingly teaching her wonderful glowing lessons, so unlike the dismal grammar ashes and cinders so long thrashed into us. Here without knowing it we still were at school; every wild lesson a love lesson, not whipped but charmed into us. Oh, that glorious Wisconsin wilderness! Everything new and pure in the very prime of spring when Nature's pulses were beating highest and mysteriously keeping time with our own! Young hearts, young leaves, flowers, animals, the winds and the streams and the sparkling lake, all wildly, gladly rejoicing together.

Muir didn't begin writing his autobiography until roughly sixty years after he arrived at Fountain Lake Farm, and it was published serially in 1912 and 1913 before it appeared in book form. We can't know how much the intervening decades of ecstatic wandering in the wilderness heightened Muir's memory of his enthusiasm for "that glorious Wisconsin wilderness." Nonetheless, it's remarkable how much of the book celebrates in considerable detail the natural world he witnessed as an eleven-year-old immigrant. Reading his account of observing a kingbird drive a "hen-hawk" away from the vicinity of his nest or of watching flocks of nighthawks hunting above the fields, one is reminded that reading Wilson's portrait of the osprey and Audubon's of the passenger pigeon had influenced Muir's bent toward natural history in Scotland. In his chapter on Scotland, Muir tells how he "stood for hours enjoying [the] singing and soaring" of skylarks. That must have helped prepare his appreciation of the courtship rituals he describes in Wisconsin for the common snipe (or "common jack snipe," as he calls it) and the partridge (possibly a ruffed grouse). Muir says, "Everything about us was so novel and wonderful that we could hardly believe our senses except when hungry or while father was thrashing us."

Lessons about the civilized world that he learned in Scottish school and memorization of the Bible that his father insisted on were "taught to the tune of a hickory stick," as the old song goes, "whipped" or "thrashed" into him. Nature's lessons, though, were "charmed" into him, "streaming into us," in large part because he had opened himself up to receiving them.

I try to imagine the natural landscape John Muir first saw when he arrived on the plot of ground his father had chosen to farm. The lake with its water lilies shone at the center of his vision, and beyond it the meadow with its grasses and sedges and, as he later came to discover, its orchids and ferns, and surrounding it the woods of oak and hickory dotting the low hills. It was open, spacious country, punctuated by oak openings but dominated by prairie and savanna, the floodplain of the Fox River not far away. The landscape historian John Warfield Simpson, standing on Observatory Hill and imagining the panorama Muir would have witnessed when he stood there over a hundred years earlier, writes, "Here he looked across a savanna-like expanse of rolling hills and prairies covered with widely-scattered trees. Here he saw broad, open marshes and lowlands stretching for miles to the east and south. To the west and north he saw more hills and prairies than in the other directions, with marshes and lowlands and a few forested spots interspersed. Above all, he saw little sign of human disturbance in any direction."

As the pace of settlement increased, the scene would soon change. The window of time through which John Muir would gaze upon and run merrily through unbroken prairie and un-plowed savanna was really limited to that first summer; in the following year his father worked hard to turn over the soil and replace the natural vegetation with commercial crops.

For a period it was possible to understand what had kept the prairies and savannas treeless, since before settlement, fires still ran freely over the prairies. One English immigrant, John Greening, who settled near Mazomanie some fifty miles to the south of Fountain Lake Farm, wrote in his October 24, 1847, journal entry, "The prairie fires are blazing around us day and night for months together. 'Tis a grand sight to see a whole forest burning and millions of feet of fine timber destroyed in a short time." Four days later he wrote, "Last night we had fires blazing, rushing and crashing in all directions, and very windy indeed all night. This morning all was burned as black as a cinder for 50 miles. The fires run through the country as fast as a horse can trot, and sometimes faster." His neighbor lost two ricks of wheat, and other neighbors lost their fences; Greening himself had no damage to his property but claims he "stayed up half the night to watch the spectacle."

The following day Greening went "across the wide marsh to the banks of the Wisconsin river all day, and to view the effects of the fire. . . . Trees 50 feet long in the trunk, and 100 feet to the top, burnt and falling in all directions, with a crash that makes the earth tremble, and sometimes into the river that makes the water boil again, while the deer and other animals plunge headlong into the water as their only protection." He felt that "it is necessary to be burnt, or else the country would be one mass of forest and does no harm when people are prepared for it" and found the fire advantageous: "The grass on the marsh and the brush in the forest being so thick, it was quite impossible to get across. The marsh grass in some places being more than four feet high, and so thick it was impossible to walk there, but now good traveling." It was the fires of autumn that had maintained the landscape on which John Muir's family had settled.

Muir's memories of his home ground are intermingled with his greater knowledge of the natural world in the years after he

began his rambles. It may be that his affection and enthusiasm
for the natural world of the farm had been heightened by his
appreciation of what was lost to the environment by European
American settlement and lost to him by his need to move out
on his own. He certainly seems, in the central chapters of the
book, to be determined to catalog the flora and fauna he encountered in those early years on Fountain Lake Farm. In the second
chapter, which recounts his family's journey to Wisconsin and
arrival on the farm, he tells of finding with his brother the nests
of brown thrashers, song sparrows, kingbirds, hen-hawks, nighthawks, whip-poor-wills, and woodpeckers. "Everything about
us was so novel and wonderful that we could hardly believe our
senses." He marvels over lightning bugs, partridge drumming,
"the love-song of the common jack snipe," the frogs and the hyla
(tree frogs), and thunderstorms at length. In the third chapter
he talks about domestic animals, snakes, and insects and item-
izes the creatures he observes in the lake: "pickerel, sunfish,
black bass, perch, shiners, pumpkin-seeds, ducks, loons, turtles,
muskrats, etc." He admires the water lily, the pasque flower, and
lady's slippers and enjoys strawberries, dewberries, cranberries,
huckleberries, hickory nuts and syrup, and hazelnuts. He opens
the fourth chapter by declaring, "The Wisconsin oak openings
were a summer paradise for song birds, and a fine place to get
acquainted with them," and then catalogs nuthatches, chickadees,
owls, prairie chickens, quail, bluebirds, robins, brown thrashers,
bobolinks, red-winged blackbirds, meadowlarks, song sparrows,
chickadees, wood ducks, Canada geese, bobwhites, loons, and
passenger pigeons.

Again and again in his narrative Muir brings alive a moment
of wonder and delight in the natural world. He opens his passage
on the brown thrasher with general praise and then offers a vivid
scene featuring it:

Of all the great singers that sweeten Wisconsin one of the
best known and best loved is the brown thrush or thrasher,
strong and able without being familiar, and easily seen and
heard. Rosy purple evenings after thunder-showers are the
favorite song-times, when the winds have died away and the
steaming ground and the leaves and flowers fill the air with
fragrance. Then the male makes haste to the topmost spray of
an oak tree and sings loud and clear with delightful enthusiasm until sundown, mostly I suppose for his mate sitting on
the precious eggs in a brush heap.

He goes on to describe the thrasher's "faithful and watchful and
daring" defense of his nest against snakes and squirrels, as admi-
rable an action in his eyes as the kingbird's assault on hawks. He
returns to their song: "Their rich and varied strains make the air
fairly quiver. We boys often tried to interpret the wild ringing
melody and put it into words."

In that brief passage Muir celebrates the bird while simultaneously teaching us something distinctive about it, capturing the
youthful excitement of discovery his boyhood study of it must
have invoked. In most of the passages on individual birds we find
not only information on the habits and behavior of the birds—the
prairie chickens "strutted about with queer gestures something
like turkey gobblers, uttering strange loud, rounded, drumming
calls,—boom! boom! boom! interrupted by choking sounds";
"the lonely cry of the loon" sounded as "one of the wildest and
most striking of all wilderness sounds, a strange, sad, mournful,
unearthly cry, half laughing, half wailing"—but also anecdotes
about his own memories of them. He tells of wounding a loon
and taking it home where it has a memorable encounter with
the housecat, of his brother Daniel catching a prairie chicken as
she sat on her nest, of Indians hunting ducks and gathering wild
rice in the marshes. In this way he transports himself back into

his youthful witnessing of the natural world and, in the process, transports the reader there as well.

Muir, writing his coming-of-age memoir at seventy, is well aware of the changes that had come over the world during the intervening decades. He knows he is writing a history of both personal and environmental losses. His long passage on the passenger pigeon is virtually an elegy for that species. It opens:

> It was a great memorable day when the first flock of passenger pigeons came to our farm, calling to mind the story we had read about them when we were at school in Scotland. Of all God's feathered people that sailed the Wisconsin sky, no other bird seemed to us so wonderful. The beautiful wanderers flew like the winds in flocks of millions from climate to climate in accord with the weather, finding their food—acorns, beechnuts, pine-nuts, cranberries, strawberries, huckleberries, juniper berries, hackberries, buckwheat, rice, wheat, oats, corn—in fields and forests thousands of miles apart. I have seen flocks streaming south in the fall so large that they were flowing over from horizon to horizon in an almost continuous stream all day long, like a mighty river in the sky, widening, contracting, descending like falls and cataracts, and rising suddenly here and there in huge ragged masses like high-plashing spray.

He describes the beauty of the birds and offers an anecdote that confirms how some of those who hunted them and decimated their number were simultaneously admiring of their beauty.

> "Oh, what bonnie, bonnie birds!" we exclaimed over the first that fell into our hands. "Oh, what colors! Look at their breasts, bonnie as roses, and at their necks aglow wi' every color juist like the wonderfu' wood ducks. Oh, the bonnie,

bonnie creatures, they beat a'! Where did they a' come fra,
and where are they a' gan? It's awfu' like a sin to kill them!" To
which some smug, practical old sinner would remark: "Aye,
it's a peety, as ye say, to kill the bonnie things, but they were
made to be killed, and sent for us to eat as the quails were
sent to God's chosen people, the Israelites, when they were
starving in the desert ayont the Red Sea. And I must confess
that meat was never put up in neater, handsomer-painted
packages."

Muir tells us that he never saw the roosting places of the passenger
pigeons "until long after the great flocks were exterminated," and
so he quotes Audubon's account of them at length, then ends
the chapter with the description of the roosts from Pokagon, "an
educated Indian writer."

> I saw one nesting-place in Wisconsin one hundred miles
> long and from three to ten miles wide. Every tree, some of
> them quite low and scrubby, had from one to fifty nests on
> each. Some of the nests overflow from the oaks to the hem-
> lock and pine woods. When the pigeon hunters attack the
> breeding-places they sometimes cut the timber from thou-
> sands of acres.

He concludes with a description of millions of birds captured and
shipped to New York to be sold for a penny apiece. That Pokagon's
remarks and Audubon's witnessing of a typically massive pigeon
hunt end the chapter suggests that, at least so far as nature is a
central focus of the book, lament is a major element.

Muir observes domestic animals, too, talking at length about
efforts to understand oxen and his pony, Jack, and he confesses his
own complicity in destruction, not only in the story of wounding
the loon but also in shooting a woodpecker and hunting muskrats,

gophers, and deer. His fifth chapter talks of muskrats, foxes and badgers, raccoons, squirrels and flying squirrels, and gophers and often steps away from reminiscence to admonish the wantonness of some hunting he observed. Here, Muir turns away from celebration and lament toward a more autobiographical recounting of what his life on the farm was like as the son of a demanding, driven father. In doing so he leads us away from the pleasure of imagining a young Johnnie Muir reveling in the feeling of having nature stream into him and leads us toward the changes he and his family and the settlers around him wrought on the land.

4

In my boyhood and youth, when I read the biographies of Daniel Boone and Davy Crockett in the Landmark series of juvenile history books or, somewhat later, when I read the N. C. Wyeth illustrated volumes of *The Deerslayer* and *The Last of the Mohicans,* I imagined colonial North America as a narrow band of British American civilization along the Atlantic coast and, to the west, vast tracts of dense forest populated mostly by wolves, bears, and deer, which eventually gave way to vast tracts of rolling grasslands where buffalo roamed and deer and antelope played.

Occasionally, I knew, a restless frontiersman might run into a primitive village of Indians, but my understanding of the New World was as an immense, open, lush, and fertile natural world, new not only because it had been a surprise to Europeans but also because it was unused, empty of everything the Old World contained. Implicit in our history is the concept of land as something wasted if not put to the service of a community or a government or a commercial enterprise. In the early accounts I've read of various state histories, the emphasis is largely on encouraging exploitation of natural resources—trumpeting the ease with which a prairie can be converted into a productive farm, the prospects available for mining or lumbering, the potential inherent in nascent villages and towns. Emigrants from the Old World came to the New as farmers, miners, tradesmen, merchants, laborers, and landowners; they brought their own, assumptions about land and saw no profit in questioning those assumptions. The consequence was virtually the total transformation of the American landscape; the changes began in each locale immediately after settlement and barely took a decade or two to complete.

Before my own emigration to Wisconsin and the rise of my own need to figure out where I was, if I thought of Wisconsin at all, I saw it as the vast dairy land it promoted itself to be, the result of converting empty prairie into productive pastureland. My obliviousness was unintentional, on par with my ignorance of most of the forty-five other states I've never lived in—I'd been as blasé about Colorado until I moved west, though there the mountains insisted I take immediate notice of my terrain—but in the interval since we settled here, I've been a little more attentive and a little more observant. I've come to appreciate the Wisconsin landscape in ways I hadn't expected.

A couple of things are clearer to me now about the landscape to which John Muir was introduced in 1849. One is that the land was being used thoroughly and well by the prairies, marshes, oak savannas, and woodlands that occupied it. The grasses, sedges, flowers, shrubs, and trees, in concert with natural or Indian-set fires, flourished everywhere. The wildlife flourished as well, all those waterfowl and songbirds, reptiles and amphibians, fishes and fauna of the grasslands and forests. The natural world had found a balance here, as it always has, among its various populations—the plants that felt most at home on this particular soil, the animals that felt most at home among those particular plants.

It is also clear that Wisconsin had been densely populated up

until the influx of European American settlement. The Menominee, Ho-Chunk or Winnebago, Ojibwa or Chippewa, Sauk, Fox,
Potawatomi, and Dakota all lived here. Other tribes had more
fleeting residence in the territory; and before all of them there had
been mound builders—Wisconsin, until Europeans routinely de-
molished most of them, had more effigy and burial mounds than
any other state, spread all across the region. When Muir tells the
story of learning to ride the pony his father bought from a store-
keeper "who had obtained it from a Winnebago or Menominee
Indian in trade for goods," his lessons began at "a smooth place
near an Indian mound back of the shanty." Though treaties had
relocated the tribes, Muir was aware of Indians passing through
the area, occasionally hunting muskrats or harvesting wild rice
and ducks in the marshes. It's evident that for those various tribes,
undeveloped Wisconsin had been home ground.

Muir tells us, in "The Ploughboy," his sixth chapter, "When
we went into the Wisconsin woods there was not a single wheel-
track or cattle-track. The only man-made road was an Indian trail
along the Fox River between Portage and Packwauckee Lake." He
claims that "in the spring of 1849 there was no other settler within
a radius of four miles of our Fountain Lake farm," yet "in three or
four years almost every quarter-section of government land was
taken up." Many of the newcomers were immigrants from Great
Britain, in addition to a few "Yankee families from adjacent states."
Muir describes the settlement process:

> All alike striking root and gripping the glacial drift soil as
> naturally as oak and hickory trees; happy and hopeful, es-
> tablishing homes and making wider and wider fields in the
> hospitable wilderness. The axe and plough were kept very
> busy; cattle, horses, sheep, and pigs multiplied; barns and
> corncribs were filled up, and man and beast were well fed; a

schoolhouse was built, which was also used for a church; and
in a very short time the new country began to look like the
old one.

His succinct account of settlement could apply across the country.
Muir's "Ploughboy" chapter is particularly rich in chronicling
the kind of labor that turned prairie and woodland into farmland.
It is in many ways a minor history of transformation in the land,
and often Muir makes clear not only the nature of the transformation but also its unforeseen consequences. For example, he
notes, "After eight years of this dreary work of clearing the Fountain Lake farm, fencing it and getting it in perfect order, building
a frame house and the necessary outbuildings for the cattle and
horses," his father bought more wild land five miles away and
"began all over again to clear and fence and break up other fields
for a new farm, doubling all the stunting, heartbreaking chop-
ping, grubbing, stump-digging, rail-splitting, fence-building,
barn-building, house-building, and so forth."

By then, nearly twenty, Muir was old enough to run the breaking plow, "turning furrows from eighteen inches to two feet wide,"
used for "breaking up the wild sod woven into a tough mass,
chiefly by the cordlike roots of perennial grasses, reinforced by
the taproots of oak and hickory bushes, called 'grubs,' some of
which were more than a century old and four to five inches in
diameter." This detail may not be one Muir appreciated at the
time but his memory of what he was transforming is vivid. He
later explains how "the uniformly rich soil of the Illinois and Wisconsin prairies produced so close and tall a growth of grasses for
fires that no tree could live on it," but once "the oak openings in
our neighborhood were settled, and the farmers had prevented
running grass-fires, the grubs grew up into trees and formed tall
thickets so dense that it was difficult to walk through them and
every trace of the sunny 'openings' vanished."

For Fountain Lake Farm, much of the transformation was the result of Daniel Muir's driven profligacy, attempting to farm as large a plot of land as he could and reap the rewards of its fertility as quickly as possible. John Muir recounts a neighbor's conversation about the misuse of the land and its consequences, which makes clear that Muir's father's approach was commonplace. Having transformed land that had limited value as cropland and then exhausting it, and having no sense of how to renew its fertility, Daniel Muir simply moved on to another plot of ground to repeat the same radical alteration there.

Looking off from the promontory on Observatory Hill nearly a century and a half after Muir first stood there, John Warfield Simpson explains that the landscape he sees "differs both from the one John first beheld and from that formed by the extraordinary change he witnessed in the subsequent few years. More forest cover exists now than when he gazed across the rolling hills and broad lowlands." He notes that two new cultural layers have been added to the original landscape, "layers that nearly erased the prior conditions." One layer was produced when "pioneers initially cut farms into the indigenous landscape," and another when those farms were themselves transformed in purpose and in productivity in the succeeding century.

> That second layer is the one I now see from Observatory Hill and as I drive the chip-sealed and paved roads around what was Fountain Lake Farm. Dairy farms dominate. Black-and-white-mottled cows graze the pastures on the drained bottomlands and the rolling hills. I also see black beef cattle, sheep, and swine. Red-painted wooden barns with crisp white trim stand surrounded by fields of wheat, corn, oats, and alfalfa.... Some scenery is charming and pastoral, neat and tidy. Other places like wetlands and marshes look disheveled with the scruffy appearance of abandonment and succession.

That second layer is the one I saw as well from that same promontory, and though I climbed the hill in order to look across
the landscape where John Muir spent his adolescence, I have to
remember that the country I saw was not the one Muir gazed
upon. But I also recall that Muir had hoped one small patch of
it would be.

5

On November 23, 1895, in an address to the Sierra Club in San
Francisco, John Muir spoke of his thwarted dream of preserving
some portion of Fountain Lake Farm.

> The preservation of specimen sections of natural flora—bits
> of pure wildness—was a fond, favorite notion of mine long
> before I heard of national parks. When my father came from
> Scotland, he settled in a fine wild region of Wisconsin, beside
> a small glacier lake bordered with white pond-lilies. . . . And
> when I was about to wander away on my long rambles I was
> sorry to leave that precious meadow unprotected; therefore,
> I said to my brother-in-law, who then owned it, "sell me the
> forty acres of lake meadow and keep it fenced, and never
> allow cattle or hogs to break into it, and I will gladly pay you
> whatever you say. I want to keep it untrampled for the sake of
> its ferns and flowers; and even if I should never see it again,
> the beauty of its lilies and orchids are so pressed into my
> mind I shall always enjoy looking back at them in imagina-
> tion, even across seas and continents, and perhaps after I am
> dead."
>
> But he regarded my plan as a sentimental dream wholly
> impracticable. The fence he said would surely be broken
> down sooner or later, and all the work would be in vain.

Eighteen years later I found the deep-water pond lilies in fresh bloom, but the delicate garden-sod of the meadow was broken up and trampled into black mire.

John Muir eventually left home, at first to try to make a career as an inventor and mechanic—his ingenious and intricate study desk is encased near an entrance to the Wisconsin Historical Society building on the campus of the University of Wisconsin in Madison—and later he enrolled as a student at the university. Eventually, though he doesn't tell us this in *The Story of My Boyhood and Youth*, he went off to Canada to avoid the draft that would have made him a soldier for the Union cause in the Civil War then raging. In the conclusion of the book he more circumspectly claims, "I wandered away on a glorious botanical and geological excursion, which has lasted fifty years and is not yet completed." He positions himself on a hill overlooking the university, saying farewell "with streaming eyes" and setting off for "the University of the Wilderness."

In time, of course, he did take his thousand-mile walk to the Gulf of Mexico, tramp through the mountains of California and across the glaciers of Alaska, and become a major voice for the preservation of the wilderness. But except for occasional trips to see his family, he seldom visited Wisconsin.

Fountain Lake Farm, which Daniel Muir had sold to his daughter Sarah and her husband, David Galloway, was sold off in increments in 1865 and 1866, and once John Ennis owned the eighty acres around the lake, it became known as Ennis Lake. John Muir later considered making an offer to Ennis to preserve a portion of the property but decided it wouldn't work and eventually gave up. Fountain Lake Farm shifted into that second layer of transformation that Simpson talks about, the alteration of the pioneer farm of the mid-nineteenth century into the farm of the twentieth. The abandoned Muir farmhouse eventually burned down and the property passed into the hands of Archie Schmitz, who replaced the house with one of his own and hoped to preserve the site of Muir's youth.

On April 14, 1948, Aldo Leopold, then a professor of wildlife management and land conservation at the University of Wisconsin, whose weekend retreat on the Wisconsin River was less than twenty miles southwest of Ennis Lake, wrote to the director of the Wisconsin Conservation Department to propose acquisition of "one of the two boyhood farms of John Muir as a state park." He recommended that those involved in making such a decision read *The Story of My Boyhood and Youth:* "It is a necessary background." Leopold had given the project some careful consideration:

> The reason I have hesitated to recommend this project in the past has been that the Muir farm is undoubtedly badly depleted floristically and otherwise, and hence any possible restoration at this time might be a pretty drab affair compared to the original farm described in Muir's book. It now occurs to me, however, that this area might fall half way between a state park in the ordinary sense and a "natural area", the objective being to restore the flora to something approaching the original. To this end the cooperation of the Botany Department would be needed, and the superintendent would have to be a botanist with a general enthusiasm for this restoration job. He should also of course be equipped with the requisite knowledge of history and literature.

Leopold knew he was advocating an "enlarged function of state parks," and he insisted that instead of being "a mere stopping place for tourists looking for something to do," such a park "might be made a public educational institution in the ecological and intellectual history of Wisconsin."

April 14, 1948, was also the day that Leopold learned Oxford

University Press would publish the book now known as *A Sand County Almanac,* one of the most significant volumes in environmental literature, the book that placed Leopold in the pantheon that included Thoreau and Muir. One week later, on April 21, Leopold died of a heart attack while fighting a grass fire. Coincidentally, April 21 was also John Muir's birthday.

Others began advocating for a Muir Park in the late 1940s, and in 1955 Marquette County established a John Muir Memorial County Park near the site of Fountain Lake Farm but not actually containing any original Muir property. In 1965 the county expanded its holdings to include the lake and the meadow, and in 1972 the State of Wisconsin established the Muir Park State Natural Area, intending to restore and maintain the fen, prairie, and sedge meadow communities around the lake. A portion of the original Muir property is still in private hands, owned by Erik Brynildson, the Muir scholar whose own house stands where the Muir farmhouse once stood and who pursues his own mission of restoration and preservation.

Brynildson spoke at the dedication ceremony in 1991 that established Fountain Lake Farm as a National Historic Landmark. Speaking of his acquisition of a portion of the farm in 1987, he told of clearcutting a "dense crop of red pine," planted in 1960 as a replacement for the fallow farmland, having the land rough-disced and fine-tilled, and hand-planting a prairie-savanna seed bed, in hopes of restoring the site to what it was in the spring of 1849. Bobwhite quail were released and nest boxes for various birds installed around the area, and at the time he hoped to reintroduce prairie grouse.

From Fountain Lake Farm, John Muir went out into the wider world, making his mark as a close observer of, and inspiring presence in, the natural world. Edwin Way Teale has written about the range of Muir's accomplishments, as a botanist, a glaciologist, and a conservationist. "Today Muir would probably be called an ecologist," Teale writes. His impact can be felt in the continuing work of the Sierra Club, which he served as its first president and presiding spirit; in the national parks, like Yosemite, Sequoia, and the Grand Canyon, that exist largely because of his efforts; and in the books he wrote, like *My First Summer in the Sierra, The Mountains of California, Travels in Alaska,* and *A Thousand-Mile Walk to the Gulf,* which are still in print a century after his death and cited frequently by a range of writers who follow in his footsteps. In *The Story of My Boyhood and Youth* he gives us a glimpse of the boy who became that man by showing us the lake, meadows, woods, and hills that prepared him to see the world in his own unique way.

All that is the landscape I walk when I try walking with John Muir.

6

The day before the autumnal equinox I drive again to Muir Park. On a rural county road I pass four sandhill cranes standing in a field, three of them foraging, one of them watching me. I slow the car but don't want to spook them so keep moving. At once I see a second, larger group of cranes on a higher terrace of the grassy field and then a third still more numerous group even farther up and back, maybe two dozen cranes in all spread out across the fields, the grass a rich green rustling beneath them. An hour and a half into daylight and for me it's already a good day.

At the park I step down to the dock where I started my walk last spring. The wind is cold and the sky overcast, low woolly clouds obscuring the sun. Lily pads float on the surface of the lake, their stems curling below the surface. They have no flowers but I remember Muir writing ecstatically of drifting on the lake and admiring "how they grow up in beauty out of gray lime mud and ride gloriously among the breezy sun-spangles." He thought the white water lily "the most beautiful, sumptuous, and deliciously fragrant of all our Wisconsin flowers."

Leaves are turning color on the bushes, thicker and higher than they were last time, some of them already a vivid dark red. I've missed the growing season, having come in early May, when it was barely beginning, and now again in late September, as it ends. A cleared path heads off from the other side of the boat ramp and I follow it, on damp and spongy ground, through an alley of high shrubs with flowers plentiful: pink thistles, deep blue and pale blue asters, white marsh asters, a bevy of yellow flowers. A wedge of geese passes overhead, honking all the way, dark shapes against light gray clouds. Glancing up I notice the oak opening on the hill above; I'd passed it on higher ground last time. The understory is dense with shrubs, bushes, flowers, and ferns. Every so often small birds fly up out of the thickets and cross the path to the thickets below the oak opening. Some find a perch on the tallest, deadest oak. Somewhere toward the lake is a hidden fen.

This path takes me to a junction with the trail, established by the Ice Age Trail Alliance, that circles the park. From this point I'll be on familiar ground, or at least on ground I've walked before, though the fullness of the summer's growth makes most of what I'm seeing unfamiliar. The shrubs give way to grasses, and the ground is firmer, dryer, no longer black muck. Grasses stretch above my head and mingled in them are intermittent stands of milkweed and thistles and tall flowering shrubs with the petals gone. The tall grasses soon give way to shorter ones I can see over. I pass the willow thicket, higher now and leafed out, denser than it was in May. More geese fly over from the direction of the Fox River wetlands to the west. I hear shots in the distance and re-member that Marquette County devotes a good deal of acreage to hunting. The Fox River National Wildlife Refuge itself is closed to visitors unless they're hunters—"refuge" strikes me as the wrong term from the wildlife's perspective. I feel a bit of misty rain and move on, finding myself now in waist-high grasses waving in the wind. More small birds flit briefly above them.

I pass the hickories, crushing the nutshells as I walk, the crunch reminding me how plentiful they were in spring and how hard they are to see now. The trail keeps me above a long stretch of fen and below an open field cleared as a sand blow but now grassed over. I climb the ridge into the oak opening again, my hands painfully cold from making notes in the wind, and as I warm them in my sweatshirt pockets, I survey the lake, particularly aware of one corner thick with lily pads. I remember the woman with the dog I'd met in May and imagine that she saw all the changes here happen incrementally over the seasons.

Along the path the shrubs grow thicker and taller and the boardwalk across the sedge meadow and the bridge over the inlet stream seem secluded. As I pause on the bridge, a woman comes briskly from the other direction along the trail. We startle one another but greet each other as if we haven't. I've been staring at

a red-leaved bush with abundant white berries, and when she says she lives nearby and loves this trail, I ask her if she knows what I'm looking at. She glances at the bush and tells me confidently it's red-osier dogwood. I thank her, immediately aware that I should have known what it was. She moves on, while I shift position to gaze across the garden meadow. I can barely locate the house that was so visible in spring.

Past the sedge meadow, the oak openings thicken and the winding trail feels secluded, the uplands rising to the east, the lake invisible because of the thickets and now because of the forest. When the trail veers closer to the lake and I can see it again, I briefly test a side path likely formed by animals, but I find the ground too mucky and wet, and I backtrack. There's more sedge meadow here at the southern end of the lake, and when I find a more promising side trail, I take it to the water's edge. The ground is a little spongy, but at the shoreline I can see the marl of the lake bottom, touch the reedy grasses growing just off shore, see another line of lily pads.

Further around the southern edge of the lake a longer side trail crosses a broader stretch of sedge meadow, tempting me again. The ground jiggles under my feet. My footsteps squelch and as I stand at the edge of the lake I realize I've weighed the ground down enough for water to rise around the bottoms of my shoes. I think of John Muir's memory of carpenters working on the house who "noticed how the sedges sunk beneath their feet, and thought that if they should ever break through the bouncy mat, they would probably be well on their way to California before touching bottom." Sedge meadow fills the space between the two side paths I've taken.

I move into oak woodlands, a forest with a high canopy, its understory now entirely filled in, bordered by high hills on the west side of the trail. As I come out of them, I watch for the pool at the center of the fen I'd seen in the spring, but the undergrowth is

too tall and I can catch only the slightest glimpse because I know
it's there and I'm looking for it. The cattails near the bridge across
the outlet stream have almost all burst open. Back in the county
park I take one last long look at the water and the distant shoreline
from the dock, then walk up to the signs at the trailhead explaining the different ecozones I've passed through. I've done better
this time at knowing what I'm seeing than I did in the spring. If
I lived as close to Muir Park as the woman I met today and the
woman I met in May, I would walk the circuit often, becoming
familiar with everything I see, not simply memorizing but letting
nature stream into me.

That essentially was John Muir's approach—to open himself
up to nature, to put himself in its midst and be willing to learn
what it had to tell him. That's what he did here and then what he
did everywhere else he went. That's what I will need to do on my
own home ground.

I'm aware, of course, that I am not walking the same place that
John Muir walked when it was his home ground—he himself
helped change it and he lamented the changes that came after
he moved out into the larger world—but, as Aldo Leopold once
hoped, what the natural area here preserves and has partially restored offers the chance to gather intimations of Muir's experience and to lightly replicate it through opening ourselves to it.

By reading Muir on Fountain Lake Farm I gain insight into an
approach to nature and to place with universal application, one
still potent and pertinent. It's important for me to acknowledge
that this is no longer the place Muir knew—I haven't really engaged in time travel here—and to develop some comprehension
of the ways in which the environment here has altered—I will be
walking my own home ground in its altered, present state, after
all—but that doesn't lessen what I can gain from letting nature
stream into me wherever I am, at the moment I'm there.

Not long after I leave the park I turn a corner and see two

sandhill cranes stalking through an overgrown field. I slow the car, then stop by the side of the road. I stay a few minutes to watch them move, admiring their patience and pace. They add to the sense of calm that has grown in me across the morning. Cranes have bookended my autumn hike in Muir's home ground; before I put the car in motion, I thank them for being there.

Interlude

Saturday, April 7, 2011. Perhaps spurred on by reading Aldo Leopold, who would have been up and out long before now, I strike out for the woods around 7 a.m. It's cold, and a light, low fog hangs over everything. Rains have raised the river level, and I can tell at first sight that the wetlands are partly flooded again. I stride down to the observation deck to gauge the water level and find it higher than the last time I saw it, but still much lower than it was a few weeks ago, when I could find no sign of land other than a couple of small, temporary islands. For once I've remembered my binoculars, and I sweep them slowly across the floodplain, following the course of the river. I stop when I notice, upriver, two sandhill cranes standing near the bank. I steady the binoculars to observe them more closely. They're too far away for me to discern their red crowns, but their tall, slender gray shapes rising above the grass are clear. They are still and silent, as motionless as the stark barren shrubs that occasionally rise above the sedges. I watch them for a while in expectation of movement and eventually—too slowly—realize they are watching me as well.

I don't want them to feel the need to take flight, so I set off through the woods to the other observation deck near the marsh. It's a brisk, winding, up-and-down walk, and I soon have no sense of the river behind me. Ahead of me I hear ducks and red-wings and, I think, peepers and frogs, see a few squirrels on the ground and first a chickadee, then a woodpecker in the trees. Through the trees I sometimes catch flickers of bird flight above the marsh, and I keep moving until I reach the marsh deck. Three mallards circle the pond at its center, and two begin to float downward to splash into the water. For a minute or two they swim in plain sight, then veer into the sedges and disappear. Red-winged blackbirds abound in every section of the marsh, and I listen to them chortle, hoping more waterfowl will appear. None do. Only after I tire of scanning the empty pond, circle around the loop toward the woods leading back to the river, and reach the rise opposite the marsh deck do I see a pair of wood ducks take flight from the pond.

The truth is I'm almost scurrying along the path in hopes of seeing the cranes again. I slow as I draw opposite the meanders and spot them once more, still out beyond the river. This time they don't seem to notice me and so I stand quietly for a few minutes trying to imprint in my memory this image of cranes in the mist.

It occurs to me now how stirred I have been by the sight of sandhill cranes in Wisconsin. When I lived in the Lower Peninsula of Michigan, it was the great blue heron that thrilled me whenever I saw it, rising from a river in front of my canoe, sailing in slow motion overhead, stalking the shallows of a marshy pond. In the Upper Peninsula, along the shores of Lake Superior, it was the common loon that would make me put down my paddle or walk more gingerly to the shoreline. In Wisconsin it's the sandhill cranes that cause me to slow the car on a backcountry road for a better view of their stately motion through a field or their languid passage across the sky.

Some portion of the regard in which I hold them may have carried over from reading Leopold. In "Marshland Elegy" he reminds us that cranes originated millennia ago, in the Eocene. "When we hear his call we hear no bird. We hear the trumpet in the orchestra of evolution," he tells us. "Amid the endless mediocrity of the commonplace, a crane marsh holds a paleon-tological patent of nobility." Leopold puts all of existence into perspective by reciting the history of sandhill cranes.

Perhaps that's what vibrates in me whenever I see a sandhill crane, some sort of sympathetic tuning with a silent chord struck by the simple fact of the bird's existence. Something tells me when I see it that, however remotely, I am connecting to something far vaster and more vibrant than I can imagine.

The Taste for Country:
Walking with Aldo Leopold

1

I APPROACH THE SHACK and farm that is the site of Aldo Leopold's
A Sand County Almanac by bicycle, on a solid but hardly sleek
model borrowed from the Aldo Leopold Legacy Center a mile
or so away. It's an ecologically sound way to get here without
prolonging my trek along Levee Road. I've already driven past the
shack, but I hope this slower approach will give me a fuller sense
of the area. On the bike I better appreciate how low the tree-lined

road is and how the bases of the trees off either shoulder are deep in standing water.

Beyond the narrow corridor of trees is a long stretch of wetlands to the south. A map in *Prairie Time,* a book about the Leopold Reserve, identifies this open water, the inundated grasses, and the flooded forest as the Great Marsh. When I drove by it earlier, I saw two sandhill cranes in a treeless opening. Now, the sight of the marsh behind the trees reminds me of Leopold's April essay, "Come High Water," about being marooned by flooding; the cranes reminded me of "Marshland Elegy," the essay centered on how changes in the marshes alter the habitat of cranes. Already I'm aware of how much I'll be influenced by what Leopold had to say about what I'll be seeing.

Past the trees I spot the shack, closed up and set back across a patch of prairie that starts near the road. From here the shack might be mistaken for an abandoned outbuilding of some kind. The terrain around it is different from the carefully maintained lawns of its neighbors on the north side of the road, where large houses and the accouterments of families give evidence of being lived in. Past the prairie and under more trees, I coast into a narrow, fenced-off parking area, wheel the bike through a gap in the locked gate, and prop it against a tree. Then I step back to the gate and lean against the wooden rail to face the dirt driveway that arches back through the trees toward the prairie. The self-guided tour, for which I have an informative pamphlet, starts here and will take me to nine numbered sites. In the pamphlet, small photographs from the earliest period of the Leopolds' occupation make clear that what the visitor will see now will be what the Leopolds transformed it into, not what it was when Leopold first began to restore it. The comments about each site end with suggested readings from *A Sand County Almanac.*

I'd like to ignore the photographs and concentrate on what

I see now, but at the center before I embarked, I saw an exhibit of pictures taken early on by Carl Leopold, one of Aldo's sons. Together with the reproductions in the pamphlet, those photos, all in black-and-white, show the setting in 1935 to be desolate and empty, especially compared to the lush green forest floor ahead of me and the clear cloudless blue sky above and sunlight illuminating everything. From the gate and from the spot not far down the driveway where the visitor is encouraged to view the pines planted by the Leopolds, it's difficult to see the shack. The woods are abundant and the forest floor shrubby and green. Tall straight pines line the driveway. We have had a snowy winter and a very rainy spring, and the water-soaked fields I saw as I drove across the state make an extreme contrast with the drought conditions of the Dust Bowl years when Leopold first began bringing his family here. It's been seventy-six years since he bought the place, and the shack may be the most constant element of the landscape.

The path follows the driveway in an arc that takes me out of the woods and across the open prairie, its far edges lined with trees from the road to the shack. I know the prairie is a prairie mostly by my pamphlet. There's green in the low grasses and light brown in the dry grasses above them. In early May the area seems to still be oppressed by vanished winter snows.

The shack looks very small across the expanse of the open field and against the backdrop of thick woods around it, the treetops four or five times as high as the peak of the roof. Without its white door, it might easily disappear into its background. I approach slowly, trying to take it in by degrees. Thoreau's cabin at Walden Pond has long since disappeared, the house and shanty at Muir's Fountain Lake Farm no longer exist, but here is the very shack fashioned by Aldo Leopold and his family, still in the family's possession, simultaneously their getaway spot and an ecological pilgrimage site. I don't want to overlook anything even as I realize that my self-conscious concentration will likely preserve little in memory.

There's scant seclusion about the place. It's entirely exposed to the southeast. The exterior walls are unpainted and weathered but sound, two windows on either side of the door are securely shuttered, and the white paint on the door is cracked and chipping from years of sun and rain. It seems hardly more than the chicken coop it started out as, low and cramped for seven people to spend a weekend in. The Leopolds had five children: Starker, Luna, Nina, Carl, and Estella Jr. All worked on achieving the changes Aldo had in mind for the place, including transforming the chicken coop into a family retreat. On my self-guided tour I have no way to see the interior, but I suspect "rustic" might be an appropriate term for it—or possibly "Spartan."

A Leopold bench rests under one exterior window, simple and solid in design, gray and long-seasoned. Two more sit on either side of a nearby fire pit, and a table and benches sit off to the side of the house, under a candelabra-shaped oak. Two large upright sections of tree trunk also stand near the fire pit, as work surfaces, no doubt. The scene in front of the shack gives off a strictly utilitarian air. Only a lilac bush, not yet in bloom, and a straight and lofty white pine, both at corners of the shack's eastern wall, suggest efforts at beautification.

One side trail leads to the Parthenon, the family's joking name for the outhouse built by Starker, the oldest son. When it was constructed, it was a stark little rectangle out in the open, but now it stands demurely in a well-shaded stand of trees. The shack and the Parthenon are on high ground, but not far beyond them the land slopes off toward a long patch of reddish-brown sand, and a sandy trail leads off at an angle toward the open banks of the Wisconsin River. I'm curious about where it leads and so follow it away from the shack.

At once I'm in very different terrain than I had been walking through. The sand at the bottom of the slope opens up into a wide swath and the trees are widely separated on areas of short grasses. The pale blue sky is open and the view of it is mostly uncluttered. Another Leopold bench is set on the border of the sand near the grass and below a cluster of sprawling cottonwoods. Here and there wide stands of low white flowers proliferate across the scruffy areas where sand and grass mingle. The thin blue line I see above the green of the grasses in the distance is the Wisconsin River and I hope that the sand will lead me to it. Along the way a Baltimore oriole high on a birch branch sings exuberantly. He picked a perfect spot for his display, his breast gleaming in the sunshine and his voice filling the air. His song cheers me as I trudge through the loose, deep sand.

The trail narrows the nearer it gets to the riverbank and ends at a small beach at water's edge. The Wisconsin is very wide here and still running high. Close to the banks grasses are submerged and trees stand up to their knees in water. The northern shore seems to be entirely forested along its length, and an island midstream is also well wooded. Here on the south shore, the bank to the west seems unoccupied, but to the east I can see houses through the trees, some prudently set on much higher ground. It's clear to me that the floodplain of the Wisconsin was broader here in earlier days, and Leopold's essay "Come High Water" confirms that it sometimes extended to the slope behind the shack. The river isn't entirely a surprise, but as I stand on the riverbank, comparing the blue of the water with the blue of the sky and feeling the sense of a powerful presence, I realize that almost nothing in *A Sand County Almanac* prepared me to see it. Leopold's interest was in the land, in the country, but I suspect that what brought those other homeowners to Levee Road was more likely to have been the river. I'm sure I could sit watching it roll by for a long time.

The breeze is strong in the open along the river and the mid-May day is cool enough for me to be glad to be well layered. The bright sun gives little warmth that the wind doesn't quickly whisk away. I head back toward the shack, warming up some once I re-enter the trees.

Beyond the shack on the other side are more designated sites. The trail leads out of the clearing and up a shaded slope on forest floor covered with low undergrowth. At the top of the hill are the remnants of the farmhouse that burned down before Leopold bought the place. Still visible around the edges of a deep hole in the ground are rows of fieldstones making up the foundation walls. The trail follows the top of a ridge and once or twice I step off to gaze at the woods below, on the floodplain, where the ground at low places near the base of the slope is saturated and ponded. I'm walking under tall oaks now, with the forest floor open between them. I pass the place where Leopold noted the draba on a sand blow, still open to the sky though the sand itself is barely visible under an abundance of oak leaves. Soon I reach the commemorative stone where the "Good Oak" once stood, the subject of the marvelous February essay. The plaque on the stone reads, "Rest! cries the chief sawyer," the line that recurs through-out the oak essay. The trail has arched around south, and at the stone I'm back near the road on the southwestern corner of the property. Rather than drop down onto the pavement, I backtrack a little and follow a diagonal trail back across pine forest until I emerge at the edge of a sparsely treed orchard and open meadow with the shack beyond it.

Drifting over to the fire pit, I settle onto the Leopold bench facing the shack. Occasionally I can hear distant traffic, but the wind in the trees tends to drown out all but nearby birdsong. The birds are plentiful and full of song. The shack is not as isolated or as remote as I have always assumed it was, even though to get to it you have to take backcountry roads across one very flat plain and over low ridges and along that low paved road with flooded forests and marshland running up to its sides. It seems quite a humble place, yet I'm aware that a great book and the most significant ecological thinking arose from it. I recognize the parallels with Thoreau and *Walden*, though one man was a bachelor and the other surrounded by his family. Both raise our awareness that where you are is not what makes the difference; it's what you observe wherever you are that does.

After gazing awhile at the closed front of the shack, not really expecting to receive any particular vibrations and not really disappointed when I don't (though I remember being stirred by John Burroughs's Slabsides when I saw it), I move to the Leopold bench just under a boarded-up window, to get a sense of what Leopold and his family saw when they looked out. To the southeast is the patch of prairie that Leopold restored; to the south, beyond the fire pit, are the pines they planted that they would have seen growing year after year; to the southwest, past the woodpile and the ring of benches, are the orchard and the wooded hills beyond them. Three-quarters of a century ago there was only a row of elms, soon to die of Dutch elm disease, and acres of worn-out, barren fields. What the Leopolds could see from the windows of the shack was the restoration of the land, growing week by week before their eyes. Reinforced by memories of what it had been, they had a different sense of place than any day visitor like me is likely to develop. I can only hope that, over time, I can gain some insight into what that sense of place might have been.

2

In some places it may be easy to avoid talking about geology, but in Wisconsin, sooner or later, you will need to talk about the glaciers. Their presence or absence has determined the nature of the terrain you see. When David Rhodes, a Wisconsin writer, published *Driftless*, everyone knew at once it was a Wisconsin novel, the title alluding to the Driftless Area of the state. The Driftless Area in the southwestern corner of the state missed the glaciation that scraped and scoured and shaped the other three-quarters of Wisconsin. The glaciers determined how far south the northern forest advanced, how far north the southern forest extended, just where the tension zone between them would be established. They determined the physical features of the landscape, creating the drumlins, eskers, kames, and moraines that form the rolling hills and the kettle lakes, fens, marshes, and bogs that fill the lowlands. If you pay attention to the rise and fall of any road you're on here, you realize that you're traveling over terrain deposited and eroded in the aftermath of glaciers.

Geologic time is always difficult for me to get a handle on. It's so vast. It involves so many varied forces working at a pace that is indiscernible yet achieving changes in landscape so huge they are unimaginable. I can look at a river and accept its meanders and shifts in channel, recognize the changes in flow and flood stage; but really comprehending the composition of the land it flows through, the soil it's wearing away or in an earlier time deposited on a scale far vaster than its present appearance indicates, is much harder to accomplish.

I live close to Kettle Moraine State Forest, an intermittent series of wooded areas preserving the debris deposited by two lobes of the last glacier to cross Wisconsin. The Green Bay Lobe to the west and the Lake Michigan Lobe to the east squeezed a great deal of till and ice between them, and when they melted they left a long stretch of medial moraine interrupted by chunks of ice that, in time, melted as well. Those vanished chunks of ice left deep depressions in the hills; some are still wetlands, others have by now dried out. My county, Waukesha County, is rich in evidence of its glacial past, especially where the Kettle Moraine and the Ice Age Trail, a hiking trail that roughly follows the last glacier's edge a thousand miles across the state, pass through it. I'm getting to the point where I constantly seem to feel the glacier's absence but haven't yet mastered a sense of its former presence.

"The sand counties of Central Wisconsin," Susan Flader observes in *The Sand Country of Aldo Leopold*, "are a legacy of sands slowly settling in the shallow Cambrian sea which covered the interior of the continent half a billion years ago." The complicated history of a place over the course of half a billion years, with all the intermittent periods of deposition, compacting, exposure, and erosion, with the appearance and disappearance of mountains and oceans, is beyond my powers to imagine, let alone trace. I'm grateful to encounter a writer like Flader, who handles that half billion years succinctly and briskly, and who expresses herself in ways that make Wisconsin's emergence comprehensible to me. She tells how, "three hundred million years ago, the landmass gently warped upward and spilled the last ocean from the state," how Wisconsin had been "part of a stable landmass gradually bequeathing its mantle of soil and rock to other seas," and how, in the same period that the Appalachian and the Rocky and the Sierra chains of mountains were rising, "Wisconsin eroded seaward." The result was the loss of "thousands of feet of sediments overlying the Cambrian sandstone in central Wisconsin and with them all trace of three hundred million years of life."

Warping, spilling, bequeathing, wearing away—the scale of all this still seems incredible, but I can somehow see this transformation. The Ice Age that followed lasted a million years and saw four major glacial incursions; the final Wisconsin stage, which lasted sixty thousand years, involved "a series of advances and retreats of a multi-lobed ice sheet." The Green Bay Lobe, in Flader's words, "molded the character of this region" fifteen thousand years ago. (She calls it "a mere fifteen thousand years ago" and in geologic terms "mere" seems an appropriate word, though hard for me to use easily.)

What we now identify as the Wisconsin River was flowing

even then, in its ancestral form, and the glacier dumped debris that dammed it. The impounded water formed Glacial Lake Wisconsin, encompassing "over eighteen hundred square miles, covering parts of five counties," and the glacial meltwater and wave action on the lake deposited the sand that identifies the region and left "isolated buttes, mounds, castellated bluffs, and pinnacles rising from a level marshy plain when the waters receded." Because of the repeated advance and retreat of the glaciers, the region shifted the boundaries of its "floristic provinces" (in Flader's term) and created that tension zone of anywhere from ten to thirty miles between them. The southern province was composed of prairies, oak savannas, and southern hardwoods, and the northern province contained pine savannas, conifer-hardwoods, and boreal forest. The tension zone marked the northern limit of the southern species and the southern limit of the northern species. Flader writes, "Some botanists consider the entire sand area as a widened part of the tension zone, its sands accentuating differences in moisture content and temperature, its low-lying glacial lake beds and river bottoms more prone to frosts, its nutrient-poor acid soils preventing any one species from taking over. The result is an intermingling of species from north and south."

In the prologue to *Prairie Time: The Leopold Reserve Revisited,* John Ross complicates that picture by describing the area as lying "within the transition zone between the native eastern forests, dense and deciduous, and the western grasslands, so fully open to the sky. Here, the natural expression is that of sweeps of prairie with oak openings. Grasses and forbs fill the prairies." Ross emphasizes the immensity of the oak savanna that dominated the ecotone between eastern forest and western grassland, covering an estimated thirty million acres before settlement. "In Wisconsin, oak savanna occurred naturally on an estimated six million acres. . . . Now only about 5,000 acres of prime oak savanna, and remnant patches of prairie, remain in Wisconsin." Two-thirds of the Leopold Memorial Reserve, a privately owned area of four-teen hundred acres, "is floodplain forest and marshland, dotted with ponds and river sloughs. The remainder is hilly moraine that has recently been covered by a mixed oak-hickory-pine forest and broken by a few fields still under cultivation. A sandy substrate underlays the entire reserve and produces an easily eroded soil of low fertility."

In order to restore the land around the shack, Leopold had to have a sense of what native, natural central Wisconsin was like before the farm was corned out and devastated. The idea behind the reserve is the restoration of that earlier country. John Muir's approach to conservation as an ecological movement was preser-vation, leaving things alone and guaranteeing that they would be left alone; Leopold's approach was restoration, undoing the devastation to the natural environment and returning it to some-thing approaching its earlier state. Both men assumed that nature had achieved a sense of balance among its various communities: Muir's efforts were directed at maintaining that balance by pre-venting its destabilization; Leopold was well aware of the effects of destabilization and the complications of restoring the balance. Although certainly Leopold's heirs have done much to put his land ethic into practice, it's to be regretted that his death in 1948 cut short the further growth of his philosophy and its execution. It would have been good to hear his voice twenty years later, when his book was undergoing a significant surge in popularity. We see in *A Sand County Almanac* the extent to which Leopold never stopped observing and growing; as much as we feel his presence in the country around the shack, we can't ask him, How do you feel about what's happened here? What do you think you might have done differently? I'm certain he would have already thought about those questions.

3

Leopold evokes the glaciers in the essay "Marshland Elegy," which
opens with these images:

> A dawn wind stirs on the great marsh. With almost im-
> perceptible slowness it rolls a bank of fog across the wide
> morass. Like the white ghost of a glacier the mists advance,
> riding over phalanxes of tamarack, sliding across bog-mead-
> ows heavy with dew. A single silence hangs from horizon to
> horizon.

The simile is well chosen in descriptive terms but also alludes to
the environmental history that accounts for the marsh's existence.
Leopold is someone who is always aware not only of where he is
but also of how where he is came to be there. His sense of place is
continuously in harmony with his sense of ecological, geological,
and social history. He writes of the marsh,

> A sense of time lies thick and heavy on such a place. Yearly
> since the ice age it has awakened each spring to the clangor of
> cranes. The peat layers that comprise the bog are laid down
> in the basin of an ancient lake. The cranes stand, as it were,
> upon the sodden pages of their own history. These peats are
> the compressed remains of the mosses that clogged the pools,
> of the tamaracks that spread over the moss, of the cranes that
> bugled over the tamaracks since the retreat of the ice sheet.

Later he succinctly gives us a history of Glacial Lake Wisconsin
and the formation of the Great Marsh:

> When the glacier came down out of the north, crunching
> hills and gouging valleys, some adventuring rampart of the ice

climbed the Baraboo Hills and fell back into the outlet gorge of the Wisconsin River. The swollen waters backed up and formed a lake half as long as the state, bordered on the east by cliffs of ice, and fed by the torrents that fell from melting mountains. The shorelines of this old lake are still visible; its bottom is the bottom of the great marsh.

The lake rose through the centuries, finally spilling over east of the Baraboo range. There it cut a new channel for the river, and thus drained itself. To the residual lagoons came the cranes, bugling the defeat of the retreating winter, summoning the on-creeping host of living things to their collective task of marsh-building. Floating bogs of sphagnum moss clogged the lowered waters, filled them. Sedge and leather-leaf, tamarack and spruce successively advanced over the bog, anchoring it by their root fabric, sucking out its water, making peat.

The story Leopold tells—and Susan Flader retells in *The Sand Country of Aldo Leopold* and John Ross and Beth Ross retell again in *Prairie Time*—is a necessary one if we are to really understand where we are—not simply locate ourselves on a map, but appreciate where and when we stand upon a patch of ground. To do that we need to comprehend where the land itself came from and what it was before we were there.

In the case of Leopold's shack and farm, the condition of the land when the family bought it was far removed from the condition of the land the Muir family settled on nearly ninety years earlier and less than thirty miles away. The story of Muir's farm portrays the beginning of settlement's effects on the country; the story of Leopold's farm begins with the results of settlement's effects. With little appreciation for the land as it was, farmers and lumbermen altered the landscape by decimating the white pines and clearing the marshes of tamaracks, plowing them for crops, and overgrazing the pastures they created on the sandy hills. As John Muir's father discovered quickly around Fountain Lake, the soils of the sand counties offered limited fertility for crops and, once cattle stripped the vegetation, reverted to sandy blowouts. In rainy years fields were too wet, but draining the marshlands, as was done on a massive scale, only created more problems. Once the water table of the marshes was lowered, exposing and drying the peat underneath them, fires were given an almost inexhaustible supply of fuel. Susan Flader notes, "Fires ran at will over the sand counties during the 1920s, eating the heart out of abandoned lands. The worst fire year of all was 1930, when three hundred thousand acres of peat were consumed." The marsh across the road from the shack burned that year, though luckily the water table was replenished by Wisconsin River floodwaters and the peat preserved.

And then in 1935 Aldo Leopold came to the patch of land in the sand counties between the Wisconsin River and that great marsh. It's in the "Good Oak" essay, the chapter for February, that Leopold provides some background for his specific 120 acres. An oak killed by lightning has aged for a year before Leopold cuts it down for fuel wood. He uses the occasion of cutting through the tree rings to not only measure the life span of the tree, which covered at least eighty and perhaps ninety years, but also to note what was happening in the natural world and its intersection with civilization almost ring by ring, year by year.

> It took only a dozen pulls of the saw to transect the few years of our ownership, during which we had learned to love and cherish this farm. Abruptly we began to cut the years of our predecessor the bootlegger, who hated this farm, skinned it of residual fertility, burned its farmhouse, threw it back into the lap of the County (with delinquent taxes to boot), and then disappeared among the landless anonymities of the Great

Depression. Yet the oak had laid down good wood for him; his sawdust was as fragrant, as sound, and as pink as our own. An oak is no respecter of persons.

The reign of the bootlegger ended sometime during the dust-bowl drouths of 1936, 1934, 1933, and 1930. Oak smoke from his still and peat from burning marshlands must have clouded the sun in those years, and alphabetical conservation was abroad in the land, but the sawdust shows no change.

Rest! cries the chief sawyer, and we pause for breath.

Leopold recounts the harvesting of the tree over the course of eight sections. The next six each begin with, "Now our saw bites into . . ." and end with, "Rest! cries the chief sawyer, and we pause for breath." The final section reaches beyond 1860 and the core of the tree, before cutting through the other side of the trunk and bringing it down.

The term "alphabetical conservation" in the passage above is a reference to the various Depression-era agencies of Franklin Roosevelt's administration that not only encouraged some restoration and reforestation projects but also helped families move to more promising agricultural areas. In "The Sand Counties," a sketch in the Wisconsin section of part two of his book, Leopold admits that "the Sand Counties are poor" in economic terms but claims that he wanted to know why the area's "sand farmers," those "benighted folk," were reluctant to move away even with government encouragement; "finally, to settle the question, I bought myself a sand farm."

His motives were not so whimsical as he suggests—he initially intended simply to lease land where he could establish a hunting camp and nurture his practice of archery—but the land he leased, however promising as a hunting camp, was in a sorry state. As Susan Flader notes, "The only building was a dilapidated chicken-house-turned-cowshed with manure knee deep on the

floor." Part of the foundation was all that remained of the burned
farmhouse, a nearby island had recently been stripped of timber,
and the open land consisted of "a corned-out field coming up to
sand burs and panic grass" and sand blows on the hills. It took
a while for Leopold to see the possibilities in the place and to
feel the need to own it. He initially bought eighty acres and later
added another forty. His family was enlisted in converting it into
a weekend retreat—cleaning out the manure, repairing the shack
with driftwood, building the outhouse—and restoring the landscape by planting pines and setting out to convert the fields back
to savanna and prairie.

In the "Sand Counties" essay, after wondering about the reluc-
tance of farmers to leave, he quickly turns to reasons to stay on a
sand farm. He cites the appearance of pasque flowers in April, the
sandwort "on the poorest hilltops," the linaria and the draba on
the sand blows, as well as the birds partial to aspects of the land,
like the sandhill crane and the clay-colored sparrow, a denizen
of jack pines, and the woodcock, whose "sky dance" he describes
in the April section of the almanac. As he does throughout *A
Sand County Almanac,* Leopold is suggesting here that there are
reasons to care about the land other than economic or commercial ones, reasons that might be aesthetic or ecological or, yes,
spiritual.

A Sand County Almanac and Sketches Here and There is a powerful, thoughtful, often lyrical book, essentially a sequence of
forty-one essays that leads a reader from a series of short observations of the natural life of the land around the shack through
reflections on encounters in other parts of the country to a short
series of philosophical articles culminating in Leopold's expound-
ing on the idea of a land ethic. The most accessible and inviting
section of the book is Part I: A Sand County Almanac; together
with the first two sketches in Part II: Sketches Here and There,

"Marshland Elegy" and "The Sand Counties," it's the almanac that makes us feel we're walking home ground with Aldo Leopold. It's a tribute to Leopold's power as a writer that we have that feeling.

4

"Each year, after the midwinter blizzards, there comes a night of thaw when the tinkle of dripping water is heard in the land." These words from Leopold's opening of his "January Thaw" entry in *A Sand County Almanac* were the first I wrote in my own journal of Wisconsin walks and wanderings on January 4, 2009. As a spur to my own contemplations, throughout the year I read monthly sections of Leopold's almanac and seasonal sections of Laurie Lawlor's splendid *This Tender Place: The Story of a Wetland Year*, a thorough evocation of Pickerel Fen in Walworth County, the county south of mine. Lawlor's is the more comprehensive study of a specific site across the seasons, an expansion of Leopold's example of coming to know where you are; Leopold's is the more compelling because of the brevity and concision of its essays. Our sense of Leopold in place is created not so much by narrative as by being given the chance to see what he sees. What he sees is informed by experience and examination, the advantage of frequent observation and wide study.

The essay that perhaps gives us the best sense of Leopold's method comes from the July section of the almanac, the essay titled "Great Possessions" (which had been Leopold's original title for the entire book). His theme, expressed as a genial pretense that he is hearing the tenants of his land declare their boundaries, suggests that the 120 acres the County Clerk records as Leopold's property are not really the natural limits of his "worldly domain." He writes:

At 3:30 a.m., with such dignity as I can muster of a July morning, I step from my cabin door, bearing in either hand my em-
blems of sovereignty, a coffee pot and notebook. I seat myself
on a bench, facing the white wake of the morning star. I set
the pot beside me. I extract a cup from my shirt front, hoping
none will notice its informal mode of transport. I get out my
watch, pour coffee, and lay notebook on knee. This is the cue
for the proclamations to begin.

It really was Leopold's method to keep scrupulous records of the
natural world around him, a habit he developed as a child. He
wrote, "Keeping records enhances the pleasure of the search and
the chance of finding meaning and order in these events." The
Leopold archives abound in notebooks he kept throughout his
life, the field observations that produced a meticulous phenology
of weather, wildlife activity, the life cycles of plant life.

In "Great Possessions" he provides an example of his recordkeeping: at 3:35 a.m. the call of the field sparrow, followed by
the song of the robin; at 3:50 the indigo bunting, then the wren,
and then "all is bedlam. Grosbeaks, thrashers, yellow warblers,
bluebirds, vireos, towhees, cardinals—all are at it." Once the sun
rises and the coffeepot is empty he and his dog "sally forth . . . at
random" and encounter a rabbit, a woodcock, a cock pheasant,
sometimes a coon or a mink or a heron or a wood duck or deer.
The sounds of neighboring farms replace the morning chorus of
birds and Leopold and his dog "turn toward home, and breakfast."

The tone is light, amiable, companionable, and the detail is
rich and engaging, so much so that the reader may end up disappointed that the sounds of the unnatural world have intruded into
and overwhelmed those of the natural world. That, of course, is
what Leopold hopes to establish. Again and again throughout the
almanac his encounters with the natural world are appreciative,
contemplative, and alive with wonder, and though the writing is

well grounded in science, the voice is conversational and neighborly. The almanac opens with a January thaw, the narrator following the track of a skunk through the melting snow. Repeatedly he is a bystander and witness in the natural life of his farm: to the sky dance of the woodcock, the arrival of Canada geese on the marsh, the return of the upland plover; to the discovery of draba in the sand blow, the quiet of fishing for trout from a rock midstream, the contemplation of the wind, the prairie grasses, the competition among trees.

The language of the "Almanac" essays is deceptively charming and relaxed. We might well feel that we are enjoying some bucolic idyll, a celebration of rural life such as other, later "cycle of the seasons" nature books provide. The seasonal approach is a sound one, since it makes the writer more observant of his home ground and helps the reader more fully inhabit that space as well, and it allows a narrow focus on particular aspects of the landscape. But in this case it doesn't provide much of an overview of that landscape. Whatever we think we understand about the terrain Leopold is walking through has come through inferences and offhand remarks, not from a thorough verbal en plein air painting.

To really understand the country Leopold observed, it's helpful to look at the photographs of the years in which he was there, 1935 to 1948. As it happens, such photographs abound, not only at the Leopold Center and in the self-guided tour booklet but also in the various biographies of Leopold and his accomplished children. When Aldo and Estella brought their children to the shack in 1935, Starker was twenty-two, his brother Luna was nineteen, Nina was eighteen, Carl was sixteen, and Estella Jr. was eight. The photos are mostly in black-and-white: Nina at twenty-one, planting a pine tree in a grassy field; all the family except Carl, the photographer, with the shack and an empty sky as backdrop in 1939; the five siblings at a rough-hewn table with dense undergrowth behind them in 1982, the year before Starker's death; one photo

of the shack from 1936 and another from ten years later, of Aldo
and a graduate student seated on a bench before it; a panoramic
photo of the property "taken from atop a hickory tree at the gate
by Levee Road, 1935"; a snapshot of the chicken coop–cow shed at
the start of its repair and renovation into the shack; a picture from
the roadside gate of a row of elm trees (now gone) leading back
to the shack and a landscape described in the caption as "treeless
and almost barren"; a picture of young Estella Jr. fetching water
from the Wisconsin River with the Parthenon a little way up the
slope behind her; a shot of her mother, Estella Leopold, carrying
a bucket of pine seedlings across an empty field.

Having walked the farm with the tour booklet in hand, I recognize only the shack and the outhouse in those pictures; they
may as well have been dropped into the present landscape from
somewhere else for all I can recognize of the terrain the photos
record. What the pictures tell me is that Aldo Leopold's almanac of essays represents an idyll in country that no one would
consider wild, or scenic, or pastoral—no landscape that evokes,
at least in photographic images, an inviting natural setting. That
Leopold found fodder for a masterpiece of nature writing there,
and that all of his five children went on to make significant contributions to the field of ecology from that setting, says a great deal
about how expansive Leopold's sense of land, of country, was.

In his essay "Country," originally published posthumously in
Round River and later, with other essays from that book, added to
an expanded edition of *A Sand County Almanac,* Leopold wrote:
"There is much confusion between land and country. Land is the
place where corn, gullies, and mortgages grow. Country is the
personality of land, the collective harmony of its soil, life, and
weather. Country knows no mortgages, no alphabetical agencies,
no tobacco road; it is calmly aloof to those petty exigencies of
its alleged owners." The theme is one he sounded in "Great Possessions" as well and in more allusive ways in other essays. He

makes some distinctions among those who encounter country, suggesting that a public preoccupation with "wilderness vistas" and "sublime panoramas" leads to a shortsighted perspective on the natural world.

> The taste for country displays the same diversity in aesthetic competence among individuals as the taste for opera, or oils. There are those who are willing to be herded in droves through "scenic" places, who find mountains grand if they are proper mountains with waterfalls, cliffs, and lakes. To such the Kansas plains are tedious. They see the endless corn but not the heave and the grunt of ox teams breaking the prairie. History, for them, grows on campuses. They look at the low horizon, but they cannot see it, as de Vaca did, under the bellies of the buffalo.
>
> In country, as in people, a plain exterior often conceals hidden riches, to perceive which requires much living in and with.

Leopold invites us to challenge our sense of where we are. The almanac is the result of much living in and with the country where he had chosen to dwell and his perceptions revealed its hidden riches. After reading Leopold, we walk out into our own country, wondering where its riches might be hidden.

5

Aldo Leopold was forty-eight years old when he purchased the farm along the Wisconsin River. Unlike youthful Scottish immigrant John Muir discovering the Wisconsin landscape eighty-six years earlier, Leopold was a native midwesterner; he had been born in 1887 in Burlington, Iowa, in a huge house on a 130-foot

limestone bluff above the Mississippi River. He grew up there and
his younger brother Frederic still lived in that house some seventy
years later. Aldo's adult life was spent elsewhere. He attended
Yale University, where he earned his bachelor of philosophy and,
in 1909, his master of forestry degrees. He joined the US Forest
Service and served in the Southwest, the background of his essays
set in Arizona, New Mexico, Chihuahua, and Sonora in part two
of *A Sand County Almanac*.

One of those essays, "Thinking Like a Mountain," records a
pivotal incident in his life, witnessing the death of a wolf he had
shot.

> We reached the old wolf in time to watch a fierce green fire
> dying in her eyes. I realized then, and have known ever since,
> that there was something new to me in those eyes—some-
> thing known only to her and to the mountain. I was young
> then, and full of trigger itch; I thought that because fewer
> wolves meant more deer, that no wolves would mean hunters'
> paradise. But after seeing the green fire die, I sensed that nei-
> ther the wolf nor the mountain agreed with such a view.

He concludes the essay by recognizing the need to "think like a
mountain," to recognize the interconnectedness of nature and the
consequences of too narrow a focus about conservation.

> Perhaps this is behind Thoreau's dictum: In wildness is the
> preservation of the world. Perhaps this is the hidden meaning
> in the howl of the wolf, long known among mountains, but
> seldom perceived among men.

The passage is often cited for its powerful evocation of a wilderness ethic and is widely admired for its literary qualities of
precision and balance and thought. When we run across it in

the book we are apt to overlook its place in Leopold's personal history. *A Sand County Almanac* carefully builds a case for a land ethic. It begins with the unthreatening passage, "There are some who can live without wild things, and some who cannot. These essays are the delights and dilemmas of one who cannot," and leads to a point of agreement with his credo, "A thing is right if it tends to preserve the integrity, stability, and beauty of the biotic community. It is wrong if it tends otherwise." It isn't only a brilliant rhetorical sequence; in some ways it replicates the process of Leopold's own evolution from simply a careful observer of the natural world to a spokesman for a complex ecological philosophy. Profound and thoughtful as the book may be, it is also a very personal and revealing portrait of the author's inner life.

During his time in the Southwest, Leopold had the opportunity as forest ranger and bureau manager to think through the policies and practices of the Forest Service. In 1922 he proposed preservation of the headwaters of the Gila River, and in 1924 the Gila Wilderness became the first wilderness area in the National Forests. That same year, Leopold, now married to Estella Bergere and the father of four children, left the Southwest for a US Forest Service position in Madison, Wisconsin; four years later he left the Forest Service altogether and worked for several years conducting game surveys for a firm manufacturing hunting equipment. In 1933 he published *Game Management* and soon joined the faculty at the University of Wisconsin teaching in the new game management program. When that developed into the Department of Wildlife Management in 1939, he became its chair. In the meantime he had been writing and publishing professional articles and keeping copious records on what he observed.

In short, the man who bought the corned-out farm in 1935 was learned and accomplished in his profession. It shouldn't be surprising that very soon he began to wonder how to reverse the damage that had been done to his land and find a way to revive it. His daughter Nina Leopold Bradley has written, "It is unlikely that Father started with a clear vision of what he was going to do with the land around the shack. But the attempt to rehabilitate it brought its own lessons, its own continuous self-renewal, and its own dedication to an increasingly sharper vision." The ensuing years were an experiment in self-discovery, in trial-and-error, in learning from experience. Thirty years after her father's death Bradley wondered:

> Did Aldo Leopold truly visualize the deep pine-and-oak forest that now, forty years later, shelters deer and provides drumming logs for grouse? Did he visualize the lush native prairie with its big bluestem grass as high as I can reach, its myriad flowers blooming in succession from spring to autumn? Did he see the return of the sandhill cranes that now dance in the big marsh? Did he anticipate the battle now being waged to prevent the aspen and dogwood he planted from taking over his prairie and marsh? Did he see a family that would never again view land casually?

The splendid careers of all five children testify to the effect of the time at the farm on Leopold's family. Whether Leopold imagined what the future of the farm would bring is difficult to answer, though Bradley speaks of what has transpired in a way that makes us realize something of the impact the family project had upon the country they worked.

The Muirs had come to wilderness, to land unsettled and uncultivated, and watched the effects of their labor alter the country—clear the trees, drain the marshes, plow the prairies; in time one form of farming replaced another and desolated land drained of its fertility was abandoned. The Leopolds had come to desolated land, the result of nearly a century of settlement and cultivation and years of drought and Dust Bowl conditions, in the wake of an era of conservation that people like John Muir had inspired and government policies concerning land use to which Leopold himself had sometimes contributed. If there's a haphazard progression here, then the question is: what next? Is the future to be an effort simply to keep things from getting worse or is it to be an effort to turn things in a different direction? What kinds of directions are possible or preferable? How do you decide which to choose? How do you decide how to achieve that direction?

Those questions don't have easy or definitive answers, but Leopold's concept of a land ethic provides an important trailhead for seeking them.

6

John Muir left Wisconsin behind him and moved restlessly out into the world, most famously through the Sierras and Alaska, founding the Sierra Club and advocating for the preservation of wilderness and the creation of national parks. Though Aldo Leopold's ideas have been widely disseminated and put into practice around the world, his enduring presence has remained centered in Wisconsin. Not only are the shack and the farm still in the family, but the Leopold Reserve preserves lands surrounding the Leopold property, and the Leopold Center, headquarters for the Aldo Leopold Foundation, is located on a moraine just down the road. The center was constructed near the place where, in 1948, trying to help put out a grass fire, Leopold died.

At the end of June, just over a month after I visited the shack on my own, my wife and I drove to the Leopold Center for a Saturday afternoon guided tour. Nina Leopold Bradley, one of the driving forces behind the construction of the center, had died exactly a month before, on May 25, at the age of ninety-three. She had lived to the west of the shack and had often appeared

at special events and tours. From the moment I'd learned about
the tours I'd harbored the hope of bumping into her, and now I
regretted the lost opportunity.

The center was once considered the "greenest" building in
America. The wood used to build it primarily came from the
Leopold farm itself or from land owned by Nina Bradley, chiefly
pine and some local oak and maple, all milled either on-site or
nearby. The pines had been planted by the Leopolds decades
earlier, a prudent bit of recycling. The lobby boasts the Rumford
fireplace, an exceptionally efficient device drawing air from floor
vents in front of it and designed to store heat. The building is car-
bon neutral, thanks to earth tubes for ventilation located below
the building, radiant floors and the occasional use of woodstoves
and fireplaces for heat, solar panels for energy, strategic placement
of overhangs, and plenty of windows for natural light. Outside,
an aqueduct channels rainwater into a rain garden. The center
that bears his name offers a very concrete example of putting
Leopold's ecological philosophy into practice.

Our tour guide was Anna Hawley, a 2007 graduate of the University of Wisconsin at Stevens Point. She told us her favorite passages in *A Sand County Almanac* were the August "Green Pasture"
essay, about the floodplain ("I know a painting so evanescent that
it is seldom viewed at all, except by some wandering deer") and
the November "If I Were the Wind" section that Nina Bradley
liked to read ("It is warm behind the driftwood now, for the wind
has gone with the geese. So would I—if I were the wind"). Both
are very lyrical passages.

We drove down to the shack, Sue and I carpooling with
Anna, the others in their own vehicles. We filled the parking area.
Among the fourteen of us were a couple from Burlington, Iowa,
who knew people now living in the former Leopold home, an
elderly woman photographer originally from Poland, two college
girls, a teacher from one of the state schools, and a family with

two teenaged boys. Some had driven from La Crosse, on the west side of the state; some had connections with Stevens Point, due north along the Wisconsin River. Anna showed us photographs of the land when the Leopolds bought it, pointed out an oak near the side of the parking area that had been there then, and led us to the prairie area, where she identified the wild indigo prominently in bloom and read a little from the book. Then she turned us toward the shack.

We stood in quiet anticipation as Anna opened the door and the front windows, like privileged visitors to a shrine, at once both curious and reverent. Then we trooped inside to sit in a back corner, across from the smoke-blackened fireplace. It was somewhat crowded for the fourteen of us and Anna, and the seven Leopolds must have found their quarters tight, especially when friends accompanied them. The interior walls were white, and the walls and shelves were filled with implements and utensils of one kind or another. Some, like a sturgeon spear used to take carp from the river to fertilize the garden and a perch for a pet hawk and pet owl, dated from the 1930s; others, because the cabin is still in use by Leopold's descendants, had been added more recently. Bunks occupied the low section of the building and a table and benches were on the higher opposite side. The kitchen area was in the back, where Anna stood near the fireplace to tell us something about the features of the building. More than one person has pointed out that, having been built entirely from found materials, heated by firewood, and lit by lantern, the shack was even greener than the Leopold Center.

Too soon, Anna closed up the shack. She led us down to the river, although it was running high and we couldn't reach the bank across flooded low areas. She emphasized the sand, explained the formation of Glacial Lake Wisconsin, and pointed out that a considerable amount of land had been added to the property by the shifting channel of the river. Earlier photos, especially one

in which Estella Jr. gets water from the river with the Parthenon visible just over her shoulder, show the river much closer to the bluff the shack sits on; now it's a considerable distance away.

Back at the shack again, Anna read the ending of "The Land Ethic" and thanked us all, letting us depart. I had come to this tour with a list of questions I hoped to get answered, mostly tied to images and occurrences in the book: How abundant are the woodcocks and is it still possible to see their mating flight as recorded in "Sky Dance"? How abundant are the upland plovers mentioned in May's "Back from the Argentine"? How abundant are the draba, the ruffed grouse, the partridge, the quail? How abundant are the sandhill cranes? Essentially I was curious about how, since Leopold's time, the variety and abundance of various fauna had changed. Anna had already answered other questions I might have asked about the river, the prairie restoration, and the woodlands. She was certain about woodcocks still being there but didn't know for sure about upland plovers. I didn't ask about the other birds because it suddenly occurred to me that what we had seen accomplished at the shack was a significant change in habitat. I mentioned to her that if you change the habitat, you automatically change what can use the habitat, and she said that one of the things the foundation might eventually have to consider was whether to remove the pines and restore the oak savanna environment that was here originally. The ecological thinking that goes on in the Leopold Center hasn't stopped trying to learn from the land.

Everyone else headed for their cars, but Sue and I decided to walk the rest of the trail so she could see the woods that the Leopolds had planted and get a fuller sense of the terrain. When we came down to the road past the Good Oak plaque, we headed back toward the Leopold Center, stopping to gaze at the oak by the parking lot, the one that had been there when Aldo Leopold first saw the farm, the one still standing seventy-five years later. Then we walked up the road, past the prairie and past the marsh, all the while pondering how we should feel about what remained and what had changed around the shack.

7

John Tallmadge, in "Anatomy of a Classic," makes a telling point about Leopold's narrator in *A Sand County Almanac:*

> Leopold loves Canada geese, sandhill cranes, and wild game of all kinds, yet he seems charmingly fond of small creatures that no one appreciates, like *Draba,* the chickadee, and the field mouse. His interest in undervalued and marginal things extends to landscape; he prefers the nondescript scenery of a sand county farm to the romantic sublimities of Muir's High

Sierra or the edenic woods and pastures of [Gilbert] White or
Thoreau. Indeed, landscape as such hardly seems to interest
him. What goes on in the land is what fascinates, and toward
this he reveals an endearing capacity for the deepest feelings.

In "Country" Leopold writes: "There are woods that are plain
to look at, but not to look into. Nothing is plainer than a cornbelt
woodlot; yet if it be August, a crushed pennyroyal, or an over-ripe
mayapple, tells you here is a place. October sun on a hickory nut
is irrefutable evidence of good country." The passage confirms
Tallmadge's assessment, although the contrast with Muir and
Thoreau may not be as sharp as he would have us think. The cabin
at Walden Pond was constructed on a woodlot, and Muir's nature
studies began around a small lake on his family's farm. Like Thoreau and Muir, as a youth Leopold tended to take long hikes from
his boarding school in New Jersey, studying birds and plants. He
had a penchant for the same kind of close observation and solitary
exploration as the earlier naturalists.

The connection between Muir and Leopold runs even deeper.
Leopold, after all, was thinking about creating a natural area at the
site of Fountain Lake Farm when he died, a scheme that reminds
us of his familiarity with *The Story of My Boyhood and Youth*, but
the connection began even earlier than that. According to Curt
Meine, author of a thorough Leopold biography, in 1934 Aldo
Leopold and his brother Carl, returning from a fishing trip to
Waushara County, stopped near Endeavor Marsh to investigate
a report of a pair of nesting sandhill cranes. A farmer "not only
told them where they might find the pair, but gave them a lengthy
history of the farm, the cranes, and the marsh." After spotting
the birds, Leopold began to research sandhill cranes both at the
marsh and at the University of Wisconsin. In 1937, in the journal *American Forests*, he published the essay "Marshland Elegy,"
which was one of the earliest essays to later be included in *A Sand*

County Almanac and a distinctive rendering of the voice of the later book. It is particularly notable for the time span it covers, giving the reader a history of the marsh as well as a history of the bird. It educates and elegizes at the same time. By coincidence, Endeavor Marsh is located along the Fox River, and it's notable that, before he purchased his shack, Leopold was already on the path to his book and that the path started near the boyhood home of John Muir.

One of the essays written much later also echoes a subject Muir wrote about in his memoir, the passenger pigeon. In "On a Monument to the Pigeon," inspired by the erection of a monument to the passenger pigeon in Wyalusing State Park in 1947, Leopold writes:

> We have erected a monument to commemorate the funeral
> of a species. It symbolizes our sorrow. We grieve because no
> living man will see again the onrushing phalanx of victorious
> birds, sweeping a path for spring across the March skies,
> chasing the defeated winter from all the woods and prairies of
> Wisconsin.
>
> Men still live who, in their youth, remember pigeons.
> Trees still live who, in their youth, were shaken by a living
> wind. But a decade hence only the oldest oaks will remember,
> and at long last only the hills will know.

In *The Story of My Boyhood and Youth* John Muir's account of seeing immense flocks of passenger pigeons overhead and watching farmers shoot them leads to a long excerpt from Audubon and a shorter quote from Pokagon. It's a memorable nine-page passage of narrative and description, and it largely serves to record the impression they made on him, among all the other birds he describes in the same chapter. Leopold takes the occasion of the monument not only to lament the extinction of the pigeon but also to tie its existence to the environment—"only the hills will know"—and to the larger issue of man's profligate nature regarding the natural world: "To love what was is a new thing under the sun, unknown to most people and to all pigeons." It's another elegy.

Of course, it's a measure of how the environment has changed that Muir is remembering what he saw and Leopold is lamenting what can never be seen again. In a sense Leopold is building on what Audubon and Muir had made memorable. The cumulative effect is to make clear that, in walking home ground, we need, in John Burroughs's phrase, to keep a sharp lookout, to really see what's there; we also need to learn what was once there before we came along and what might not be there in the future, in order to preserve the memory of what's lost and, perhaps, to impede the loss of what might disappear; and, finally, we need to know what we can preserve and what we can restore. Once we know these things, we have a better idea of what we need to do.

8

It's quiet here this September day, the prairie grasses taller than they were in June, the path mown and separate from the restored plants. Having seen sandhill cranes earlier that morning in the course of my autumn tour of Muir terrain further north, I suspect that it's the influence of "Marshland Elegy" that makes me revisit Leopold terrain around noon. By now I've learned that the Leopolds recorded no cranes in their observations during the thirties, and that the cranes of the essay were inspired by the ones at Endeavor Marsh, not the marsh across the road from the shack. But I'd seen cranes there on my first visit to the shack and the thought of cranes will likely always make me think of Leopold, just as loons always make me think of Thoreau. I have no expectations as I stroll through the pines and across the prairie and note how high grasses now obscure the sight of the shack in the background. The shack, of course, is closed up and as I stand before it and slowly survey the area, I find a humble serenity in the moment.

Remembering how high water kept us from the riverbank in June, I again follow the path behind the shack, trudging with some effort across the brown rusty sand. The river's lower now and I make it easily to the sandy beach area. Across the river I see more exposed shoreline and bare sandbars with gulls spread out across them; further downstream, a dozen or more egrets wade calmly. Midstream the river flows briskly.

Everything I've walked on since coming down the slope from the shack has been added by the river since Leopold bought the place, building on earlier deposits of sandbars and islands. To one small island, one of his daughters repeatedly made a bridge, but it's likely that most of what's here—the grasses and sand and trees and riverbank—are what he never saw, the river's restoration project. No doubt the opposite northern bank of the river has changed a lot as well since Leopold's time. Thoreau wondered about the succession of forest trees; Leopold attempted to heal and restore land where natural processes had been interrupted and human intervention had added to the process of succession; here, the river, aided no doubt by dams upstream and powered by floods in spite of dams, has made its own choices about succession and intervention.

I take my time returning from the riverbank and once more sit calmly on the Leopold bench in front of the shack. I think I'm trying to burn a disc of memory of the setting but after a while I realize I'm simply sitting, which, for a few more moments, seems enough to do. When I set off again to follow the trail past the old house foundation and the sand blow to the Good Oak plaque, I realize for the first time how many of Leopold's pines I'm walking through, along with all the volunteer oaks. Their height and their sturdy, erect stance makes it hard to imagine that, when Leopold came here, none of them existed.

Once on the pavement I amble to a side road into the reserve. It's a short distance to the end, where lowered water levels have exposed the pilings of a wooden bridge that once crossed the stream there. Someone has dumped trash in the parking area, a hostile form of human intervention. As I step closer to the water, a kingfisher flies up from the pilings and finds a limb on the opposite shore where he can scold me for startling him. I apologize but continue to stand there a few more minutes, trying to take in everything around me. Then I walk slowly up the road back to my car, pleased to have been alone at the shack, at the river, on the trail.

I drive away distractedly, still sorting out the effect Leopold's home ground has on me. Off the shoulder of the road leading away from the river I see cranes in the periphery of my vision. I drive on, but I continue to look for them in my rearview mirror until the road turns.

Interlude

SATURDAY, MARCH 26, 2011. Winter seems reluctant to leave Wisconsin. The pond near our complex, which has finally been open water for several days, has a skin of ice over two-thirds of its surface this morning. I notice the ice as I walk past on the bike path, heading toward the ball field in the park just north of the pond. For months I've been aware of a bend in the river upstream visible through the bare winter trees and shrubs on the far side of the park, a bend mostly hidden from view in more verdant seasons. Startled that I hadn't seen it before—or at least acknowledged it—I've been intending to take a closer look at it. The idea became more insistent after the February blizzard, when the stark brown trees stood out against the white snow, and the Fox River, still running open, glowed a deep blue behind them, flowing at first perpendicular to the park and then parallel to it.

From then on I looked for the bend each time I drove past. Driving by gives me a more elevated perspective that makes it easy to locate the bend, but on foot I'm not certain exactly where it is. The park is at the bottom of a ten-foot slope and the trees and undergrowth are thicker at ground level, obscuring any view of the river. When I tromp down the slope and cross the grass toward the line of trees, I thread my way through them a little too soon, coming out well below the bend. A rough path along the riverbank takes me to a point where a huge oak sprawls thick trunks in four directions close to the ground. From here I have a view of the river bend.

My arrival startles a nearby pair of mallards, who fly off complaining. In the distance two more ducks leave the water to rise up into the trees. I pull out my binoculars for a closer look and find myself staring at the first wood ducks I've ever seen in the wild. On the water I discover half a dozen more, and then I spot some buffleheads, some common goldeneyes, a pair of common mergansers, and more mallards—a surprising variety of waterfowl. It seems to be a popular spot. Except for the mallards, I've seen none of these birds on the river before. Red-winged blackbirds fly into the grasses on the shore and chickadees call from deeper in the woods. My presence causes no more alarm and I watch through binoculars as long as I can stand still in the cold. Then I find an easier, more direct path out of the woods.

I cut back across the ballfield, the grass flecked with snow, and climb the slope. The sun at 9:30 has begun to affect the edge of the ice sheet on the pond but, as cold as it is, I'm sure it won't shrink much.

I follow the paved path between the pond and our complex back toward the river. Last weekend we had two days of heavy rain, and with the melting snow and the rain, the river has been running high. The floodplain glistens from the water spread across it, and I am certain that the path will be flooded near the observation deck. We've had several dry days and very cold nights and the hummocks of sedge between the path and the river seem separated by ice rather than by water.

Still, as persistent as winter is, the birds are ready for spring. I see robins and red-winged blackbirds and hear birdsong all along the path. Once I have a close-up view of a singing song sparrow and pause to listen to him warble and trill. A few other birds are too fleet of wing for me to identify, but they are distinctive enough for me to realize they aren't anything I've seen or heard already this morning.

At the entrance to the woods the path runs closer to the flood-plain and I begin to see more signs of flooding the closer I get to the observation deck. The foremost pilings of the deck are now in water and the platform seems to overlook a lake. The river here meanders through the wetlands, swings east and then west and then east again, approaching the deck and turning abruptly south to glide away from it. The sedges are usually high and dry and the channel of the river readily visible. Today, except for a few slightly higher parcels of land that have become islands, it is almost impossible to tell where the river usually runs. Around one of the islands I see a pair of mallards, as well as Canada geese in pairs or groups of three or four, no more than a dozen altogether. At one point a gander on one island storms across the shore of another to chase off two geese that were calmly standing there. The other geese ignore the fracas and drift around the island calmly.

The sun is bright, the wind brisk, and snow flurries persistent, sometimes so light as to be barely noticeable, sometimes so intense as to cloud the air. When my hands become too cold to write notes or to hold my binoculars steady, I head home, well contented. I didn't set out to have a lively birding day and I appreciate how lucky I've been. All I wanted was to become better acquainted with the river and, with the help of the birds, I've gotten that as well.

The Pattern of the Seasons:
Walking with August Derleth

1

I END MY FIRST day trying to walk in the footsteps of August Derleth at the Ferry Bluff Natural Area, along the Wisconsin River southwest of Sauk City. A dead-end dirt road brought me into thick woods and a place to park at road's end, where Ferry Bluff towers above the road; a trail to the south led me through shady forest on a steep climb up to the open space of Cactus Bluff, a lower prominence. From here I have a panoramic view of the Wisconsin River. I supposedly can see the Wisconsin Heights battlefield of the Black Hawk War across the river and, to the southwest, Blue Mound, at 1,716 feet the highest point in southern Wisconsin. It's possible I do, but it's hard for me to tell. Mostly I take in these 500,000,000-year-old bluffs and the hawk's-eye view of the Wisconsin River.

Downstream, grassy and occasionally well-wooded islands interrupt the broad river; upstream near the east bank is a long, narrow island with young trees throughout two-thirds of it. The river seems very wide here and forest covers both shores as far as I can see in either direction, though beyond the woods to the north and east I also discern narrow strips of cultivated or cleared land and some very tall structures.

I'm trying to sort out what to make of the kind of day I've had, what I've learned and what I've seen and what I've been unable to see in my rambles around Sauk City and Prairie du Sac. It hasn't been a day like those first days tracing Muir and Leopold. Walking their home grounds at Muir Park and the Leopold Center, I was in specifically circumscribed locales, places expressly preserved to allow me to do that. The Sac Prairie setting that was August Derleth's home ground is less accommodating.

It's not because Derleth has been forgotten in the twin villages of Sauk City and Prairie du Sac. One entrance to Sauk City is the August Derleth Bridge across the Wisconsin River; a historical marker stands at the entrance to August Derleth Park; August Derleth's image is included on a sesquicentennial mural by the side of the road. The Sauk City Public Library has an August Derleth Room in its basement, housing material from the August Derleth Society, and the Tripp Memorial Museum in Prairie du Sac contains an August Derleth exhibit, complete with Derleth's chair, writing table, and one of his old typewriters, with photocopies of typescript scrolled around its platen and piled nearby. (The Concord Museum has a similar display for Henry David Thoreau, a parallel that would surely have pleased Derleth.) In Sac Prairie, August Derleth's presence is inescapable.

But the challenges to walking Derleth's home ground are multiple. For one thing, it's so encompassing. He was a habitual walker not only of woods and river bottoms and bluffs but also of residential streets and business blocks. He recorded his wanderings in a voluminous private journal, numerous essays and poems, and six books of personal nonfiction. Some of the books handily have endpaper and interior maps locating the sites mentioned in the books. There's no shortage of material to draw on.

In the Sauk City Library's August Derleth Room I found an article declaring "Derleth was Wisconsin's Thoreau" and encouraging readers to walk the land that Derleth walked, just what I came here hoping to do. Another article provided locations that figure in Derleth's books: his birthplace, his boyhood home, his girlfriend Margery's house, the *Freie Gemeindehalle*, and the Schwenker harness shop. An article posted in the Tripp Museum exhibit gave addresses for houses specifically mentioned in one book, *Walden West*.

I mapped a tour for myself of Derleth-related sites. The birthplace house looked to have been entirely renovated or possibly replaced; the boyhood home was well cared for on a quiet street, as was the girlfriend's house. Other buildings, like the *Freie Gemeindehalle*, built in 1884 by German Freethinkers who had come to Sauk City as early as 1852, was interesting in its own right, and some of the other houses were suitable for a tour of home design. However, none of the buildings is specifically preserved as a Derleth-related site. I found myself agreeing with a brochure for a walking tour of Prairie du Sac that advised tourists to view the homes from the sidewalk and to maintain the privacy of the current residents—it would serve no purpose to do otherwise.

Derleth often walked the streets of Sauk City and Prairie du Sac, observing the lighted interiors of houses as he passed, claiming, "Each house has about it atmosphere of time past, and this atmosphere of houses is the atmosphere of towns, the ceaselessly changing aspect of time and age." The theme emerges in several of his books, including *Walden West*, but in autumn midday sunlight, I could read very little atmosphere of the houses at which I gazed.

Searching for something more tangible, I drove out to Lueders Road, where the place he started out from on many of his walks and the place he finally ended up are across the road from each other. At St. Aloysius Cemetery, on the outskirts of town, I easily located Derleth's grave. The grave marker isn't large, but it's distinctive: a marble bench with a seated cherub leaning against the square support of a sundial, intently reading. A small garden gnome stands at the base, and on a metal pole beside the bench hang a wind chime with a butterfly to activate it and a golden sun medallion with twin metal spirals below and small cups to catch the wind. At times it is likely the liveliest grave in the cemetery.

Inscribed in the top of the bench is Derleth's favorite quote from *Walden:* "I wished to live deliberately, to front only the essential facts of life, and see if I could not learn what it had to teach and not, when I came to die, discover that I had not lived." As with the other places Derleth quotes it, here too Thoreau's opening phrase, "I came to the woods because . . . ," is missing, and its absence gives Derleth the broader implication he took from it. The epitaph reinforced my sense of Derleth's sense of connection with Thoreau.

Across the road, Derleth's house, Place of Hawks, stood in deep shade behind thick trees and a high, gated metal fence. From the shoulder of the road I could barely make it out. I saw no signs of life around the place. Together the grave and the house seemed to emphasize Derleth's absence.

I looked again at the photocopies of those endpaper maps and tried to decide where to go. The oldest map I had dated back more than seventy years, and Derleth had been dead for forty of those years. Sac Prairie had changed considerably during those decades, which led to the other great challenge to walking Derleth's home ground—discovering today anything that could give me a sense of his yesterday.

I'd come here prepared to visit several sites in particular, but when I asked the curator at the Tripp Museum about them, he told me that at least two were no longer accessible. What Derleth referred to as the Big Hill across the river had been quarried into oblivion by a gravel plant; a railroad trestle Derleth is pictured near in a well-known photograph, on which he often crossed the Wisconsin River to reach what he called the Spring Slough, now had a long impassable gap midchannel—apparently flood-waters pushed the rails out of alignment and an effort to realign the trestles with dynamite destroyed the center of the bridge. I had envisioned myself climbing that hill, ambling across that trestle, gazing out at the view from places Derleth sat, and dili-gently journaling my impressions of the terrain and the feelings the moment inspired. I suddenly remembered driving out on Cape Cod once to visit the Outermost House that Henry Beston had written about and arriving at a sign that told me the house had been swept out to sea years before. As then, I was more than a little disconcerted now.

On the old endpaper map I could see where the trestle would be and the route Derleth must have taken to reach it, so I drove to the trestle, hoping the curator was overly pessimistic about the chances of getting across the river there. He wasn't. I parked in a hardware store lot, crossed the street to the narrow gravel shoul-der above the river, and stood looking at two trestles end to end. One foundation was below me on the west bank, another was in the middle of the river, and a third was on the east bank. A rusty, gated fence closed off the western trestle. When I peered through it directly down the center of the trestle, I could see the space where the far end had fallen away and the second trestle began. Grasses grew on the section of trestle still suspended above the river. Clearly I'd have no chance of reaching the Spring Slough trestle and Bergen's Island from this direction, and neither trestle was the one behind Derleth in that familiar photograph.

By the time I eventually came to Ferry Bluff, I was all too aware of how disconnected I felt to everything I'd seen. Sac Prairie, his name for this area, continued to be well aware of his former presence; but, as I reviewed the day's wanderings, I didn't know how any of it could help me understand what it was like for August Derleth to walk his home ground.

Getting ready to leave the bluff and head for home, I happen to glance up. A hawk hovers and glides high overhead, his broad wings outstretched, his white underside bright in sunlight. He almost seems to be circling my location. I vaguely remember Derleth remarking once that after death he'd come back as a hawk. I wonder if this hawk is him. When you're needing encouragement, any possible sign can provide it. I give the hawk a little salute. He's as good a sign as I'm likely to get today.

2

In the opening pages of *Walden West,* varying a description he had given twenty years earlier at the start of *Village Year,* his first "Sac Prairie Journal," August Derleth locates Sac Prairie "on the edge of the great driftless area, on a fertile, outthrust paw of land in a fine unbroken curve from west to north pushing out to west by south."

He helps us get a sense of the terrain: "The Wisconsin River is its eastern edge; to the west and to the north the undulant prairie rolls in a succession of slowly rising terraces to the foothills and the bluffs; to the south, the bottoms border the river to the Ferry Bluff range in the southwest. Across the river is the soft line of the moraine where the glacier stopped."

The moraine he mentions is the Johnstown Moraine, not so pronounced opposite Sauk City as it is elsewhere in the area, but actually the formation that marks the limit of the Green Bay Lobe's advance during the Wisconsin Glaciation, the final time the Laurentide Ice Sheet crept into the area. The moraine angles northwest toward the Baraboo Hills; everything to the east and northeast of it bears the marks of that glaciation, including the land where the Muirs established Fountain Lake Farm and the Leopolds restored the shack; and everything to the west falls into the Driftless Area and the Central Plain, where outwash and melt-water created Glacial Lake Wisconsin.

The Wisconsin River flowed a different course before the gla-cial lake was formed. But in time, a catastrophic flood emptied the lake and the Wisconsin River formed a new channel, carving in the process the sandstone formations of the Wisconsin Dells. The river flowed east and then arched around south to eventually head southwest to the Mississippi. Aldo Leopold's shack is on the southern bank of the eastbound section, and roughly thirty miles directly south—at least forty miles or more if you travel by river—is August Derleth's Sac Prairie, twin villages on the western bank of the river.

The two writers have in common the river and the history of agriculture in its floodplain, but the terrain around Sac Prairie has a different feel to it. From the east you descend to the river to cross into either Prairie du Sac ("Upper Sac Prairie" in Derleth's label-ing) or Sauk City ("Lower Sac Prairie")—both villages named for the Sac, or Sauk, tribe that US expansion displaced from the prairie stretching west from the river. If you continue west you cross a long stretch of flat land before you reach the bluffs and hills in the distance. As Derleth summed it up: "It lies in a setting of great natural beauty, in a kind of valley, with the slow river flowing broadly past, surrounded on all sides by low, wooded hills—near on the east, far on all other horizons."

Derleth's home ground is essentially that encompassing the hills east of the river, the marshes and bottomlands along the Wisconsin River, the floodplain forest and the islands accessible by way of railroad trestles and railroad tracks, the bluffs and banks lining the west side of the river, and the streets that led him past the houses and shops of the twin villages where he spent the entirety of his life.

The duration of his wanderings there adds a different dimension to our sense of his home ground than we had with Muir's dozen years at Fountain Lake Farm and Leopold's dozen years at the shack. Muir came to his home ground when it was untrammeled wilderness; Leopold came to his farm after it had been depleted and long abandoned; Derleth was born into the fourth generation to have occupied and developed those villages along the river, and he rambled around his stretch of territory for sixty-two years, taking in changes not only in the land but also in the community the land surrounded. He walked through the natural world and recorded what he saw and heard and smelled in tandem with his walks through the social world of his community. His journals preserve his accounts of flora and fauna, as well as accounts of personalities and behaviors and interactions with townspeople. Everything he recorded was potentially of use in his writing, be it fiction—neighbors and acquaintances were accustomed to identifying one another in the characters inhabiting Derleth's novels and short stories—or poetry—in his journal books he often mentions locations where he wrote specific poems, some published in those very books or in his own

subsequent collections—or nonfiction—the journal books are
full of conversations and encounters with local people, particularly at Hugo Schwenker's harness shop, and vignettes of his walks
to various locales.

Derleth never published a nature book per se—the only one
that fits that description, *In the Course of My Walks,* is actually a
posthumous editing and reprinting of the nature interludes in
Return to Walden West—but he did publish a great deal of nature writing in literary and outdoor magazines throughout his
career, material taken from his journals and often included later
as segments of his journal books or as elements of *Walden West*
and *Return to Walden West.* He contributed short prose vignettes
and longer essays to *Trails* from 1933 through 1934, to *Outdoors*
from 1934 to 1942, and to *Country Book* from 1942 to 1948. From
1945 to 1953 he published a quarterly series of nature essays in *The
Passenger Pigeon: A Magazine of Wisconsin Bird Study,* first under
a seasonal title ("Sac Prairie Winter," "Sac Prairie Spring"), and
later under the title "Country Calendar." Notably, the series was
interrupted in 1950 and 1951 by eight contributions under the
title "*Walden West* (Excerpts)"; an explanatory note claimed that
Walden West was "a spiritual autobiography" and "a logical out-
growth of the Sac Prairie Journal." Seven of the excerpts appeared
ten years later in the published book. In the same period he published three pieces in the literary journal *Prairie Schooner:* "Lives
of Quiet Desperation" (Spring 1948), "Excerpts from Walden
West" (Fall 1950), and "Passages from Walden West" (Summer
1953). All these excerpts give some indication of both how Derleth found multiple venues for his work-in-progress and also how
long *Walden West,* unlike most of his other books, was in progress.

The Sac Prairie Journal, as Derleth referred to his daily journal keeping, ran continuously from 1935 up until the end of his
life in 1971, and though many of the entries might emphasize
town characters or personal business or musings about writing

in progress, the nature entries were a continuous element of the writing throughout those thirty-five years. Reading the entirety of Derleth's journal, most but not all of it available in the Wisconsin Historical Society Library archives, would be a mammoth undertaking. But the four journal books—*Village Year: A Sac Prairie Journal* (published in 1941), *Village Daybook: A Sac Prairie Journal* (1947), *Countryman's Journal* (1963), and *Wisconsin Country: A Sac Prairie Journal* (1965)—which collectively cover the period from 1935 to 1942, contain a great deal of material revised and edited from those journals, material that may be thought of as Derleth's idea of the highlights. They are amicable and accessible and atmospheric.

Walden West and *Return to Walden West* are in some ways sequels to those journal books, drawing on much the same source of material, but neither is bound to the calendar and each endeavors to stay true to the intentions announced in their early pages: "An Exposition on Three Related Themes. I. On the persistence of memory; II. On the sounds and odors of the country; III. Of Thoreau: The mass of men lead lives of quiet desperation."

When I look for a way to walk August Derleth's home ground, it's to the nature interludes in the Walden West books that I turn.

3

"A memoir of my interior life," as August Derleth called it in the autographed first edition copy I own, seems a fair description of *Walden West*. Although the journal books that preceded it, *Village Year* and *Village Daybook,* and the ones that followed it, *Countryman's Journal* and *Wisconsin Country,* are largely casual and conversational, they aren't as intimate or as insistently reflective about his life as *Walden West* is.

Those "three related themes"—"the persistence of memory,"

"the sounds and odors of the country," and "The mass of men lead[ing] lives of quiet desperation"—run throughout the book. Derleth's epigraphs for the book are the quote taken from Thoreau about living deliberately, later carved onto his tombstone, and a line from *Pluies (Rains)* by Saint-John Perse, who won the Nobel Prize for Literature in 1960: *"Innombrables sont nos voies, et nos demeures incertaines"* ("Innumerable are our ways, and our dwellings uncertain"). Both epigraphs speak to the intentionality behind the book and behind its author's life. In the prologue, explaining his decision to return permanently to Sac Prairie after a mere six months away, Derleth sounds a Thoreauvian note:

> I set about to write so that I might afford the leisure in which to improve my acquaintance with the setting and the inhabitants—hills, trees, ponds, people, birds, animals, sun, moon, stars—of the region I had chosen to inhabit, not as a retreat, but as a base of operations into a life more full in the knowledge of what went on in the woods as well as in the houses along the streets of Sac Prairie and in the human heart.

The book proper begins with an italicized section—these interludes, usually reflecting on nature, occur throughout the book—recounting something of Sac Prairie's past and declaring it to be, in essence, a microcosm of "countless other villages" throughout the country. It is a country, he writes, "to be explored . . . by a walker in its lanes and byways, . . . a walker bent upon knowing the least bird as well as the least fellowman, an explorer of past time as well as of today." The figure he's portraying is himself, of course, someone "determined to know the patterns of the world of which he himself was an integral part by choice," yet someone well aware "that what every man knows about himself and his world is but the most infinitesimal part of knowledge, and what he can know about someone else and someone else's world is even less than that." Walking home ground for August Derleth was a different experience than it was for John Muir or Aldo Leopold because Derleth was tied to its past as well as to its present, and to its community as well as to its environment.

Derleth's ancestors had come from Zinl, Bavaria, to the United States in 1839 and to Sauk City, Wisconsin's oldest incorporated village, in 1852. His great-grandfather established a blacksmith shop, which his grandfather and his father ran in their turns, and which was an important site in Derleth's upbringing. In the early sections of *Walden West* he talks about the childhood influences of family and teachers, Grandfather Derleth prominent among them. His grandfather often took him fishing at Lodde's millpond southwest of town and talked to him about life: "He preached honesty and honor and truth, he spoke of the value of money and the need of man to work, which were lessons I never forgot." Derleth credits Sister Anaclete at St. Aloysius Catholic School with inspiring him to be creative and Sister Isabelle with fostering his interest in both nature and writing. A spinster named Annie Maegerlin gave him clippings of Thornton W. Burgess's nature stories from which he traces a path "straight to Thoreau by way of Ernest Thompson Seton and John Burroughs." Derleth in essence charts the path of his creative life in those early segments.

It was his high school teacher, Miss Frieda Schroeder, who entangled him with Thoreau and Emerson. Derleth admits to having had a crush on the young, attractive woman and being inspired to read classic American literature to win her approval. "I took up Emerson's *Essays,* and what I read there and in *Walden* profoundly influenced the course of my life," he claims, perhaps because "I was already then conditioned to accept without question what I read in Emerson and Thoreau." He felt, "There is in every life the right time for enlightenment . . . and I had come to it, and the door had been opened for the light to flow in . . . only such a light as to illumine my own path through the years ahead." He wrote that what he "found profoundly true in Emerson, I found even more true to my nature in Thoreau's *Walden*," where he discovered "justification for my dawning belief that . . . Sac Prairie was the microcosm that reflected the macrocosm of the world." These are sentiments that occur elsewhere in his writing, often in almost the same words.

The section on Miss Schroeder is followed immediately by a long profile of Josephine Merk, the librarian at the public library, who was his friend for many years and whose slow death is recorded in entries of *Village Year*, and finally by a section on H. P. Lovecraft, who was a correspondent and an influence on Derleth's work in genre fiction. Derleth claimed that Lovecraft "had found his private Walden, near rural areas of his childhood's city, Providence, Rhode Island" and had written that "a man belongs where he has roots—where the landscape and the milieu have some relation to his thoughts and feelings, by virtue of having formed them." Derleth credited Lovecraft, along with Frieda Schroeder and Josephine Merk, with guiding his reading and reinforcing his decision to write about Sac Prairie, "to remain in this western Walden and draw from it my sustenance and strength."

Long before Derleth began the conscious effort to compose *Walden West*, he was practicing the principles it espouses: commitment to native terrain, close observation of natural and social events and behaviors, meticulous recordkeeping of daily experiences. One can read Derleth's personal journal as a kind of phenology of Sac Prairie, not only of its wildlife but of its citizenry as well. As early as 1939 he published *Atmosphere of Houses*, a forty-five-page book he claimed was taken from *Evening in Spring*, a novel that wouldn't be published until 1941—actually it's an expansion and enlargement on a theme sounded at only a few different places in the novel. *Atmosphere of Houses* is nonfiction, centering on houses as a way into the lives of their occupants. In

Walden West Derleth returns to that theme: "Often, walking the streets and lanes of Sac Prairie, I have been made to think that houses exist on an extraterrestrial plane—not merely as structures of wood or stone, of glass and brick, but as edifices created by people and events, the people who have lived in them and the events of their existence." He explains,

> This atmosphere of houses becomes in time an integral
> part of the night life of the mind of the village dweller; as
> for instance when one nears a park conscious of the deeper
> darkness there is in that part of town, so one nears and passes
> houses with cognizance of their existence in an aura or atmo-
> sphere of past time inextricably linked with the present. And
> in Sac Prairie this was all the more so as the years passed.

He recalls one summer when he habitually walked from the back street to the main street of Upper Sac Prairie and felt "the atmosphere of houses was as inescapable as the very air I breathed, and indeed a part of that air."

This is the distinguishing characteristic of Derleth's version of *Walden*—profiles of individuals he encounters are as central to his writing as the natural terrain he wanders. Sometimes the profiles are admiring or affectionate, often they confirm the quiet desperation with which these people lead their lives, but always they are compassionate and empathetic, partly because Derleth himself, for all his gregariousness, feels a bond with the isolated and the solitary. Of such a figure early in the book, Joe Lippert, the riverman who "was a solitary by inclination," Derleth claims, "when he died at last, he left behind him a legacy so strong that I never walked into the islands along his old paths without the conviction that I might meet him at any moment." In the houses he describes, the Keysers live and die alone; Harry Mills kills

himself over his thwarted love affair with Jenny Baker, who, de-
nied his love by her parents, never marries; Ella Bickford pines
away for a lost love; and a son-in-law in the Cummings house
shoots himself and his son is institutionalized. Relatively few of
the people Derleth observes without befriending end happily or
live without desperation.

To walk August Derleth's home ground, then, is not only to
walk the hills, prairies, and riverbanks but also to walk village
streets and lanes and country backroads. And yet the nature writing in *Walden West* has a particular intensity and drive. Thirty-six
italicized segments break up the profiles and narrative reminis-
cences in roman (unitalicized) type. As Norbert Blei has observed, in a very shrewd article on the book, "approximately four
of these sections appear only indirectly concerned with nature."
He cites the opening interlude, one about a single-track train, one
about Christmas cookie cutters, and one about watching Hugo
Schwenker at work. The thirty-two interludes concerned with
nature tend to concentrate on wildlife—purple martins, grack-
les, woodcocks, veeries, whip-poor-wills, hawks, peewees, song
sparrows, frogs, snakes, the wind—or on odors—the "musk" of
the river, the smell of grass, the perfume of spring—or on seasons—autumn, winter, spring, summer, the vernal equinox—or
on locations—the Spring Slough, the bottoms, the marshes, the
Big Hill.

Often in these interludes the hour is late, evening or night;
usually the narrator is a solitary walker, content to be an observer
of the natural world, content to be alone in his sauntering. The
italicized segments make up less than a fifth of the book—yet,
mixed within his reflections and narratives about his own life
and the lives of fellow townspeople, these interludes bring a restorative sense of calm. What Derleth notices and records in his
ramblings on the outskirts of his town helps center him. He identifies with the lives of quiet desperation his neighbors lead, but

the natural world he goes out into makes him feel less solitary, more connected to something lasting, something less desperate.

4

When you read the works of a single author, it's often easy to isolate that writer from the community of writers to which he belonged. I'm struck by the proximity of Fountain Lake Farm, the shack, and Sac Prairie to one another and curious whether these writers affected one another. John Muir arrived in Wisconsin two years after Henry Thoreau left the woods at Walden Pond; and when Thoreau died, in 1862, Muir was a sophomore at the University of Wisconsin. Muir studied with James Davie Butler, who, according to Edwin Way Teale, was a friend and disciple of Ralph Waldo Emerson, introduced Muir to the writing of Emerson and Thoreau, and encouraged Muir to keep a journal. Muir came to know Emerson and in later years visited the graves of both Emerson and Thoreau, whose portraits he kept on the mantel of his home in California. References to Thoreau pop up in Muir's writing; one of Muir's early essays seems particularly indebted to the essay "Walking," and Muir biographer Frederick Turner claims that Muir "could quote whole passages from [Thoreau's] works, especially *Walden*." Emerson reportedly had said, "Muir would be the perfect man to edit Thoreau's works."

When John Muir died in 1914, Aldo Leopold was twenty-seven, a Yale graduate in forestry working for the US Forest Service in New Mexico, who would come to Wisconsin in 1924. Leopold was familiar with the writing of both Thoreau and Muir. He cites each of them in *A Sand County Almanac*, and, shortly before his sudden death on Muir's birthday in 1948, he proposed that Muir's boyhood farm site be designated a state natural area. One curious concurrence of events was Leopold's study of cranes on Endeavor Marsh along the west bank of the Fox River, several miles from where Muir grew up. We can't make too much of that coincidence except to note that in 1935, years after Leopold wrote "Marshland Elegy," the earliest piece in what became *A Sand County Almanac*, he found his own farm site along the Wisconsin River and began the work that might restore his land to the condition in which Muir had first encountered his.

That same year, farther downstream on the Wisconsin, August Derleth, a twenty-six-year-old graduate of the University of Wisconsin, where Muir had gone to school and Leopold was teaching forestry management, had settled into a life centered in the community into which he'd been born and raised, his Sac Prairie. During the time remaining to Leopold, roughly twelve years, Derleth's nature writing would appear scattered across various magazines, in two books drawn from his journals, and in *The Wisconsin: River of a Thousand Isles* (1942), his contribution to the Rivers of America series.

The two men seemed to have had contact only during one short period. On May 27, 1943, Leopold wrote to Derleth complimenting him on *The Wisconsin* and mentioning a few individuals he thought worthy of Derleth's attention as "notables" from the Wisconsin River region. Leopold also enclosed correspondence from Louis Clas. Leopold had been charged with evaluating Clas's proposal to donate to the University of Wisconsin land on Bergen's Island, across the river from Sauk City. Leopold wrote to Derleth, "I wonder if you would tell me by scribbling one sentence at the bottom of this letter whether you see in his island any notable or biological values." He specifically assured Derleth that he needn't explain his reasons but, "if your reply indicates a doubt," Leopold would be willing to withhold judgment "until we can talk the thing over."

There seems to be no record of Derleth's side of the correspondence, but Leopold's letters to Derleth are archived, and Derleth's conversation with Clas is mentioned in Derleth's journal. The entry for June 6, 1943, remarks that Clas, then eighty-two, walked out to Derleth's house that morning "to discuss the disposition of the Class [*sic*] acreage on Bergen's Island, which had been offered to the University of Wisconsin, and about which Aldo Leopold had written him. He had also written me." Clas claimed that he had persuaded various nieces and nephews to renounce any claim to the property and expressed an eagerness to be rid of it before he died. The man stayed an hour and a half, giving a rambling account of his memories of the island, and when he left, Derleth only commented, "Thereafter I returned to my work, considerably behind."

Apparently, though, Derleth did respond to Leopold. On June 8, Leopold wrote back to thank Derleth for his willingness "to take a look at the place with me" and promised to write "shortly, proposing a particular time." In an undated handwritten note to Derleth on the same letterhead stationery as the typed letters, sent on a Thursday, Leopold promised he would call at Derleth's place that Saturday, "in the hope that you can show me Mr. Clas' island." Leopold likely would have been on his way to or staying at the shack over the weekend.

Derleth makes no mention in his journal of having met with Leopold or visiting Bergen's Island with him. But on July 9, Leopold wrote to Clas, turning down his offer. "I have looked over the island in company with Mr. August Derleth, who kindly showed me the property lines and the vegetation," Leopold wrote, mentioning that "Mr. Derleth pointed out to me that even in the absence of any immediate use, the maintenance costs would be negligible" and assuring Clas, "Personally, I am keenly appreciative of the things the island has on it, particularly the wahoo, woodcock, and partridge." Derleth received a copy of this letter, and Leopold sent him a further explanation a few days later: "I found that the University has a fixed policy against accepting gifts of land for which it has no foreseeable use. That knocked out our island."

No further mention of Derleth shows up in Leopold's archives, but in Derleth's I find the review he wrote of *A Sand County Almanac* for his "Minority Report" column in the *Capital Times,* dated November 5, 1949. It's a very positive, enthusiastic review of both the book and the writer. Derleth wrote, "All genuine conservationists throughout Wisconsin and the Midwest generally realized that in the death of Aldo Leopold Wisconsin lost one of its most able men in the field of conservation." Leopold's book was "one of those rare volumes to which sensitive and intelligent readers will turn again and again," a book "certain to become a minor nature classic, and a milepost in conservation literature." He admired the way Leopold "makes one see and hear the aspects of earth he sees and hears—the skunk coming from hibernation in dead of winter, the carp exploring the inundated land, the gabbling of migratory geese, the sky dance of the woodcock, the upland plover, trout fishing, etc." He quotes liberally from Leopold's foreword, letting the author's words carry the most weight, and concludes that the book deserves a place on bookshelves beside Thoreau and Burroughs and other nature writers.

Though Leopold was clearly the more learned and scientifically educated of the two men, Derleth was thoroughly knowledgeable about the flora and fauna of Sac Prairie and the islands and bottomlands along the Wisconsin River. I suspect that, on the occasion of their tour of Bergen's Island, they made amiable company, the tall, burly writer in his thirties and the slender, solid professor in his fifties. They likely followed Derleth's route from his house on Lueders Road to the railroad trestle and crossed to the island that way. I can imagine them standing on the trestle looking off at Bergen's Island and wish someone had been around to photograph the moment; I'd also like to see a picture of Derleth at the shack, taking a look at what Leopold and his family were up to, sitting with Leopold on a Leopold bench against the front wall. As of this moment, however, I have no evidence that Derleth ever visited the shack.

There's no reason to think that Derleth had any impact on Leopold's writing. But it's possible that Leopold's writing had some impact on Derleth.

Derleth tended to write and to publish as quickly as he could. His prolific output of historical novels, mysteries, horror stories, juvenile books, biographies, histories, and poems is virtually the first fact anyone ever learns about him. He had an outsized ambition in regard to his Sac Prairie Saga, which at one point was to comprise fifty novels, and he drew upon his voluminous journals for some of the nonfiction books he compiled. To read the journal books consecutively (though not in the order published) is, in essence, to cover the years 1935–1942 in Derleth's life and the life of his community: *Village Year* covers December 1935–December 1938; *Village Daybook,* January 1939–December 1940; *Wisconsin Country,* 1941; and *Countryman's Journal,* 1942.

The difference between the Walden West books (*Walden West* and *Return to Walden West*) and the journal books is not simply a change in format—the Walden West books don't follow the journal sequence—it's also a shift in focus. *Walden West* and *Return to Walden West* are much more reflective, philosophical, chastened. Both are a series of segments alternating between meditations on nature around Sac Prairie and profiles of individual citizens. Derleth doesn't always make clear when things happened, but I feel the stories he's telling in *Walden West* often are set in earlier decades, about people from the previous century who expired in his youth. In *Return* some of the characters from the journals are the subject of the profiles, Derleth more observant, analytical, detailed about their backgrounds and their fates than in the journal books. Memory runs through both books, the memory of outings around the river and of the individuals he's met in his solitary walks around town; the nature entries often focus on sounds and odors; and almost all the profiles document lives of quiet desperation, though in *Return* the subjects aren't always neurotic and solitary. A number of critics have commented on the slower, more conscientious pace at which Derleth worked on these books, which accounts for their greater power, lyricism, and reflection.

I can't help but wonder whether *A Sand County Almanac* contributed to Derleth's desire to exercise more craft in these books. In his review Derleth emphasized that "*A Sand County Almanac* is divided into three parts, the first of which is a kind of journal of life on the author's sand farm weekend refuge, month by month, an account of things seen and heard. The second part consists of random sketches designed to show how Leopold learned that most people were out of step and how he became the ardent conservationist he was. Finally, the third part sets forth a philosophy of conservation." There is something of a correspondence here with Derleth's identifying each Walden West book as "An Exposition on Three Related Themes." Reading Leopold may have inspired Derleth to raise the level of his game in his nonfiction.

Obviously Leopold wasn't the only influence. Throughout his career Derleth consistently drew upon models from other writers: his Solar Pons series of mysteries were "pastiches" of the Sherlock Holmes stories of Arthur Conan Doyle; his horror stories expanded what he termed the "Cthulhu Mythos" of his friend H. P. Lovecraft; his attention to local characters and community bore resemblances to the midwestern focus of Edgar Lee Masters and Sherwood Anderson—certainly echoes of *Spoon River Anthology* and *Winesburg, Ohio* can be heard in his profiles of individual characters. Derleth's best works in nonfiction seem to merge the perspective of Masters in particular—he was a friend and at one point, when Derleth was engaged to Marcia Masters, a prospective father-in-law—with the perspective of his most persistent influence, Henry David Thoreau. While Thoreau's influence on Muir led to a life in wilderness and nature advocacy, his influence on Derleth was more pervasive, even if Derleth's focus in his nonfiction wasn't as contained as either Thoreau's or Muir's. After all, the Walden West books are titled after Thoreau's great book, their third theme is a quote from Thoreau, and Derleth even named his son Walden. Among his other books are two poetry titles centered on Thoreau and Walden, *And You, Thoreau* and *Rendezvous in a Landscape;* a biography, *Concord Rebel: A Life of Henry D. Thoreau;* and *Walden Pond: Homage to Thoreau,* a compilation of three journal entries from trips to the pond in 1938, 1947, and 1965. Thoreau and Walden have significant presence in Derleth's view of himself and of his world.

Derleth's reading of Thoreau reinforced both a fondness for nature and a tendency to feel connected to his home ground. His regular contributions to magazines like *Trails, Outdoors, Country Book,* and *The Passenger Pigeon,* totaling more than a hundred pieces between 1933 and 1953, are all based on his nature walks around Sac Prairie and the journal entries he compiled about them, as Thoreau's *Walden* was. Derleth may have been a novelist, poet, editor, and publisher, but throughout his career he also saw himself as a regional nature writer with a strictly local focus.

Not a man much given to travel—he spent six months in Minneapolis before giving up his editing job to return permanently to Sauk City—he made his first pilgrimage to Concord and Walden Pond in September 1938, but he had been keeping a daily journal, as Thoreau did, from much earlier. His archive in the Wisconsin Historical Society Library maintains typed entries from December 14, 1935, to January 11, 1970, a thirty-five-year span. He published his books based on his journals after his first visit to Walden; *Village Year* also included items from the *Outdoors Magazine* series between 1934 and 1939, and *Village Daybook* included more *Outdoors* items from 1939 to 1941. The second visit to Walden Pond may have incited his interest in really writing a *Walden* of his own. In *Walden Pond*, his revised journal entry for September 12, 1947, declares:

> For every one who finds his private Walden, there are many thousands who never know a refuge, whose existence is mere resignation, who never learn that the universe is wider than their view of it. To Thoreau his Walden, to me Sac Prairie—a sort of Walden West, in which I have traveled no less widely than Thoreau at Concord, and in which I am involved as much as if not more than he in his village, each taking time to explore his private seas, as well as to improve his acquaintance with the setting and its inhabitants, learning what goes on not only in the woods but also in the hearts of men.

He likely had made that connection years before, but the passage here sounds very much like the moment he felt inspired to write *Walden West*. Apparently he worked on the book throughout the 1950s, continuing to write and publish other work at his usual prolific pace but also steeping himself in Thoreau.

Derleth's biography of Thoreau, *Concord Rebel*, was published in 1960, a year before *Walden West*. The author's bio, likely contributed by Derleth himself, makes clear Derleth's identification with Thoreau: "Derleth's interest in Thoreau began in his high school days and has been the shaping influence of his life. He lives in Sauk City, Wisconsin, very much in the same way that Thoreau lived in Concord, teaching, lecturing, and writing. He is as familiar with the environs of Sauk City as Thoreau was with those of Concord." The book's foreword includes a somewhat curious but rather revealing passage:

> "The cost of a thing is the amount of what I call life which is required to be exchanged for it," [Thoreau] wrote, and he

went his way through life determined to exact the most from
every moment at the least cost in living, and this, despite his
limitations—for he was a bachelor, and he made his sacrifices
only for himself, which is considerably easier than making
sacrifices which might involve dependents in deprivations—
he did.

Derleth by this time was a divorced father with custody of his
two children. He had married in 1953 and divorced in 1959. One
senses in this passage Derleth's defensiveness over having chosen
a life less dedicated to the ideals he felt he drew from Thoreau, a
common insecurity among Thoreau's admirers.

In *Walden West*, finally completed and published a year after
the biography, Derleth gave free rein to his most Thoreauvian
instincts, letting the spirit of Thoreau pervade the book's nature
interludes even as he brought a deeper, more lyrical perspective
to his familiar observations of community life.

5

August Derleth turned fifty-two in 1961, the year *Walden West*
was published. He had been walking his home ground for five
decades and working on the book intermittently for more than a
decade. It's not surprising that the passage of time is a constant
theme in its pages. In an interlude titled (in the table of contents
but not in the text) "The Process of Renewal," he talks about one
of the "many things we do every spring," spending afternoons "on
the moraine east of Sac Prairie on the far side of the Wisconsin."
He goes there, he claims, "not alone to inspect familiar paths and
corners, long-known slopes and valleys, but also to take pleasure
in a renewal of acquaintance with places with which some of my
earliest memories are acquainted." The place not only gives him a

thorough overview of Sac Prairie but also, through those memories, connects him "to these slopes so firmly that I mourn the loss
of every tree felled by the woodsmen, each invasion of every turn
of the hillside path by the encroaching river, and the alteration of
every portion of the landscape there."

Prior to this he has dwelled on his childhood and his associations of people with place; the nature interludes have focused
on the onset of night and the stirring of memory in the odors of
the seasons. This interlude on the eastern hills is something of a
pivot point. It ends by musing about the way "this place which
changes very little from year to year" offers "that illusion of permanence which we all seek so diligently in one form or another
throughout life." The onset of spring in the hills suggests to him
"that some aspects of individual existence are immutable" and
there he feels the "conviction of continuity," but he acknowledges,
"I know the illusion, I know the infinite erosions and decayings
which go on ceaselessly from moment to moment, and to which
the mind adjusts so imperceptibly as to obviate them, so that
it seems that they have not taken place at all." He concludes: "I
come to a kind of spiritual rebirth on these hills every spring,
and I renew it each year despite increasing awareness of death
inherent in that rebirth, an awareness which exists independent
of volition or conscious act."

The moments of celebration in *Walden West* are almost always for the recurrence of events in nature—the migrations and
behaviors of birds, the regeneration of plants, the return of familiar seasonal odors in the air—while empathy and elegy seem to
dominate the profiles of the individuals that populate the social
segments of the book. The shift into an italicized nature interlude
is a welcome one after a segment on the quietly desperate life of a
Sac Prairie citizen, a moment of meditative calm before a return
to the people of the community. Derleth muses: "It is significant,
I sometimes think, that the facets of nature which quicken my

pulse with that awareness of both life and death are inextricably associated with the loneliness of man's mote-like existence in the cosmos—and acceptance of man's essential solitude on earth, or by love, or both together, for they are different aspects of the same face."

Derleth's home ground, in addition to the villages of Sac Prairie, largely consists of locations along the river. Easiest to access in his youth was undoubtedly what he calls Ehl's Slough, "down the slope immediately behind the house, east of the street, and comfortably west of the river." He thinks of it as "almost wilderness country," because village sounds were muted and the area was surrounded on high ground by trees—maples, poplars, alders—and in the low places by reeds. As he observes, "the slough was all that remained of what had once been a channel of the Wisconsin," but had been filled in over time until the terrain had formed what everyone referred to as "the Islands"—First Island, Second Island, and Third Island, each cut off from one another by channels that in high water separated them almost entirely and in low water were more like tapering fingers of land reaching out into the river. It was a more accessible and popular location than others where Derleth walked.

A location he speaks of more often is what he refers to as "the marshes." He reached it by walking along the railroad tracks that arch through Sauk City and cross the river to turn south toward Mazomanie. His approach varied, coming at the location by way of the river bridges or the highway or the east bank of the river. He tells us the area was lowland, with "a rewarding diversity of woods, sloughs, meadows, and marshland, where great fields of Joe-Pye weed shone lavender in later summer and autumn, meadows flamed green in spring, oak groves vied with willows and osiers, and the whole was framed by a low moraine just east of the rounding trestle." He notes a number of specific sites along the tracks that he and his friend Hugo or earlier others had named:

Dead Dog Hole, the Ice Slough, the Spring Slough, "over which curved the long trestle, the brook and the Brook Trestle, . . . the Mid-Meadow Trestle, the Triangle Lane Crossing, and finally Heiney's Crossing," this last a turning place to begin the walk back.

The Spring Slough was a special place, "the magnet that drew me afternoons and evenings in the spring, and early in the morning hours of many summer days." It was on the Spring Slough trestle that Derleth would "read and write and dream, . . . watching the years pass, at first slowly, and then with passing swiftness, and never counted a moment there ill-spent." In the journal books especially, Derleth records a great deal of byplay with neighbors and acquaintances and fellow townspeople, and the need to have these almost daily moments of solitude in the hills or the marshes is particularly marked. But those journal books have an air of immediacy about them, in part because they are closer in tone and energy to the actual daily journal entries they are drawn from, that *Walden West* doesn't have, in part because of its long gestation and in part because of its more reflective perspective.

Derleth perhaps senses that aspect of *Walden West* when he concludes the book with a final interlude.

> Sometimes of evenings there is in the air a quality which makes for the temporary illusion of timelessness. A subtle transference is effected by a fragrance, a scene, a familiar face, a pattern of light and shade, so that the present falls away and seems to merge into those aspects of the past first associated with awareness. Usually it is a fragrance related to change which effects this reversion—the smoke of burning leaves marking the turn of autumn to winter, the indescribable musk of thawing snow, presaging the spring, on which turns the experience of walking into the past.

In the paragraphs that follow, as he walks the streets in the present he muses on the feeling of being the adolescent who walked these streets in the past, on the sense that figures from the past might readily appear before him, on the way the slightest sight or sound or odor might trigger memory. "Perhaps these moments are integral in an existence close to the familiar scenes of childhood and youth, wherever there is a continuity of living," he writes. "They do not come with nostalgia, they come without warning; suddenly the chance of the moment, the place, the scene, the familiar sensual experience combine, and the present becomes fleetingly once more the past." He concludes the book pondering the reason for such recurring experiences:

> Perhaps it is the subconscious yearning for past time, for a time of irresponsibility, which lays traps for the unwary, the longing for a return to the dark, enclosing place, the intimacy of being lost to alien eyes, of being secret and alone, which may be another expression of the desire to be merged with all things, with earth itself, an awareness not of timelessness as such, but of the obliteration which is both death and the merging into time, the moment behind is the moment that has died, as were it knowledge that death always lurks behind, and before, the unknown, and beyond the unknown somewhere death at full circle, life and death being one.

Walden West, in its profiles of Sac Prairie townspeople, is largely a book of the dead. It makes sense that Derleth, who is aware at the time of his writing the book that Derleths have been in Sac Prairie for more than ten decades and he himself has passed half a century there, would be unable to avoid thinking about losses. In spite of his tendency to focus so much on his interior life, August Derleth's home ground is not centered on the natural world but encompasses it along with the life of the community he has been bound up with. In that sense, unlike John Muir and Aldo Leopold perhaps, August Derleth is someone very much more like all the rest of us.

6

Return to Walden West claims to be an exposition on the same three themes as *Walden West*, but its shifts in tone and emphasis make it more of a "spiritual autobiography" or "memoir of my inner life" than the first book was. Very much a valedictory book, *Return* places Derleth himself among those leading lives of quiet desperation by adding a preoccupation with change, loss, and isolation to its themes. Sounding more Thoreauvian throughout its interludes, at book's end Derleth offers a kind of metaphysical summing up by measuring himself against Thoreau's example.

The profiles of townspeople in *Return to Walden West* include individuals familiar as living characters in the journal books, but from the "Apologia" that opens the book, it's clear Derleth sees himself as someone who, from childhood, "was lost forever to the world in which men engaged life in momentous concerns and affairs, charmed away by the world intimately near to my senses." He claims the whole of his life was an effort "to live out that special enchantment and explore that world where the major concerns of other men did not matter—not fame or wealth or the pursuit of other phantoms conjured up by hope or love, valor or avarice."

In the book's first interlude, Derleth tells us, "In the course of my walks in the hills or marshes," he sometimes felt "a sense of utter harmony with all things," as if "I was one with the least grain of sand and the hawk soaring aloft, one with the mouldering log and the blossoming violet, . . .—and one, too, with an invisible anima, a spirit of place and time knowing neither beginning nor end." The ending of the interlude is elegiac and mournful, referring to "those brief periods of ecstasy that made me one with all earth and sky, dust acknowledging dust in all the shapes into which dust is moulded from one state of being to another, season to season, generation to generation."

The expectation of impermanence sounds throughout the interludes. For example, walking the streets at night with a view of the village in one direction and the prairie and night sky in the other, Derleth feels as if city lights and stars marked "in a real sense the limits of my universe," but adds, "there was so much to be learned in the small universe of Sac Prairie, and so little time in which to learn it." In another interlude, on night sounds, he writes of "the step of the night-walking solitary marking off another moment of his allotted time before he returns to dust." The nature interludes are, as in the earlier book, observant and celebratory, focusing on plum trees, maples, cherry trees, wild crabapple, field sparrow, nighthawks, killdeer, bittern, hawks, swamp owl, frogs, toad song, morels, stars, snow, and fog; but, particularly in those instances where he dwells on the places familiar to him in his wandering, he emphasizes his sense of solitude in tones that suggest isolation.

Though his walks still take him to the Brook Trestle and the hills across the river, Derleth describes other places where he can most thoroughly be alone, places that inspire some of his most lyrical musing. For example, of Baxter's Hollow, a secluded area on Otter Creek where he sometimes went to read and write, he claims, "Its isolation exactly suited my solitudes." Of the Brook Trestle, he says, "It was a good place to be alone. . . . The water flowed past as time ticked away, reminding me unceasingly of my own mortality, until it seemed that in that solitude I grew from youth to middle age, and nothing of change came to that little corner of Sac Prairie." He tells us the Genz Pocket, west of

Ferry Bluff, where he walked in late evenings, "offered the kind of solitude necessary after a day at my desk," and let him feel himself "an integral part" of nature. In such a secluded place, "I came often face to face with myself, without artifice or mask, a confrontation necessary for that renewal so vital in middle age." Derleth's confrontations with memory seem to lead him ever deeper into contemplation of himself. He writes of the Breunig Hill across the river that "once on the hill I was lost in nature, and thus as well in myself." The passage sounds particularly Thoreauvian and makes clear Derleth's sense of the linkage between solitude in nature and greater contemplation of himself.

Much of that contemplation arises from his sense of time passing. Early in the book Derleth tells how Sac Prairie "came almost reluctantly into the twentieth century," but in his youth, during the 1920s and 1930s, "slowly, slowly, the atmosphere of the village changed, its pace quickened, and the leisurely *Gemütlichkeit* once so integral to life in Sac Prairie faded with the passing generation." The profiles in the Walden West books are largely devoted to the generations that have passed; in *Return* Derleth not only commemorates them but also connects to them more personally, as one who will be joining them.

His sense of loss is particularly heartfelt in regard to the terrain he has wandered almost daily, the places like Baxter's Hollow where "time had its way with it" and "something of the sylvan magic . . . was lost forever." He writes with nostalgic fondness of Lodde's millpond, four miles west of Sac Prairie, where he often fished with his grandfather. "The millpond was a place of unalloyed delight. Its setting was sylvan—great soft maple trees lined all the east bank, where we fished, and not far from the edge of the water on the west shore, rearing above the falls, rose the almost sheer hill that was always known as the Mill Bluff." In Derleth's memory the millpond "had all the shimmering beauty of a mirage on a summer day. It seemed to be always summer there," "a place of undeniable magic for a child." In *Walden West* his reminiscence might well have ended on that note of celebration, but in *Return* he adds one more paragraph:

> But inevitably change came upon it, too, as upon all things—
> the mill ceased its operations, the store closed and was torn
> down, and the mill after, and one day after torrential rains
> the swollen Honey Creek burst out the weir, and the pond
> washed in flood down to the Wisconsin and was lost in that
> greater stream for all time.

Throughout the book Derleth is constantly aware of change and inevitable loss, the alteration of landscape that changes the atmosphere of the place. His sense of loss arises repeatedly and he takes the losses personally.

At the end of an interlude celebrating his hunting of morel mushrooms, he gives us a picture of what he gained in the course of walking his home ground—his discovery of whip-poor-wills' and red hawks' nests, woodcocks with their young, lady's slippers, Indian pipes, and orchids, badger digs, mating blue racers, gyrfalcons, and a great gray owl. "I knew where the brook was at its most amiable, from what heights the countryside was most gracious to the eye in its sweep over fields and mounds, past farms and hamlets, to the hills along the horizon." Surely in such passages, drawn from the journals where he captured the immediacy of his days, Derleth felt a deep kinship with Thoreau.

Near the end of the book, discussing the ten-acre homestead that made him, at thirty, "a man of property," Derleth begins an extended comparison of himself with Thoreau. "The house was no pond-side cabin, no Walden; Sac Prairie was that, in its entirety; and it had no more solitude than the solitudes within me, solitudes that never faded and were never wholly plumbed." In the passage that follows, he deliberately echoes Thoreau's language in *Walden.*

> When the house was built and enclosed, I had little more means than Thoreau; but I had more varied ambitions, wider horizons, and many debts and obligations. My foundations were as solid; I had been building them in Sac Prairie for three decades; like Thoreau I had been for as many years walking forest paths, cross-lots routes, rail-beds, and wood-land lanes; marking the comings and goings of hawks, terns, wild geese, owls and whippoorwills—and here, at this new post, once heard one persistent whippoorwill cry his name 1,507 consecutive times; keeping a record of wilderness talk as well as of the multifarious concerns of my fellowmen; listening to what was in the wind; and keeping my presence at the rising of the sun each morning and its setting in the evening; playing calf to the moon; and observing the morning and the evening stars.
>
> I sought this house in the country to transact some private business, too, but with all the more obstacles a century of time and human experience could bring about; all my occasions were not within, but almost as much outward, and here in the open country I was closer to the stars. I did not intend to live meanly here, but to live within my limitations, and to pursue a modest career with my pen at a suitable distance from my neighbors, and toward this goal I advanced with as much confidence as Thoreau had toward his, living a life perhaps not quite as I imagined, and meeting a modest success which was hardly more than I expected or sought, knowing that such goals as fame and wealth and social status were altogether too shabby to be held up as on the same plane as peace

and love and truth, all as implicit in the gentian's blue and the
song sparrow's threnody as in the drone of the bee, the cricket's churr, the peewee's invitation to come into his woods,
in trees, blossoms, grasses, in the thunderheads forever on
the horizon, the tints of the dawn and the afterglow, as in the
higher laws that govern the universe. I knew that the universe
was wider than my view of it, and would always be, and I
learned that if the mass of men lived lives of quiet desperation, too often they were, for want of confidence or courage,
the authors of that desperation.

The passage is finely wrought to spark echoes of Thoreau's own
prose in *Walden*. It strikes me as one of the more self-revelatory
passages in Derleth's writing, and it explains one of the major
themes of the Walden West books, a theme not emphasized in
the journal books. Derleth had often associated his Sac Prairie life
with Thoreau's Concord life, but here he fleshes out the distinctions he felt obliged to make between them, as if clearing the air
of any confusion of motive or identification.

The segment is one of the longer ones in the book, and it's
followed by three striking segments. A one-page interlude on "the
first batrachian voice announcing winter's end and the advance
of spring" recounts Derleth's habit of going out nightly around
and on the vernal equinox to hear the first spring peeper or spring
cricket frog. It ends partly in memory and perhaps partly in anticipation: "I have waited under many a clouded heaven, in vain,
under new moon and evening star, beside the still leafless trees
black on heaven, in the quiet, windless, chill air to hear that first
frog call, to know renewal once again, to meet one more spring."
I can't help feeling that the ending of the passage is something
close to a prayer.

The concluding profile of the book, about Judge Jim Hill, is

one of the most positive profiles in the two books and, in its conclusion, about the ways Hill faced the end of his life, suggests a
kind of identification Derleth felt with the man.

> Though he withdrew a little from some of his activities as
> he grew older, he never retired. He came to his office and
> listened to the tribulations of his clients until illness struck
> him down, and again, after his recovery, until a further illness
> forced him to his final bed, still tranquil, uncomplaining,
> knowing as he had always known that death is as much a part
> of life as joy and sorrow, birth and love.

Before *Return to Walden West* was published in 1970, Derleth suffered a long stretch of illness arising from complications following
gall bladder surgery in August 1969. His illness was severe enough
that a single journal entry covers a two-month span. His final
entry is dated January 11, 1970. He died of a heart attack on July
4, 1971, at age sixty-two. I don't know if he had premonitions of
his death when he wrote the final words of the Hill profile, but
he had written often enough of the end of solitary lives, and it
strikes me that in this final profile he was stepping back from his
focus on himself but not entirely avoiding a last expression of his
own values, perhaps an imaginative rendering of what he hoped
his own end would be.

Certainly throughout *Return to Walden West* Derleth is very
much discouraged by encroaching change but seemingly accepting of the ends to which the passage of time leads us all. His final
one-page interlude begins:

> I never found that nature failed me in the continuity of time
> and place so essential to my well-being. While the condition
> of man on his planet slowly worsens, the pattern of the sea-
> sons changes not at all, however much nature's aspects reflect

the damage wrought by man in his avarice and his devotion
to false, unnatural values.

Here he sounds like an environmentalist for our own times. In the
next paragraph he celebrates the continuity of the natural world
with an account of the change from winter to spring, and in the
third paragraph he muses about the social world:

> In the village as in the country, birth and death know no win-
> ter; here life is more patently unceasing change. Familiar faces
> vanish, long-known voices sound no more, gone to ground.
> The young grow up to confront a life ever more complex,
> and in their time are harried to the grave, scores of men and
> women who may never see the beauty of the earth they live
> in, who may never know themselves as integral to nature.

In the final paragraph he locates himself in his home ground:

> I walk among them, it often seems, increasingly an alien, in-
> formed by compassion and understanding, but less content
> among my fellow men than in the marshes or the hills, on the
> river or along a country road at night, where I am closer to
> coming full circle, to awareness of that ultimate darkness that
> is the merging of the self with time and the inevitable dust.

It is a somber ending to the book.

In his conclusion to *Walden,* Thoreau tells us, "I left the woods
for as good a reason as I went there. Perhaps it seemed to me that
I had several more lives to live, and could not spare any more time
for that one." In his professional activities and personal relationships Derleth sometimes seemed to live several lives simultaneously, but his role as Sac Prairie's own Thoreau seems to have
been central to him. *Return to Walden West* ends his nonfiction

Sac Prairie Saga with a mixture of resignation and acceptance that attempts to let him come to terms with the life he had chosen for himself, walking his home ground.

7

I come back to Ferry Bluff in early April, about a year and a half after my first visit. The sun is out, the trees are greening, and the new grasses overwhelm the dead grasses of the previous season. The forest canopy is thriving but not yet thick; light penetrates the floodplain forest along Honey Creek and illuminates the face of the bluff along the road. Across the empty parking area at the end of the road, I walk down to the riverbank to inspect a border of mud, thick with animal tracks, between the dry ground and the shallow, clear water of Honey Creek. The creek moves slowly above the bare, light-brown bottom on its way toward the Wisconsin River.

The trail runs along the base of the bluffs on one side and along a drop-off of several feet to the floor of the floodplain forest on the other. It arches away from the creek where willow brush or alder brush grows ever more thickly closer to the river, until it's impossible to see the creek. I keep glancing at the vertical walls of the bluff, with their indentations and openings visible now through the trees in ways they won't be once spring turns to summer. Past Ferry Bluff, the highland recedes into a U-shaped recess where a dry wash bisects the slope. One side trail leads off toward the base of Cactus Bluff and a distant canoe landing site, passage along it impeded by fallen trees hanging upside down off the bluff face onto the path. I start the climb up the main trail.

The trail Derleth walked was surely not a carefully demarked route like this one, with wooden borders on either side like high curbs, leading upward and inland, then switching back to rise along the slope of Cactus Bluff to the height where the surface of the bluff emerges out of the woods. This trail bears the hallmarks of the DNR and the Nature Conservancy, who got the place designated a state natural area seventeen years after Derleth's death.

I emerge into the open on the shoulder of the bluff and follow a partial boardwalk downhill toward the edge facing the river, near a row of informational displays, most in disrepair, and some benches under some low cedars. I edge around them onto the sand and stone of the exposed cliff and gaze out upon the river. It's a cool day, clear, the sky almost cloudless, the river a deeper blue than the pale blue sky. I take some time to consider where I am and where I've been.

~

In the past year I've sometimes needed to drive across Wisconsin to and from Minnesota and sometimes routed myself through Sac Prairie. I would usually swing by the western end of the railroad trestle to gaze at Bergen's Island and the tracks disappearing into thickets on the eastern bank. I drove to Heiney's Crossing, the turnaround point in Derleth's railroad walks, and saw for myself how impassably overgrown the tracks had become; I pulled into Snuffy's Campground, just off the August Derleth Bridge, in hopes of a footpath to the trestle and was told that none exists and that the woods are now thickly overgrown and rampant with poison ivy; I learned that trying an approach by canoe would be no more likely to help me reach the Brook Trestle further inland. Each detour into Sac Prairie added little to my knowledge on the ground and, despite the consolation of some good cheese and good local wine, I drove away discouraged.

In time I came to feel that the inaccessibility of the Brook Trestle was the essence of the story in the twenty-first century. In Derleth's time the railroad still ran up the tracks from Mazomanie and across the trestles, above the Wisconsin, and through Sauk City.

The trains kept the tracks clear. Now the rails rust and the ties rot and thickets grow in the spaces between the ties. Had Derleth lived to see the railroad end and the western trestle be destroyed, he would have lamented the change. As inspiring as it might have been to visit a spot near the Brook Trestle where someone might have erected a Leopold bench in Derleth's memory and where a visitor like me might have sat to read what he wrote there, it may say more about time and change that it can't happen.

Unlike Muir at Fountain Lake Farm and unlike Leopold at the shack, Derleth's home ground wasn't so much his as it was a landscape through which he moved without restraint and without impact. Place of Hawks, his fenced-in ten acres, was his workspace and his social space and, because of the demands of being a prolific author and an editor and a publisher, the space that housed "the prosaic events of the day" that he needed most to find solitude away from. Whatever becomes of that house—his daughter April Derleth, its most recent occupant, died in March 2011, and when I passed the house a year later it was silent and empty—Place of Hawks would be the logical place to commemorate Derleth the

Wisconsin author. Walking with Derleth the solitary rambler will be a more complicated matter.

Nevertheless I decided to try again, after calculating what present settings might give me echoes of Derleth's Sac Prairie. I began with a favorite site from his childhood.

August Derleth Park slopes down from Water Street into a vast green open sports area with two parking lots and occupies the area Derleth called Ehl's Slough, where First Island, Second Island, and Third Island were separated from one another and the mainland by sloughs, along the Wisconsin River. At the time I visited, members of the August Derleth Society had been working to restore native plants, remove invasive species, and bring the area back to what it was when Derleth walked here. On a cold March day, I parked in the lot closest to the river and followed a paved path north into the trees. The paved path and solid dedicated benches made me aware that now is not then.

Not far along the path a mixed group of juncos and gold-finches were preoccupied with pecking at the pavement. They gave me hopes for spring. The trail divided, to form a loop, and a bridge above a dry slough took me toward the riverbank. A long, flat, open stretch was bordered with a low fence above a bluff, and more heavy benches faced the river. But for the cold I might have sat for a while to watch the river flow or to scan the eastern shore, where scatterings of new greens in the trees livened the winter grays of the woods. It would have been a good use of my time on a warmer day. Soon I reached the midpoint of the loop and began to follow a footpath leading off along the riverbank, high above the water. A fisherman, well bundled up, stood on his boat near the shore, watching his line in the current, and didn't notice me pass quietly above him. A fisherman just like this could have been observed on the river at any time over the past few centuries. I wove through scrubby growth, then took a side trail leading to the remains of a campfire littered with cans and other debris, a setting hard to date, and finally broke into the open above a sandy slope and a clear view of not-so-distant houses on Water Street. Until that moment I hadn't been aware of the nearness of the street or the traffic moving on it.

Soon after I began retracing my steps, I heard croaking voices overhead and stopped to scour the sky. Two sandhill cranes appeared above the trees, heading east across the river, calling back and forth as they went. They alternated the beating of their wings, as if deliberately taking turns. I watched them until they grew faint above the distant woods, somehow reassured by their flight—cranes were crossing the river long before fishermen floated on it or campfires burned above it. Back on the paved path I completed the loop, noting where the sloughs had been, now well grassed over and filling with trees and shrubs.

I thought that, as a memorial site to celebrate Derleth's walks, the park was a pleasant place. It's good to stand on high bluffs on the west bank and gaze across the blue expanse of the river at the lower banks and beaches and sandbars on the eastern side. I'd been the only one here and, in my solitude, despite the lack of feeling in my hands by now and the windburn on my face, I appreciated how peaceful the park could be. Still, as one who has read his nature writing, I found it hard to imagine Derleth in it. I couldn't help thinking how unlike the places he usually wandered this park had become.

The intervening decades had wrought a good many other changes in the ways the environment along the Wisconsin River has been managed. Several designated state natural areas have been created close to Sac Prairie, including Lodde's Mill Bluff west of Sauk City, Mazomanie Bottoms on the east bank of the river opposite Ferry Bluff, and Ferry Bluff itself. An extensive Lower Wisconsin State Riverway preserves locations across seven counties, a stretch of the river Derleth traveled for his book *The*

Wisconsin: River of a Thousand Isles. Near Sauk City, the riverway encompasses the Spring Slough and Brook Trestle area, though it's not as readily accessible as other areas designed for recreation.

The Lodde's Mill Bluff Natural Area sits near the site of the millpond Derleth remembered so fondly from fishing outings with his grandfather. I drove out to the cemetery for a quick look again at Derleth's grave, paused again before Place of Hawks, from where Derleth would have set out on his rambles, and headed for Lodde's Mill Bluff. I spotted it almost at once after I turned onto River Road, straight ahead less than two miles west from Place of Hawks, rising around three hundred feet above Honey Creek. I was startled to think I'd barely noticed it before—now it seemed so prominent. The road led directly to the spot below the bluff where the millpond once sprawled.

When I crossed Highway 60 on River Road, on the opposite side of the creek from the bluff, I found myself at a dead end, in a cul-de-sac circled by a few houses. As I turned around, I saw an elderly woman by the side of the road, near some mailboxes, watching me. Hoping to seem harmless and inoffensive, I pulled over, rolled down my window, explained I was looking for places Derleth wrote about, and asked her about the millpond. She stepped over closer to my car and told me she was not a Sac Prairie native, but her husband had family ties to the Loddes and their house was on family land. As she gestured toward the house, I recognized the name on a sign near her driveway as one I'd read on Derleth's endpaper map of seven decades earlier. She said the mill and the millpond were gone by the time she came to Sac Prairie, but she remembered attending a lively Christmas party at Derleth's Place of Hawks when she and her husband were courting, more than forty years before. In fact, she told me, there were still a good many people in Sac Prairie who could recall interacting with Augie.

Following her directions, I drove south across Honey Creek, turned onto a dirt road at the base of the bluff, parked, and walked back along the road. The bluff was an impressive mass on my right, its cliffs formed of Cambrian sandstone, its cap Prairie du Chien dolomite, all of it hard to see through the trees on the leaf-covered slope below it, birch, oak, hickory, and basswood. Entrance to the bluff itself was farther south, access restricted by its owner, the University of Wisconsin, because of diverse and uncommon flora and a stretch of vanishing dry prairie on the summit. Derleth likely climbed the bluff at some point in his youth, but in *Return to Walden West* it's the millpond he reflects on and eventually laments. Looking off to my left I saw long stretches of flat grassland. Much of that flatland had been underwater when the millpond was here. Now a wide, level patch of green grass stretched out toward distant trees. Soon I reached a point where Honey Creek meanders from the north and turns near the road to head east under Highway 60 and due south to the Wisconsin River near Ferry Bluff. The brown water flowed briskly through plentiful young trees on either bank, some shrubs just beginning to leaf out, promising to obscure the view of the creek by summer.

I'd come to Sac Prairie this time armed with printouts and photocopies of plat book and DNR maps, and I had thought often of finding a way, if not to reach the Spring Slough and the Brook Trestle themselves, then to at least locate someplace equivalent, someplace that might feel like the next best thing to having walked them. And so, when I left Lodde's Mill Bluff, I headed for the Mazomanie Bottoms Natural Area on the east side of the river, off a county road linking Sauk City with Mazomanie to the south. It struck me as the same kind of landscape that the river bottomlands across the trestles must be.

I parked in an empty lot a little way down a gated dirt road and set off on foot, trying to distinguish the trees of a Wisconsin River floodplain forest—mostly silver maple, elm, basswood, and

ash. In another season I might have heard some uncommon warblers, but today the only bird sounds came from woodpeckers and
turkeys. The road seemed to go a long way, paralleling the river
through the middle of the woods. When I spotted a clear side
trail, I took it a short distance to an intersection with a footpath
running along the riverbank.

Ferry Bluff and Cactus Bluff filled the skyline across the river;
a low island with a scattering of trees and a solitary goose floated
in the water near the eastern shore. I remembered seeing the island before, looking down from Cactus Bluff. For a little while
I followed the footpath in either direction, first south and then
north, but soon returned to the place where I first emerged from
the forest. With my binoculars I slowly scanned the island, hoping
to see at least another goose, and then turned my attention to each
of the bluffs, surveying in turn the exposed layers of light-brown
sandstone that form their cliff faces, trying to gain a better sense
of their summits. Everything I saw was as motionless as if it were
a landscape painting. I had no idea how much time I was taking;
but I knew that, however slowly I gazed at each part of the scene,
I would still take in very little of it.

A little upstream, a flicker of motion at skyline caught my attention. An eagle had spread his wings and was launching himself
off a tree. I saw him circle effortlessly above Ferry Bluff. A hawk
appeared and began circling about the eagle, then dove down
closer to him. Hawk and eagle maintained a parallel circuit, and I
could vaguely hear the hawk's cries. A second eagle began to hover
far above them, keeping its distance but obviously aware of them.
I watched the hawk and the eagle circle one another high above
the bluff for a long time, every moment wondering what might
happen, until finally the eagle veered away and disappeared over
the woods to the north. The second eagle, still at height, paced the
first in that direction, and the hawk remained a moment longer
before gliding out of sight beyond the bluff.

I recalled seeing a hawk hovering above me the first time I climbed Cactus Bluff and the coincidence got my attention. I had no way of knowing if it were the same hawk and didn't speculate. What I'd seen was what you hope to see when you're out wandering the riverscape, something that seems more urgent than what may await you back where you live, something that helps you lock the moment securely in memory.

~

The view of Cactus Bluff and Ferry Bluff across the river stayed with me in the following weeks, and so I find myself again on Cactus Bluff, gazing east and remembering the place I stood the month before looking at these bluffs from the Mazomanie Bottoms. From this height, the twists and bends of the river are more pronounced and the sand bars more distinct. I hear distant geese, something rustling below me in the woods, but mostly the wind, sometimes rather brusque but mostly mild. I'm pleased not to have layered on as much as I first intended. Glancing up at the empty sky, I try to imagine what it would feel like to be here on a cloudless night, taking in the universe, as Derleth so often did. I stand quietly alone for many minutes, my gaze sweeping slowly along the river in either direction, aware of how much there is to take in, afraid that too little of it will register.

Though I'm alone here, I judge from the wear of the ground this must be a popular locale, easy to reach despite a persistent, relentless ascent; it's broad and open and relatively flat. The edge is unprotected but not unnerving. I remember seeing a footpath near the boardwalk that winds more steeply uphill. My last time here, when grasses were thick and the direction of the path uncertain, I didn't follow it very far. This time I'm sure it must lead to Ferry Bluff, the higher bluff, and I force myself away from the view to follow it. The grasses now are low and the path clear, snaking upward toward a wooded prominence. The sand changes from tan above the ledge to gray, all ground from the rocks prominent ahead of me. The path grows steep and, as I rest on a small level spot, I notice two deer a long way below me on the slope, beyond a stand of leafless bushes, stepping slowly and making the rustling sound I heard earlier. I climb the path up a narrow ridge and emerge onto the summit of the bluff, a rounded, wooded, grassy open space. In the distance I see blue sky through the trees—the summit is not very wide.

The footpath winds inland, away from the river, and then arcs along the heights over to and out onto Ferry Bluff. The farther I go, the thicker the woods become, with more underbrush and more frequent deadfall across the path. I swing west, then north, then back east, rising gently all the while, until I see the point at which the trees stop and the sky opens up beyond them. At the limit of the trees the path narrows further, becomes more of a dirt path winding out into the open on a sharp grade down toward the edge of the bluff. Some undergrowth hasn't yet filled in this season, but the bluff is more exposed and open, far narrower and more abrupt than Cactus Bluff. It gives me a truly magisterial view of the river, the shoreline forests, the agricultural lands beyond them, the expanses from northwest to south. From here I can see where Honey Creek empties into the Wisconsin River. I have a better sense of sandbars and islands, can almost see the process of their forming, the water directly below sometimes brown from silt and sometimes red from sand just below the surface.

I have only a few minutes to take it all in before another hiker, younger, more fit, in his forties, brandishing a straight, home-made walking stick, appears behind me and slowly descends to the top of the grade. I suspect we're both disappointed to find another person here, but we greet one another with smiles and chat amicably for a few minutes. He tells me he's a Sauk City native who never followed the trail all the way up here before, though he frequently fishes and hikes along the river and has often been on Cactus Bluff. When I tell him I'm from near Milwaukee, he helpfully points out distant Blue Mound, the highest point in southwestern Wisconsin; through my binoculars I locate its tower. He also mentions the nude beach to the south, on the east shore, formerly accessible by car at the end of Conservation Road but, since Mazomanie Bottoms became a state natural area, reachable now only on foot. We stand gazing into the distance for a moment or two, and just before I'm about to offer to change places with him—I think I have the better vantage point—he turns to leave. As he steps away he warns me about ticks, especially abundant this season, perhaps because of the mild winter and the early spring. I wave good-bye, sit down to take notes, immediately find a tick on my pants leg, and flick it off.

Dawdling some to give him a head start, I watch as a downy woodpecker works a tree for a few minutes, then start my own slow return. The descent is relatively easy, backtracking all the way, though a few places are steep and I try to be cautious. As I walk, I wonder how much of it Derleth saw, though I'm certain the expansiveness and the remoteness of it were elements of Ferry Bluff he felt especially. In *Return to Walden West* he wrote that "Ferry Bluff and its sister hills were little changed through the decades," but for a widening of the road in a government project and the loss of some trees, including those that fell across Honey Creek, "adding new water voices to the day and night." The changes didn't bother him much because he tended to walk there at night, when little was visible. For him, "the Ferry Bluff range, the road, the hillside path . . . remained unchanged, offering by day the grandeur of the river valley and the Sac Prairie country on both sides of the broad Wisconsin, and by night the intimate, enclosed space in which to treasure my solitudes." Having had some solitude in my wanderings on the bluff and across the river in Mazomanie Bottoms, I feel as if I know something of what he felt.

Back down on Cactus Bluff I take a moment to scan the sky in case there's a hawk hovering overhead; I'm only a little disappointed when none appears. By now I've walked August Derleth's home ground enough to know that there's little to be gained by searching for symbols. Any confirmation you need can be had simply by paying attention and knowing where you are, in just the way Derleth walked his home ground.

PART TWO

Interlude

SATURDAY, NOVEMBER 18, 2012. I should have known, long before now, that the Retzer Nature Center, on the west side of Waukesha, is located on a glacial drumlin, a long, narrow hill shaped like an inverted spoon. We've been here before, cross-country skiing on its winter trails and walking through its autumn woods, and a week ago I staffed an Ice Age Trail information table at the Apple Harvest Festival (made apple-less by this year's drought). But it's only today, on a family outing on our son-in-law's birthday, that I recognize the drumlin beneath our feet.

We amble through the woods, chatting amiably, hoping to keep the grandchildren's attention on their surroundings. It's a sunny day, but the November air has little warmth in it. Emerging from the trees onto a slope that rises through the dry grasses of an autumn prairie, we pass numbered sites on a yellow trail loop without the interpretative pamphlet that would explain what we're seeing. Beyond the high brown grasses, a long stretch of mown green falls away to the south.

We leave the restored prairie and walk down the grassy slope toward a side trail that would take us to a fen, but it's hunting season and the trail is closed to hikers, so we climb back up the hill to a fenced area just at the crest. This is the vista overlook, the high point on the drumlin. Walking down and up the slope, we've gained a sense of the drumlin's scale. From the overlook we can see a long way off to the east, the south, and the west. While Lilly runs through the tall grass with her parents and grandmother behind her, her brother, Louie, and I step up to the overlook fence. I point out the water tower in the distance near where our house is located, and we both note a large house nearly due west, on the crest of a neighboring hill, positioned to obtain a magisterial view.

We complete the circuit, view exhibits in the visitor center, then separate and head for home. Our drive back into Waukesha takes Sue and me past Glacier Cone Park. Glacier Cone is a moulin kame, a cone-shaped mound of glacial sediment, its base hidden on three sides by trees and shrubs and a well-populated neighborhood. It's open on the north, near the street, but from that side it simply looks like a grassy hill. If you start up the mown path on the west side, however, you discover a steep climb through high grass to a summit with a random quartet of oak trees and a mown space with a fire circle littered with cans, bottles, and scraps of paper.

I climbed it last June, on a spur-of-the-moment outing, but Sue hasn't seen it, so we backtrack, park on a side street, and cross to the entrance. Today the grasses are pale and bent low, but the path and the open area at the top are still green, and though it's a cool day and the climb is steady work, it's pleasant on top of the kame. I look to the west and locate the open space on the drumlin that Retzer occupies, more than a mile away, and beyond it the silhouette of the gigantic house Louie and I noticed. I face south. Our condo is about three miles south-southeast as the crow—or, preferably, the sandhill crane—flies, and invisible to me from this location. The River Place subdivision rises on slopes to the east of our complex, and other housing extends on the heights beyond it, and they all provide an indicator of where we live. Our complex is set on a terrace just above the floodplain of the Fox River as it flows out of Waukesha; we're situated at the lowest point in the community, and from here on the kame, I can't even see the Fox wetlands that spread out behind us.

I can't help but ponder this juxtaposition of high and low. Newly aware of this kame here and that drumlin at Retzer, I begin to recognize, in spite of all the residential and commercial development that covers the landscape, how much the glacial past is still present. Glacier Cone Park is officially 25.09 acres of oak openings and prairie grasses, undeveloped (except for that mown path and circle) and intended to remain a natural area. Paths through the grasses leading off from the summit suggest that people in the neighborhood climb the kame often; it's demanding enough that one could stay in good shape walking it a few times a week. If I've read topographic maps correctly, the kame rises to 1,120 feet, and the floodplain of the Fox behind my condo is at an elevation of 780 feet or lower. That's a 340-foot change in elevation. In the neighborhood around Glacier Cone Park the elevations tend to be around 850 feet, 270 feet lower. From the top of the kame I have a better sense of the lay of the land. If we lived in this neighborhood, I'd likely be up here at the summit often.

Walking back down the path, Sue and I talk about how this kame came to be here. A moulin kame is created by the steady dropping of glacial debris through an opening in the glacier, creating a cone. Other, lower kames surround Glacier Cone. We both look overhead and try to imagine how high above us the glacier's surface must have reached to have formed a kame this high, in steady increments over time. We imagine that mass of ice melting down below the top of the kame, below the slopes, below the base, all that meltwater eventually carried away by the postglacial ancestor of the Fox River—flowing, that is, over and then finally past the terrain on which our home stands. Suddenly the high and the low of our home ground seem intimately connected.

The White Ghost of a Glacier:
Walking the Ice Age Trail

1

IT'S NEAR THE END of December, but southeastern Wisconsin has yet to see much snow so far this winter. The day is gray and overcast and the temperature persistently stable at thirty-two degrees. Bundled up and well layered, Sue and I set out to hike a segment of the Ice Age Trail, the thousand-mile-long National Scenic Trail that winds through Wisconsin from near Lake Michigan in the east to the Minnesota border in the west. We're starting what our Ice Age Trail Alliance chapter calls the "Walk the Wauk" program.

By this time next year—or quite a bit sooner, we hope—we'll have walked approximately forty-five miles of the Ice Age Trail here in Waukesha County at least once and, given the likelihood of our hiking out and back, probably twice. The seasons will have changed considerably by the time we've covered our county's portion of the trail.

We won't hike the county segments in order, in a determined march from one end to the other, though we do start at the northern limit, near Monches, at the Washington County line. A sign at the northern trailhead for the Monches segment tells us we're about to enter the Carl Schurz Forest, named for an early Wisconsin conservationist. Carl Schurz was born in Germany and in 1855 settled in Watertown, Wisconsin, in nearby Jefferson County. There his wife, Margarethe Schurz, founded the first kindergarten in North America, modeled on that of Friedrich Fröbel in Germany. Schurz was a lawyer and politician in Wisconsin, a major general in the Union army during the Civil War, a US senator from Missouri, and secretary of the interior from 1877 to 1881.

As secretary, Schurz decried the depletion of forests on public land by private lumbering companies and initiated the first federal forest reserves, essentially starting the movement toward a national forest service and a national park system. During Schurz's childhood in Germany, his father had managed the forests of Count Metternich, and Schurz once declared, "I learned to love the woods and to feel the fascination of the forest-solitude, with the whisper of the winds in the treetops." I don't know whether Schurz ever saw this stretch of forest—probably not—but I like the fleeting sensation of this forest harking back to forests across centuries and continents.

We leave the trailhead and climb a slope, traipsing through a narrow wooded corridor. Open farmland is hidden to the west by the top of the rise and obscured to the east by trees lower down the slope. Soon the woods expand into oak forest, generations of oak leaves making the forest floor a tan and brown kaleidoscope. The canopy, open now in winter, is high above us. Often we descend into a swale, or depression, with high ridges cutting off the horizon, the trail winding through the forest, rolling up and down. We hear no wind in the treetops, but the forest solitude is enough to make me think Carl Schurz might have liked walking here.

It takes a geological imagination to recognize what we're hiking on as the result of glaciation ten thousand years ago, and part of the point of walking the Ice Age Trail is to get acquainted with the glaciers and what they wrought. I've consulted *The Ice Age Trail Companion Guide* to briefly prepare me for where we'll be and *Geology of the Ice Age National Scenic Trail* to keep me thoroughly apprised of how it came to be there. The latter book, by David Mickelson, Louis Maher, and Susan Simpson, is particularly thorough and conscientious, and, even if my grasp of glaciation or geology always seems tentative and superficial, I'm gaining an awareness of what glacial forces shaped the landscape under the Ice Age Trail.

The Monches segment begins in the valley of the Oconomowoc River, which meanders through what once was a wide glacial meltwater channel. The river itself is not visible from the forest but arcs around the eastern side of Monches, through the inevitable millpond marking where the village began; the Ice Age Trail won't cross it until about a third of the way through the segment. The oak forest has grown on what the geology book identifies as "high-relief hummocky topography." This means that, when glacial ice melted, sediment that deposited on top of it, in varying thicknesses, settled onto earlier deposits to form an uneven landscape, sometimes in high relief, sometimes in low relief. The meltwater channel cleared and leveled the ground it passed over, and the river that succeeded it carved its own channel lower into the floodplain, leaving relatively flat terraces on either side. Of course, to see all this occurring would require time-lapse pho-tography covering thousands of years—the scale and scope of Ice Age glaciation would never be obvious to a bystander in any of those millennia.

Eventually we come down out of the forest, veering through a grassy field and into denser, younger forest as we near the Ocon-omowoc River. The water is clear, shallow, and undoubtedly cold, often interrupted by dead trees and fallen branches that teeter across exposed boulders. The riverbed in some places is thoroughly rock-strewn, and the banks are low enough that they don't drain well. In wet years a long stretch must be persistently waterlogged. Though we've had little snow, we've had plenty of cold—in some places small ponds are simply iced over and in others, water flows from beneath rugged canopies of ice. Just be-fore a long narrow agricultural field, a high wooden bridge arches over the river and a series of boardwalks and puncheons extends through the floodplain forest on the eastern side. The bridge and boardwalk are new, a restoration project by a volunteer work crew of the Ice Age Trail Alliance. It's easy to see that a combination of heavy snowmelt and spring rains could make the lowlands mucky and saturated. A low terrace that will take us to the end of the segment gives us drier footing, and more puncheons sometimes guide us over the lowest parts of the trail.

Except for occasional yellow blazes on trees to mark the trail, until we reach the bridge we have little sense of a world outside the forest. But coming out of the lowlands, the forest narrows again and we notice houses not far beyond the top of the slope, perched on a higher terrace. Often driftwood, tree limbs, and trunk sections are piled at the border between the private yards and the woods; a couple of times we pass overturned canoes. We've seen few other people on the trail, but those we have—a couple of mothers with their children—make us realize that the Ice Age Trail, at least in this segment, offers some very accessible recreation for nearby homeowners. The women and children were lightly layered, all of them in sneakers, chatting casually as they ambled along, comfortably strolling what to them was home ground. With our hiking boots and daypacks and steady, determined pace, we felt a little melodramatic about our appearance, our outsider status uncomfortably obvious.

Past the houses the wooded corridor narrows still further, even as the river widens. Fields and farmlands spread off to the east; west of the woods the floodplain opens up into sprawling wetlands filled with thick, tall, tangled brown grasses. Exposed to the sky, the river takes on a placid, bright gray gleam as it curves through the grasses into the distance.

Soon we come to another expanse of oak forest, younger than the Schurz Forest, more studded with saplings. We cross a small creek on a low, flat bridge and pass a Leopold bench with a memorial marker: "These Woods Are Where My Spirit Lies . . . When You Are Lost, Come Here And You Will Find Me." We started the walk at the sign honoring Carl Schurz, so it doesn't surprise me to find another memorial on the trail, but I keep thinking about it as we walk on. Something about this personal commemoration seems more difficult to achieve in the commemoration of a public figure. Whether the man memorialized in the bench marker ever said anything close to what's inscribed there, the memorial has a reciprocal effect: it honors not only the man but also the place that mattered to him. There's something elevating in the association for man and forest alike that cemetery headstones and public monuments can't capture. To his friends and family, some part of him is still here on what he felt to be his home ground.

We are close enough to County Highway Q, a stretch of the Kettle Moraine Scenic Drive, to hear the traffic. It pulls us away from glacial reflection. Soon the trail curves around a high embankment for the railroad and emerges in view of a long concrete overpass that the train tracks cross. One of the three arches in the overpass, close to the trailhead, serves traffic on the road, and another serves the river, which continues on its way south. We stand near the sign for the southern trailhead of the Monches segment, sipping water and noticing local traffic. In that moment it's clear that, no matter how much it's the glacial terrain that lures us out onto the trail, the present is too much with us for us to imagine for long that we're walking in the past.

2

It's humbling to confess, after spending more than four-fifths of my life in glaciated Great Lakes states, a good portion of that time writing and teaching the literary nonfiction of place, that I have only lately begun to pay attention to glaciers. In spite of their having left Wisconsin around ten thousand years ago, I seem to be constantly aware of them, constantly struggling to tune my senses to their former existence upon my present home ground.

I've tried to anchor my understanding more solidly by taking Marlin Johnson's continuing education class in the glacial geology of Waukesha County; I've heard David Mickelson, an author of the book I constantly consult, lecture on the glacial geology of the Ice Age Trail; I've tracked down some of the sources that Johnson and Mickelson have drawn upon, like Lee Clayton's *Pleistocene Geology of Waukesha County, Wisconsin*. Clayton's abstract for his Wisconsin Geological and Natural History Survey Bulletin very succinctly sets the stage: "Waukesha County, in southeastern Wisconsin, straddles an area that was the junction of the Green Bay and Lake Michigan Lobes of the Laurentide Ice Sheet during the Wisconsin Glaciation. Most of the topography of Waukesha County formed during this glaciation." I may not always know what glacial remnants are beneath my feet, but I'm constantly aware that they are there.

The eastern two-thirds or more of Waukesha County was once beneath the Lake Michigan Lobe of the Wisconsin Glaciation. This is the lobe that crossed what is now the Wisconsin shoreline of Lake Michigan and the Michigan Basin to the east and reached into northern Indiana and Illinois. In Wisconsin, the cities of Sheboygan, Milwaukee, Racine, Kenosha, and, further inland, Waukesha all rose on the outwash of the Lake Michigan Lobe. The Green Bay Lobe of the Wisconsin Glaciation flowed more southwestward from what is now Green Bay, crossed present-day Waukesha County from roughly the north central portion to the southwest corner, and continued only a short way beyond. Its terminal moraine, the elevated ridge of glacial debris marking its furthest progress, curves around to the west and up the central part of the state, looking on the map like the shaky outline of a chubby forefinger. In the eastern counties of Wisconsin the Ice Age Trail largely follows the line where the Green Bay and Michigan Lobes met, and from where they diverged, the trail follows the terminal moraine of the Green Bay Lobe. If we were to hike the trail's entire thousand-plus miles, from Potawatomi State Park on the Door Peninsula to Interstate Park on the St. Croix River, we would pass near August Derleth's Sac Prairie, Aldo Leopold's shack, and John Muir's boyhood lake. The more northern terminal moraines of other lobes that descended only a third of the way down the state—the Langlade, the Wisconsin Valley, the Chippewa, and the Superior—lead the trail the rest of the way to the border with Minnesota. South of those lobes a relatively narrow band of terrain shows evidence of earlier glaciation prior to the Wisconsin Glaciation, and south of that band is the large southwestern quarter of the state known as the Driftless Area, with no sign of glaciation. When you think of Wisconsin's landscape, you think in terms of either the glacier's presence or its absence.

The Ice Age Trail grew out of the desire to preserve evidence of the Wisconsin Glaciation and to encourage people to explore glacial features and learn about glacial geology by walking through the terrain it formed—in essence, to enhance people's connection with their own home ground. The idea originated in the 1950s with Ray Zillmer, a Milwaukee lawyer and avid hiker. Zillmer's advocacy of the Wisconsin Glacier National Forest Park led to legislation that eventually supported aspects of his concept. August Derleth was one of the prominent figures in Wisconsin who supported the idea.

Zillmer died in 1960 and didn't see his idea come to fruition. But in 1964 the Ice Age National Scientific Reserve was established, as Henry Reuss, the Wisconsin congressman who authored legislation to create the reserve, points out in *On the Trail of the Ice Age,* to "assure protection, preservation, and interpretation of the nationally significant features of the Wisconsin glaciation, including moraines, eskers, kames, kettle holes, swamps, lakes, and other reminders of the Ice Age." By 1973, nine units around the state, consisting of state parks, recreation areas, and forest and wildlife preserves, had been created to protect glacial landscapes and landforms, and the reserve was officially dedicated. Zillmer's dream had been a thousand-mile-long national park; the Ice Age Reserve was hardly that, since its separate locations were scattered across the state. But the reserve sites were located in places along the line formed by the limits of the Wisconsin ice sheet's final advance, places that would have been part of the Wisconsin Glacier National Forest Park; the idea of linking them by means of a thousand-mile trail arose readily. Eventually, through the work of volunteers, enough progress had been made on the trail that in 1980 Congress renamed the IAT the Ice Age National Scenic Trail, giving it equal status with the Appalachian and Pacific Crest National Scenic Trails, under the aegis of the National Park Service. In the thirty-five years since then, almost seven hundred of the proposed thousand-plus miles of the trail have been completed, some of them running through national and state forests and state and county parks, some of them running across private lands, all of them maintained by dedicated volunteers in twenty-one different IATA chapters scattered across thirty counties. More than 130 people have officially walked the entire length of the trail (compared with more than twelve thousand on the Appalachian Trail and nearly five thousand on the Pacific Crest Trail).

Sue and I likely will not be among those who complete the thousand miles, but we have been among those working and walking on the trail segments in Waukesha County. A phrase of Aldo Leopold's sometimes comes to mind when I'm on the trail. In "Marshland Elegy" he described a dawn wind rolling a bank of fog across the marsh "like the white ghost of a glacier." It seems to me that, when we and the others we sometimes work and hike with walk the Ice Age Trail, we're walking with the white ghost of the glacier, the glacier forever out of sight, of course, but on the best hikes, still somehow companionably, impressively present.

3

In the Monches segment the Carl Schurz Forest is a definite woods on definitely glacial terrain, and the Oconomowoc River floodplain is more or less enclosed and self-contained. Despite occasional houses and yards at certain points along the trail, it was easy for us to concentrate on the landscape and the forces that shaped it, easy to develop a sense of where we were. The next few segments will give us little chance to feel the same kind of seclusion. It will be like moving abruptly from Muir's Fountain Lake or Leopold's shack to Derleth's Sac Prairie, from a mostly natural setting to a mostly developed one.

On a January afternoon, walking from an ice-coated parking

lot near the southern end of the Monches segment, we pass
through the stone arch below the railroad trestle just as a freight
train rumbles across overhead, as if to confirm the continued need
for the overpass. At the nearby trailhead for the Merton segment
we follow the trail up a steep slope into the woods, paralleling
the Oconomowoc River in the distance for a way, then veering
off and descending onto the bed of the defunct Kettle Moraine
Railway. The tracks were laid down in the nineteenth century by
the Milwaukee and Superior Railroad, which intended to cross
the state to the Lake Superior ports of Superior and Duluth. But
they only got as far as North Lake, four miles west of Merton, and
for a while carried mostly gravel and ice to Milwaukee. The Kettle
Moraine Railway, an old-timey tourist train running between
North Lake and Merton, used the tracks more recently, until pressures from subdivision development, objecting to a loud, smoky
historic locomotive blocking backroad traffic, forced the business
to close. Rather than agricultural or vacation areas, Monches and
Merton have become bedroom communities for commuters as-
piring to a more suburban way of life.

To the west a fence closes off the wooden trestle over the
Oconomowoc; to the east the rail bed is level and straight and
walled in on either side by trees and higher ground. We follow
the yellow-blazed Ice Age Trail path running along the southern
slope parallel to the railway, as if it were more legitimate than
the converted tracks, but when we near the top of the slope, we
realize how narrow a strip of woodlands we're walking through.
The sunken bed of the railway makes the first stretch of this trail
segment somewhat secluded, but we soon emerge onto the outskirts of Merton.

From here on we feel rather conspicuous following the trail
in the open, sometimes on the rail bed, sometimes along a thin
line of trees that makes us look incompetently furtive. We pass
open farmland, a power station, the backs of houses and garages,

on a flat, straight run to Dorn Road, the first of the off-trail connecting routes we'll have to hike on the shoulder of the road, cars
whizzing by in either lane. The road runs up and over a rise, and
we descend to a bridge over the Bark River. We've crossed into
the floodplain of a different river than the one we started near.

A throng of Canada geese floats on the surface of the river,
backlit by late-afternoon sunlight and stretching off around the
bend. There are too many to count, most of them barely moving.
The trail almost immediately leads into the woods along the river
and its wetlands. For a while, weaving near to and away from the
river, seldom in sight of it, we continually agitate the geese. They
can hear us clumping through mud and over stones and loudly
comment on it. The stream is rimmed with ice and the eddies
sometimes have a thin coating, but otherwise the water is clear
and open. Eventually the trail winds away from the river, first into
tall trees and then through dense thickets, and we no longer hear
the geese. Wooded slopes rise in the distance on one side of us
and on the other we often can't see the sedges of the wetlands.
In a little while we enter a broad meadow, brown grasses high on
either side of the trail, and walk in sunshine along a glassy, ice-
covered path. We emerge onto an open field heading toward a
distant barn and a low roadside fence, where the river goes under
another bridge. The river seems to widen here and flow serenely.

We're nearly to the limit of the completed trail in the Merton
segment. Across the road, after a short walk through some woods
and over a bridge, we'll enter a subdivision that takes us back to
Dorn Road and a two-mile walk to the next trailhead. Connecting routes like this link completed segments of the Ice Age Trail.
Sometimes they pass through quiet residential neighborhoods,
sometimes along country roads, sometimes along crowded four-
lane highways. The IATA continually negotiates for easements
through more natural environments and continually works to
complete new segments of the trail and to reroute older ones as

development encroaches, but as yet it still needs the connecting routes.

Our walk in the Merton segment alters our sense of the Ice Age Trail from what the Monches segment implied it might be. Monches was entirely woods and riverbank, essentially a nature hike; Merton is largely the abandoned railway bed and passage through town and across and along roads, at best a rural walk. Only along that short stretch of the Bark River floodplain, where we saw sunlight gleaming off the breasts of the geese and listened to them murmuring about our passage, did we feel isolated enough to concentrate on our surroundings. We're not eager to reach the subdivision and roadside connecting route and put it off for a month by heading back the way we've come.

In early February, sunshine and temperatures around forty degrees inspire an impromptu hike of the Hartland segment, the next section to the south, which also passes through glacial terraces of sand and gravel outwash. From the northern Hartland trailhead in Centennial Park, a paved path parallels the Bark River behind a heavy growth of slender trees on a narrow strip of riverbank. It makes me wish the trail from Merton had stayed close to the stretch of the river Milton J. Bates describes canoeing in *The Bark River Chronicles*.

In the nineteenth century, rivers were the sites of choice where villages sprang up, exploiting the water's potential for dams, mills, and commercial transportation. But after highways and railroads and other shifts in local economies diminished the water's advantages, communities turned their backs on the rivers, building away from them and using them as drainage for sewage and refuse. Reuben Gold Thwaites, canoeing the Wisconsin River in 1887, thought the Sauk City of August Derleth's parents' day "a shabby town" of "squalid back yards" where "slaughter-houses abut the stream." It led Thwaites to muse about the differences among river towns: "Some of them present a neat front to the water thoroughfare, with flower-gardens and well-kept yards and street-ends, while others regard the river as a sewer and the banks as a common dumping ground, giving the traveler by boat a view of filth, disorder, and general unsightliness which is highly repulsive." Only a downturn in manufacturing and a late-blooming recognition of the aesthetic appeal and commercial potential for tourism, recreation, and real estate of rivers inspired efforts to restore and even celebrate them. Such seems the case in Hartland. We pass many people out walking the paved paths along the river that the Ice Age Trail follows. Once again, in our hiking clothes we feel as conspicuous as voyageurs blundering into a civilized settlement.

From Centennial Park the river flows strongly through snow-lined banks and substantial cottonwoods. The trail soon arcs through a corridor of trees at the base of sloped lawns leading to a higher level of residences, sternly designated as private property. We clatter over a solid, well-built boardwalk, cross an arched wooden bridge, and walk another narrow corridor of trees above a flat, leaf-covered riverbank. At Hartbrook Drive, we face the raised embankment of State Highway 16 and detour through an underpass. The cars whooshing overhead sound more frenzied and determined than the train crossing the Oconomowoc overpass. The trail heads away from roads to follow the Bark all the way to downtown Hartland. There we leave the river, rise onto the main business street, and begin an urban stroll, down village streets and over city bridges, into Nixon Park. Misinterpreting signs, we head south on Cottonwood Avenue and discover ourselves at the Hartland Ice Age Wetland, an extensive marsh along the Bark River.

Hundreds of geese congregate in open water deeper in the marsh, away from the road. The brown grasses and the blue water and the multitudes of geese replay the scene we admired at the end of our Merton hike, as if the geese had all floated downstream over the course of a month. The wetland stretches a long way off on either side of the road, occupying the lowlands created by a glacial spillway, overlooked by housing on the highlands above it. Across the river and across the road, in a little cleared space, a sign like the one for the Carl Schurz Forest commemorates John Wesley Powell. Four years older than John Muir, Powell grew up on a farm in Walworth County, just south of Waukesha County, and, like Muir, really made his mark in the American West. Powell's exploration of the Colorado River was memorably epic, and his contributions as the head of the US Geological Survey were significant. His connection with Wisconsin marshland is tenuous, but as a Wisconsin-born conservationist Powell merits recognition, though the sign is easy to ignore by passing drivers on Cottonwood Avenue and a little challenging for hikers to reach.

In Hartland, the Ice Age Trail takes us by two other commemorative sites for Wisconsin conservationists. From the Powell site we backtrack a little through a residential area to get to the Aldo Leopold Overlook, above the eastern end of the marsh. At the top of a forty-five-foot glacial hill we find, appropriately enough, a Leopold bench with a view of the marsh. Below us is a frozen pond, with a couple of nesting boxes jutting up out of the ice. Beyond a stretch of tall sedges we see the geese crowded along the open water of the Bark. This is not the marshland that inspired Leopold's "Marshland Elegy," but it will do, and for a conservationist whose writing is intimately connected with the Wisconsin environment, it seems an inviting place to read that essay.

From the Leopold Overlook, the Ice Age Trail skirts the wetlands on one side and housing developments on the other and rambles to the Hartland Marsh–John Muir Overlook. A sign at the top of a rise quotes Muir's description of Fountain Lake and refers to this marsh as an Ice Age wetland. A footpath loops deeper into the area. Two years earlier, on our first hike with our IATA chapter, Sue and I took a tour through the marsh led by

Paul Mozina, who had been laboring for years to remove invasive plants crowding out native growth. He'd burned six hundred
piles of brush, mostly buckthorn, cleared the forest floor, and
planted native flora. We saw red oak, white oak, bur oak, cottonwoods—some trees were magnificently huge—white wild
geraniums. After long walks on boardwalks around the marsh
we hiked to an old homestead, only a totem pole and a stone
bench and fireplace still standing, and crossed the Bark River. We
startled a great horned owl that flew off while we stood watching.

It was only much later that I began to link the Wisconsin Conservationists Hall of Fame signs for Schurz, Powell, Leopold, and
Muir with Mozina's work on the Hartland Marsh. The memorial
signs for those historic ecologists are meant to be affirmative and
perhaps inspiring, a link between the volunteers who serve as
stewards and work crews for the Ice Age Trail and the pioneering
figures who advocated for the land. But in their out-of-the-way locations, they testify to the tangential presence in the public mind
of the people they commemorate; those commemorative overlooks would be easy to bypass for anyone not following the blazes
for the Ice Age Trail. But almost anywhere on the completed and
conscientiously maintained sections of the Ice Age Trail—off the
connecting routes and on the trail itself—or here in the restored
areas of Hartland Marsh, a person would be at once aware that
some contemporary volunteers share the spirit, the passion, of
those earlier figures and perhaps sense that their connection to
their home ground is deep and thoughtful and strong.

I felt hints of that on our first Ice Age Trail outing, not only
in Hartland Marsh, but also in a section of woods that Sue and I
now routinely hike as IAT stewards. South of the Muir Overlook,
through an open corridor between commercial buildings and residential areas and across a busy road and near more housing, the
trail enters an open field, where summer grasses grow higher than
hikers' heads, and arcs through it to dense woods. It wanders west

along a slope, some farmland visible on the lowland to the north, a tony residential neighborhood out of sight beyond the top of the rise. For the most part this stretch is secluded and closed in, with huge oaks standing along the trail. The trail here essentially crosses the till settled on the western edge of the Niagara Escarpment, which underlies the upland to the east of the trail through Hartland, most notably just east of the Leopold Overlook, and much of the Kettle Moraine from this point on. The escarpment isn't exposed here, but on our first hike through this section—the one that took us to Hartland Marsh—I was aware of its submerged presence and liked sensing it. At some places on the trail I'm more attuned to the gray ghost of the escarpment than to the white ghost of the glacier.

Trail stewards help maintain the trail by walking their sections often, picking up trash and debris, hacking back obstructions, removing fallen limbs or trees. I've come to this section on chapter workdays when volunteers rerouted the trail around an eroded slope, unblocked a flooding stream, yanked out buckthorn and garlic mustard, leveled the tread. Ice Age Trail volunteers share a sense of responsibility not only for the condition of the trail but also for heightening the connection hikers or casual walkers might feel for the terrain they pass through. Like the Monches segment or that stretch of the Bark River in Merton or the wetlands in Hartland, this one-mile stretch of woods lifts me out of time and immerses me in the moment, in my sense of where I am.

That feeling of connection dissipates quickly when I leave this stretch of woods. The trail winds past huge houses and vast lawns, passes behind a huge church, and follows the edge of a golf course to a junction with the Lake Country Recreation Trail, a paved bike trail it shares through the city of Delafield.

We return in March to the junction of the Hartland and Delafield segments, at a busy intersection on State Highway 83. On the ups and downs of the Delafield trail segment, we're too aware of walking a paved path under towering power lines to concentrate on the terrain. We walk amidst an abundance of other walkers and bikers. Soon we descend onto the streets of Delafield, pass historic buildings like the 1846 Hawks Inn and a busy, bustling downtown, and stride out along the bike path until the Ice Age Trail separates from it. The Delafield segment is essentially an urban stroll through an appealing-enough town, if you enjoy taking a stroll through a town. All along the way I'm reminded of my wanderings—and August Derleth's—in Prairie du Sac and Sauk City and I suspect that only someone with Derleth's expansive sense of home ground, his feeling for both town and terrain, will connect to this segment in the way he connected to Sac Prairie. By the time we're climbing away from the Lake Country Recreation Trail toward the trailhead for the Lapham Peak segment, I realize that at almost no point in the day have I thought about the glacier that formed the terrain all this disguises.

4

At the intersection of Highway 83 and Golf Road, where the Hartland and Delafield segments meet, a drugstore occupies one corner, a shopping plaza another, and a park-and-ride lot a third, while multiple lanes of traffic rush in between. The highway slopes down toward exit and entrance ramps for Interstate 94, which spans the bottom of the slope, then rises up the other side of the valley toward more shopping centers. Within a half-mile stretch there are five traffic lights. For his course on Waukesha County's glacial geology at the University of Wisconsin–Waukesha, Marlin Johnson took his class, me among them, to a parking lot near a coffee shop on the southern slope and asked us to survey this congested area and imagine everything on it gone. A pleasant idea, if difficult to achieve. Johnson was explaining the complications of land formation here, the way the glacier would have dammed the nearby lakes—Nagawicka to the west, Pewaukee to the east—in different places at different times and forced meltwater to find different routes away from the basins. One ancient river channel that resulted was likely formed by a catastrophic collapse of an ice dam that sent a massive amount of meltwater scouring the landscape to the south and coming to rest in the lowest areas it could find. Later, when we drove south on Highway 83, we could see the floodplain of peaceful, placid Scuppernong Creek, the quiet inheritor of that wide, flat channel; and on Highway 18, when we parked at one of the southern access points for the Lapham Peak section of the IAT, we noted the flatness of the land to the east and the wooded rise of the land to the west. For those few minutes at least, we seemed to be connected to the ghost of a glacier.

The challenge for anyone trying to comprehend glacial geology is imagining the scale of past events in light of the physical world you stand on while you search for it. Marlin Johnson's class and my efforts to walk this portion of my home ground are centered on one relatively small area affected by the Wisconsin glaciation, one county out of more than fifty that were covered by the ice, and one of seven counties on the dividing line between the Lake Michigan and Green Bay Lobes.

The Kettle Moraine, which dominates the remainder of the Ice Age Trail across the rest of Waukesha County, extends to the north through Washington and Ozaukee Counties and south through a corner of Jefferson County into Walworth County. The Niagara Escarpment, which underlies much of the Kettle Moraine in Waukesha County and is usually credited with dividing the Lake Michigan and Green Bay Lobes, reaches northeast to the end of Wisconsin beyond the Door Peninsula, arches through the Upper Peninsula of Michigan and down the Bruce Peninsula of Ontario, heads east to form Niagara Falls, and crosses western

New York state. Fifty counties, 120 miles of Kettle Moraine, nearly 1,000 miles of Niagara Escarpment, glacial deposition dating back 16,000 to 22,200 years—this is what I mean by scale.

And then there's the matter of how complicated it can be to explain events that took place over millennia, and how difficult it is, first, to unravel what evidence still exists and, second, to compose an explanation comprehensible to a layperson—say, to a person like me. Glaciers advanced and melted back and advanced again, and streams ran below and through them and around their edges, and what formed at one time got altered at a later time and that got altered still later in a way that exposed a portion of what was there before the earlier alteration. And so on.

Meltwater stream sediment ran across open surfaces, but ice buried beneath the open surfaces could be covered by till; when that ice melted, the sediment could sink and form kettle depressions and turn the sediment around the kettles into "hummocky" hills and ridges. Lee Clayton, in *Pleistocene Geology of Waukesha County, Wisconsin,* tells us, "The Kettle Moraine consists of a nested series of partly collapsed outwash fans and eskers, overlain by till in places, and formed at the apex of the angle between the Green Bay and Lake Michigan Lobes." Outwash fans are the sediment deposited by meltwater at the glacier's edge; eskers are the meandering ridges formed from the sediment in streams flowing within the glacier; till is the debris on top of the glacier that settles when the ice melts. I find it bewildering to try to sort out the sequence of any of those things happening.

You say a term like "kettle moraine" and, because you have an idea what a "kettle" is and an idea what a "moraine" is—and may even be able to explain the differences among "lateral," "terminal," "recessional," and "medial" moraines—you have a single uniform image in your head. That kettles here might sometimes be "kettles" (formed by the settling of debris on melting blocks of ice) and sometimes be simple depressions on either side of a hummock (it's the buildup of the hummocks that creates the depressions); that "moraine" here might not be an accurate geological term (Clayton claims "the Kettle Moraine is more nearly an esker than a moraine"); that marked differences in terrain exist along the length of the Kettle Moraine—all these tend to fracture that uniform image.

Mickelson notes that, throughout the Kettle Moraine, very little till can be found and "nearly all the sediment is sand or a combination of sand and gravel that was deposited by meltwater." For that reason, Mickelson argues, "the Kettle Moraine is not a moraine by most definitions but instead is an interlobate zone where supraglacial and subglacial streams deposited sand and gravel." Somehow, "supraglacial and subglacial interlobate deposit zone" doesn't have quite the ring to it that "Kettle Moraine" does, but Mickelson's description is a good one to keep in mind when you're trying to figure out what you're traveling through on these segments of the Ice Age Trail.

"The Kettle Moraine has no borders," Laurie Allman asserts, in *Far from Tame: Reflections from the Heart of a Continent.* "There is no precise moment when one can be said to pass into or out of it." Instead, she says, it "runs in a snaking and discontinuous line."

When preservation of the Kettle Moraine as a geological feature of the Wisconsin landscape was first proposed, it was envisioned as an unbroken state forest, something that, like the Ice Age Trail, one might walk through from end to end without ever leaving, but the state was unable and often unwilling to push for that vision. The Kettle Moraine State Forest today consists of a large Northern Unit, a large Southern Unit, and three small units in between, Pike Lake, Loew Lake, and Lapham Peak. The separation of the units has been made permanent by the development of communities around and in between them. The Ice Age Trail passes through every unit, and Mickelson and his coauthors divide its path through the Kettle Moraine into northern, middle, and southern sections. In Waukesha County the Monches, Merton, Hartland, and Delafield segments are assigned to the Middle Kettle Moraine, and the Lapham Peak, Waterville, Scuppernong, Eagle, and Stony Ridge segments to the southern Kettle Moraine.

From the southern end of the Delafield segment on, Sue and I will be hiking in terrain somewhat more familiar to us. All the Kettle Moraine State Forest units have other trails in addition to the Ice Age Trail, some for summer hiking and winter skiing, some for mountain biking, some for horseback riding, and we've walked such trails in Lapham Peak and the Southern Unit. Often, in our early hikes, the trail we followed would cross the Ice Age Trail and we would wonder what it was and why it was different from any of the color-coded loops we were walking. Now we'll be crossing those other trails and adding a disoriented feeling of familiarity to the sense of discovery the Ice Age Trail often provides. We'll also have to broaden our viewpoint. From here on we'll have to take in not only the Ice Age Trail but the Kettle Moraine as well.

5

On the second weekend in March, on a gorgeous, sunny day with temperatures in the low sixties, we hike the Lapham Peak segment of the Ice Age Trail. Its northern trailhead occupies a corner of a vast, open, grassy area atop a steep rise a hundred feet higher than the surface of a small lake half a mile west. The trail wanders across rolling terrain beneath a uniform field of brown grasses and a pale blue sky, passes an isolated parcel of oak trees, and crosses toward more extensive woods on a slope to the east.

Laurie Allman, who wandered the area in November, observed that "with the leaves mostly down it is easier to see the contours of the land that make the region a showcase for the work of the last ice age." Until the foliage thickens, we'll find that statement true.

We wind our way up into a stretch of woods with an under-growth-free floor and a sense of spaciousness. From a ridge we spot an observation tower in the distance, rising above Lapham Peak itself. Back again in the grasses we pass preserved savanna, century-old white oaks, and restored prairie, all of it still winter dormant but full of wildflower promise for the warmer seasons. Our meandering course makes the grassland seem more extensive and broad than it is, almost as if we're walking across presettle-ment prairie early settlers would recognize. The trail turns east and eventually dips toward wetlands, the hummocky shallows still ice-coated in places but the ponds open water. On one large pond two geese float serenely. Memories of the landscape sur-rounding Muir's Fountain Lake flash across my mind. A long, tilt-ing boardwalk takes us across the wetlands around the pond, and then we enter the forested stretch of the Lapham Peak segment.

The trail is level here, circling a large pond fringed with cattails and marshland and a viewing platform jutting out on one side. We angle back into the trees, the forest floor open and the trees relatively young and widely spaced, and climb the western slope of Lapham Peak. Soon the trees give way and our view of the wooden tower opens up. It's forty-five feet high, rising above the leafless oaks that surround it. The tower and the trees stand starkly against the empty blue of the sky, above the scruffy brown grasses.

We've been up the tower before. On one of our earliest out-ings in Wisconsin, we wanted to stand on the highest point in Waukesha County and compare its 1,233 feet of elevation with the 14,000-foot elevations of the peaks we'd climbed a few months be-fore in Colorado. The difference in vistas was obvious, of course, and Lapham Peak couldn't inspire anything like the awe that Longs Peak had. It took me a while to realize that it didn't have to. Now I have a richer sense of where I am and what I should

be looking for; namely, the distinguishing features that identify
my home ground—the drumlins formed by the Lake Michigan
Lobe visible to the east toward Waukesha, the drumlins formed
by the Green Bay Lobe to the west, the flat bed of Glacial Lake
Scuppernong to the southwest. The "peak" itself is a glacial hill,
and roughly twenty miles off to the north, if the day is particularly
clear, it's possible to see the basilica on the top of Holy Hill, a
moulin kame in Washington County a hundred feet higher than
Lapham Peak. (A "moulin" is a vertical shaft in a glacier through
which debris spills to form a conical hill, or "kame.") With binoculars I can usually locate the basilica's towers, even through
midafternoon haze, but picking out the drumlins is more challenging now that so much of the terrain is tree-covered—I rely on
occasional farmlands to make their shapes more visible. It's hard
to imagine away the visible evidence of the twenty-first century
when we stand at the top of the Lapham Peak tower, but if we try
we might be able to glean a sense of our glacial origins.

I was drawn to Lapham Peak, even before I knew about the Ice
Age Trail, because of Increase Allen Lapham, one of the most fascinating figures in early Wisconsin history. He had a relentless curiosity and a wide-ranging intelligence, and his accomplishments
are impressive in their breadth and scope. Considering what he
contributed to botany, geology, zoology, history, archaeology,
engineering, surveying, education, conservation, and meteorol-
ogy—I hope I haven't overlooked any area of his interests—it's
startling to realize that he was essentially self-taught in all those
fields.

I also feel a personal connection, though in reality there is
none. Lapham was born in Palmyra, New York, in 1811, the son of
a canal contractor. At the age of thirteen he was employed cutting
stone for the locks of the Erie Barge Canal in Lockport, New York.
That's where my personal connection comes in—and reveals its
remoteness: Lockport is the town where my parents met and

married and where I was born, none of which would have happened if locks hadn't been constructed at that section of the canal.

Lapham's experience with canals brought him to Milwaukee in 1836, just before Wisconsin Territory separated from Michigan. He'd been hired as the chief engineer on the Milwaukee and Rock River Canal, intended to skirt lake traffic around Chicago to the Mississippi. The canal plan fell through but Lapham stayed on, married, and settled in Milwaukee. For nearly forty years he was active in the social and cultural life of Wisconsin: the Milwaukee Female Seminary (which later grew into the University of Wisconsin–Milwaukee), Carroll College (now University) in Waukesha, the Wisconsin Academy of Science, Arts and Letters, the State Historical Society of Wisconsin, the Young Men's Society (whose book collection grew into the Milwaukee Public Library), the Milwaukee Public High School, the Natural History Society, and the Milwaukee Public Museum—all these are indebted to his energy and intellect. For a man with no formal schooling—his doctorate from Amherst College in 1860 was honorary—he seems to have had great zeal for learning and for opening doors to knowledge for others.

Lapham's publications were varied and essential. In 1836, the year he arrived, he published the first scientific pamphlet in Wisconsin, *A Catalogue of Plants and Shells Found in the Vicinity of Milwaukee on the West Side of Lake Michigan.* In 1844 he published *A Geographical and Topographical Description of Wisconsin,* the first book about the territory, later titled in the second edition, *Wisconsin: Its Geography and Topography, History, Geology, and Mineralogy; Together with Brief Sketches of Its Antiquities, Natural History, Soil, Productions, Population, and Government.* It was widely distributed and is credited with spurring emigration to the territory. As early as 1836, as deputy surveyor for the new Wisconsin Territory, he surveyed effigy and burial mounds throughout the region, and in 1855 the Smithsonian Institution published *The*

Antiquities of Wisconsin as Surveyed and Described, Lapham's thorough review of the existing earthworks he had encountered and recorded. Worried about the potential "loss of those records of an ancient people," he argued, "Now is the time, when the country is yet new, to take the necessary measures for their preservation." In the end Lapham's book served as a catalog of what would be destroyed by cultivation and settlement in the century and a half since the book was published. To me, what Lapham's *Antiquities* still records is its author's powers of rational speculation and, even more strongly, his powers of foresight, both found throughout his writings.

In 1867 Lapham, J. G. Knapp, and H. Crocker published their *Report on the Disastrous Effect of the Destruction of Forest Trees, Now Going On So Rapidly in the State of Wisconsin.* The epigraph for the report comes from *Man and Nature* by George Perkins Marsh: "Man has too long forgotten that the earth was given to him for usufruct alone, not for consumption, still less for profligate waste." Lapham and his coauthors warned that removing the forests would have a detrimental impact on the environment, making summers hotter, winters colder, winds stronger, ground dryer, springs and rivers more likely to dry up, floods more extensive, "the soil on sloping hills washed away; loose sands blown over the country preventing cultivation; . . . the productiveness of the soil diminished"; and thunderstorms, hail, and rains more frequent and more intense. I don't know to what extent the ecological history of Wisconsin since their report confirms the accuracy of these predictions, but certainly Aldo Leopold's account of the sand county farm he first occupied bears witness to some of the effects they forecast. The report also foreshadows the Dust Bowl and perhaps our own era of climate change and harks back to the history of the Muirs' Fountain Lake Farm. It perhaps confirms a tendency in people to concentrate on the promise of immediate rewards rather than on the potential for eventual catastrophe.

Lapham was a thorough record keeper. This thoroughness extended to his observations about the weather. According to Martha Bergland and Paul G. Hayes, in *Studying Wisconsin: The Life of Increase Lapham,* soon after Lapham's arrival in Milwaukee he began "calculating the length and severity of Wisconsin winters by recording the dates each year when the Milwaukee River froze over and thawed." He installed his instruments on the west shore of the river, "little more than a block east of the Lapham home," and recorded temperatures, barometric pressures, snow and rain fall totals, and high and low water levels of both Lake Michigan and the Milwaukee River. When Lapham was away from home, his wife and sons continued to add to his records.

The results of this methodical recordkeeping, like Aldo Leopold's phenological records on his sand county surroundings, led Lapham to speculate on the practical possibilities of weather observation. In 1850 he unsuccessfully urged the Wisconsin legislature to establish a state weather bureau. But twenty years later, in 1870, Congress approved Lapham's proposal, thereby establishing the National Weather Bureau. The United States Army Signal Corps created a system of twenty-four observer network stations. Signals sent from Pikes Peak in Colorado were received by telegraph at the station on Government Hill in Wisconsin and relayed to headquarters in Chicago. Lapham wired the first published national weather forecast on November 8, 1870, reporting high winds in Cheyenne and Omaha and predicting, "Barometer falling and thermometer rising at Chicago, Toledo, Cleveland, Buffalo, and Rochester. High winds probable along the lakes." A marker commemorating this first national weather forecast was erected at Lapham Peak in 1955, and I stop to read it every time I visit the tower. And each time I hear the radio telling me the National Weather Service station in Sullivan has issued some warning or other—Sullivan is a little farther west of Lapham Peak—I think of Increase Lapham and what he accomplished.

In 1875 Lapham died of a heart attack in a rowboat on Ocon-omowoc Lake, in northwest Waukesha County, shortly after he'd completed writing his final scientific paper, "Oconomowoc and Other Small Lakes of Wisconsin Considered in Reference to Their Capacity for Fish Production." After nearly four decades in Wisconsin, he apparently never tired of learning about the state and passing on what he learned. I admire that about Increase Lapham. He certainly merits being commemorated as a conserva-tionist along with Muir, Leopold, Schurz, and Powell, not simply with a sign but with a state park. Like Muir, Leopold, and Derleth, he reminds me that, wherever we are, there is always something more to learn about what we make our home ground.

And so I try to pay attention as the Ice Age Trail descends a long, steep set of stairs on the east side of the tower hill. The woods close in around us, thicker and denser than on the western slope. We trudge a long way through deep woods, the path often narrow, continually rising and falling, bending and turning; we can seldom see far ahead or far behind or very deep into the trees and shrubbery on either side. Occasionally we cross a few of the other, wider park trails used for winter snowshoeing and skiing and I strain to recognize them as ones we've been on before. At times we notice kettles below us off the trail, a few of them dry, many of them still ice covered, a blur of white at the bottom of brown, leaf-coated slopes. Near the eastern boundary of the park we begin to meander south, reaching ever-lower elevations until we move out of the close packed trees and onto a terrace above a flat floodplain, with good views of wetlands further east. We pass through an open meadow, with an occasional sprawling bur oak that stops me in my tracks from admiration. I wonder from their size if any are older than Leopold's Good Oak.

We soon reach the trailhead on US 18, where Marlin Johnson took his glacial geology class to view the south end of that gla-cial meltwater channel. Scuppernong Creek flows through the channel now, a spring-fed "underfit stream" too small to have originally cut it. I think about the Scuppernong Creek floodplain on one side of Lapham Peak, the restored prairie, oak opening, and savanna on the other side, the tower on the hilltop, and the flourishing forest we've wound our way through, and I realize that being able to hold it all in my mind means I'm getting closer to being at home in it.

6

One thing I don't keep in mind often enough is the difference between the Kettle Moraine as a geological feature and the Kettle Moraine State Forest as an official natural resource. Established in 1937, the state forest, in all its units, has distinct borders, but the geological entity, as Laurie Allman observed, hasn't. When I leave the Kettle Moraine State Forest I'm still in the Kettle Moraine itself. In the same way, though it's handy to break the Ice Age Trail into identifiable sections with distinct trailheads to mark beginnings and endings—handy, that is, for those who prefer to hike the forty-five miles in Waukesha County or the thousand-plus miles in Wisconsin in short spurts rather than in one continuous march—the Ice Age terrain the trail traces is vaster than its outline in our hiking atlas. When someone writing about New Jersey or New England mentions the extent of the Wisconsin Glaciation there, I'm grateful for the reminder: the Wisconsin Glaciation wasn't just for Wisconsin. If I grant myself a moon's-eye view of the northern hemisphere more than a hundred centuries ago, I gain a richer perspective on what the trail we walk is connected to.

Here and now, of course, my perspective is most often narrowly focused on the ground where I place my hiking shoes, and my peripheral vision extends no farther than the edges of the trail. Even so, as I follow the Ice Age Trail through both the geological and the governmental Kettle Moraines, I continually encounter cues that send me across time, in connections both tenuous and temporal.

The temporal comes in flashes of memory from places we've hiked before. In our first year in Wisconsin, looking for nearby hiking trails, we were drawn first to Lapham Peak and then to trails in the Southern Unit of the Kettle Moraine State Forest. The John Muir Trail in northern Walworth County, popular with mountain bikers in dry, warm weather, introduced us to the forests, ridges, and kettles of the Kettle Moraine. We took it in March, when the leaves were down, the contours exposed, and the trail too muddy or intermittently snowy and icy for bikers. Other than the trickiness of the footing, I remember most vividly the view from high on a narrow ridge into a leatherleaf bog at the bottom of a large kettle and reveled in the seclusion along the trail.

The trail had originally been intended by the Sierra Club to be mostly undeveloped. The former Kettle Moraine trails co-ordinator Ray Hajewski explains, in Candice Gaukel Andrews's *Beyond the Trees,* that it was meant to be "a walk through the wild woods. If a tree fell down across the trail, so be it. You'd walk over it or around it." At first, it could be imagined as a trail someone like John Muir would want to walk; but over time, to accom-modate cross-country skiers and mountain bikers, all the trails in the southern Kettle Moraine State Forest were widened and rerouted, and their crowded use sorely altered the terrain. Some careful redesigning has since ameliorated some of the damage, but as any hiker who has walked a trail shared with bikers knows, the pleasure of a walk in the woods is ferociously detonated by the headlong rush of a mountain biker hurtling a rise or explod-ing out of a curve—bikers usually ride the woods for speed and challenge, not for solitude and serenity. Once the ground dried out and the snow evaporated, we avoided most loops on the John Muir Trail.

A year later we hiked the Emma Carlin Trail in southeastern Jefferson County, again too early for bikers, and we were entirely alone on the trail. We started out from a glacial sand plain and walked through hardwood forests to a vista over Lower Spring Lake and a potential sighting of distant Holy Hill, but I didn't appreciate sufficiently what we were seeing or realize that, because the Ice Age Trail skirts both the John Muir Trail and the Emma Carlin Trail, I had learned where the trail and the Kettle Moraine both go when they leave Waukesha County.

My interest in knowing where I was grew slowly. Closer to home in Waukesha County, I hiked the Scuppernong Trail a couple of weeks after we'd been on the Muir, and I still recall the impact the terrain there had on me. If you think that brown and gray are two colors that ought to dominate a landscape, the view on every side was a study in their use. Walking alone, meeting no one else, all I heard was the wind rustling dead leaves on the bare trees and my own feet shuffling through leaves on the trail, which often skittered around me in the wind. Sometimes sand was underfoot, sometimes gravel, but mostly leaves and, under towering pines, thick layers of pine needles.

Often the trail would climb a ridge alongside a deep bowl, sometimes one on either side, and I would wonder about the glacial forces that had been at work there. When I got home I reread Laurie Allman's chapter on the Kettle Moraine and looked in *Home Ground: Language for an American Landscape* for definitions of *moraine, drumlin, esker, kame, outwash plain,* and *kettle* (I was delighted to learn that Walden Pond is a kettle). I made sure I brought Sue with me back to the Scuppernong Trail, crossing the Ice Age Trail with only a little curiosity and unaware that Scuppernong is the northernmost IAT segment in the southern Kettle Moraine State Forest.

The more tenuous connections grew out of my discovery that, in the IAT's Waterville segment, between the Lapham Peak and

Scuppernong segments, and in the Eagle segment, just south of
the Scuppernong, it would be possible to see outcroppings of the
Niagara Escarpment if I walked the Ice Age Trail.

I was born on the Niagara Escarpment. It's the geological feature that the Erie Barge Canal had to climb using the same locks
Increase Lapham helped build in Lockport. I've driven often
along the escarpment in Southern Ontario, hiked some of it on
Ontario's Bruce Peninsula, run into it inadvertently on Michigan's
Upper Peninsula, and vacationed on it on Wisconsin's Door Peninsula. The Niagara Escarpment is the geologic feature I relate
to most, a feature that begins not far from where I did and ends
(more or less, by not surfacing again beyond it) here in Waukesha
County, where I likely will.

The escarpment is some four hundred million years older
than the last Ice Age. To simply say the name transports me at
once back to the Silurian Period, in the middle of the Paleozoic
Era, and simultaneously back to the mid-twentieth century and
a view of the Lockport locks. It's an inevitable and irresistible act
of time travel.

Sometimes, similar though less intense moments happen as
a result of having taken that glacial geology class. We took a field
trip around Waukesha County, stopping on Highway 18 to gaze
at a very clear example of a drumlin, following the glacial channel from its source at Nagawicka and Pewaukee Lakes down the
floodplain of Scuppernong Creek to the end of the Lapham Peak
unit, and wandering a portion of the Scuppernong Springs Nature
Trail in the Kettle Moraine State Forest. At Scuppernong Springs,
where Paul Mozina, our guide at Hartland Marsh, leads an effort
to restore the marshland and return the Scuppernong River to
its original channel, we saw evidence of multiple eras of time.
The marsh there once was mined for marl, the chalky, lime-rich
deposit laid down in glacial lakes and excavated to use as fertilizer
and mortar—the same substance that lines the bottom of Muir's

Fountain Lake. In addition to that early-twentieth-century enterprise, at varying times there were a nineteenth-century trout
hatchery, a hotel, a sawmill, a cranberry bog, and eventually a
brewery on the site. A Native American encampment preceded all
of them. Scuppernong Springs is presently on its way back to its
presettlement state, but to walk it is to intersect with half a dozen
time periods in ways that may not be so obvious in other places.

As I wrestle with that moon's-eye view, zooming in and zooming out as on a satellite map, I try to remember that I should also
attempt to see things at various moments in an immense timeline,
even if it means also trying to somehow see the invisible and the
vanished.

7

On the summer day we set off from the northern Waterville trailhead, after a short walk through woods and along a meadow, we
have to trudge for more than a mile along the shoulder of Waterville Road to get back onto the trail. Then we're in woods, soon
taking a long solid boardwalk through lowlands, passing under
tall trees and through thick undergrowth. The forest seems broad
and high. We're just off the western side of the Kettle Moraine,
angling along terrain on its Green Bay Lobe side and following
the edge of the Niagara Escarpment, crossing rolling terrain with
some steep slopes. It's quiet in the woods and I often gawk at the
older, larger oaks, until I sprawl headlong on the trail from not
watching my feet. When I stand up, Sue points at a deer running
away from us, no doubt alarmed by the whoomp of my fall. When
we cross a subdivision street where I parked a few years before
and enter the longer, more secluded stretch of the segment, I start
recalling moments from that earlier hike.

On that autumn day I passed through what my hiking guide

described as "remnants of pre-settlement vegetation: oak forest, oak openings, prairie and wetland" looking for "a small exposed section of native dolomite bedrock," part of the Niagara Escarpment. It was a short hike, generally downhill, through forest almost all the way. Generally the forest floor was closed with undergrowth, though occasionally the darkness from the canopy kept it clear of growth but dense with fallen trunks and limbs. I constantly tramped over acorns and oak leaves. At one point the trail wound its way along the edge of a field and then took a turn that brought me into the open. A large hayfield spread out before me, newly mown, with scattered wheels of hay standing here and there. Three sandhill cranes idled in the middle distance, moving with that stately slow-motion strut, occasionally lowering their heads to the ground. This was one of my first crane sightings in Wisconsin, and I gazed at them for several minutes. Eventually one of them complained about my standing there and, rather than prompt them to flight, I moved on.

The trail went lower and crossed some wetlands and another field, and when I could hear cars on the road again, I assumed I wasn't far from the southern trailhead and turned around. On the way back I noticed the outcroppings of buried dolomite under my feet and located some off to the side of the trail, but I found no especially pronounced formation. Except for the cranes, a few other birds invisible in the foliage, and the occasional squirrel, I'd seen no signs of wildlife; occasionally I heard distant voices from nearby farms or the sound of machinery but only near the end of the hike did I meet a man in a bright yellow vest, pumping walking sticks, coming the other way. Otherwise I'd been on the trail for an hour and a half alone.

Now, walking the Waterville segment again, I look for familiar places.

Soon enough we top a rise and parallel the edge of the spacious hayfield where I saw the cranes my first time through; it's empty now, but I can't help scouring the field in hopes of spotting them. After a few minutes of fruitless gazing, we keep walking. As we descend steeply, wind through more woods and out along a grassy and uncultivated field, cross low wetlands on some rather unstable puncheons, and make the slight rise up to the southern trailhead on a county road, I keep thinking about the cranes I saw almost three years earlier, when cranes were not so familiar to me; images from Leopold's "Marshland Elegy" arise as well. There's a long chain of connection between the birds and the land, and my awareness of it makes me less disturbed than I once might have been by the abrupt appearance of a hayfield in the midst of my woodland walk.

On that earlier fall hike the Niagara dolomite was harder to spot, covered in moss and leaf litter. This time through I notice more rocks exposed on the trail, their color and shape familiar to me now from other escarpment sites I've visited. I like the idea that the ground I'm walking on here is an extension of the home ground I walked all through my childhood.

~

The connecting route between the Waterville and Scuppernong segments is the last one in the county. From the northern Scuppernong trailhead on we'll be in the Kettle Moraine State Forest all the way to the county line. On a cool June day we start out between two pastures, one fallow, the other filled with stunted stalks of corn and vast rectangles of hay. The trail is straight and flat until we enter the woods where the land rises and angle south on a continuous upslope. These are ice-contact slopes, gravel deposits once lower than the surrounding ice but, once the ice was gone, now higher than the surface the ice rested on. The climb takes us onto a mostly level area along a red pine plantation and into the sprawling Pinewoods campground. From now on we expect to cross wider, more open trails that we've followed on other hikes. The Ice Age Trail is narrow and runs through ground cover, with alternating stands of red pine and oak overhead, though at one point we pass a stretch of low white pine. A couple of orange signs with large black letters advise: "**Don't Shoot This Direction ↑ Houses Ahead**." We wonder how close the areas open to seasonal hunting are. The only people we see in this section of the Scuppernong are a woman and two teenaged girls, each with a large, aggressive dog on a leash, following one of the broader hiking trails. The dogs pull on their restraints and lean in our direction, but the women yank them back and keep talking without overtly noticing us. Until now we've seemed to have the woods to ourselves.

We are enclosed in green, the trail a narrow corridor through underbrush, sunlight dappling it through a high, thick canopy. The high point of the trail is at 1,066 feet and the trail soon becomes a series of ups and downs, elevations changing between 50 and 100 feet. The southern trailhead will be 200 feet lower than that high point. We gain a ground-level appreciation of what the geology guide means by the term "high-relief hummocky topography." We continually climb and descend, at one moment on top of a slope, at the next winding through a densely overgrown gully or swale bottom. The forest undergrowth is generally so thick that it's hard to see very far into it, but I'm continually aware of slopes falling steeply off on either side of us or, in the low sections, rising high in all directions.

The ground beneath our feet keeps changing, sandy at times in the lower regions, packed mud in other low sections, flat needle-covered sections under the pines, and on the slopes unsorted or undifferentiated rocky till. I recognize plenty of oaks as well as pines, and other hardwoods, such as maple and hickory and probably basswood, black cherry, and aspen. At times we find ourselves passing among towering red pines, sometimes in a seemingly endless plantation, other times down a mostly clear narrow corridor beneath them, the trail largely carpeted with pine needles. On a winding turn in the trail we find a middle-aged man in an Iowa Hawkeyes T-shirt and a baseball cap, standing off to the side, reviewing scenes he's shot on a large digital camera. He glances up at us, smiling, and says, "This isn't a forest preserve— this is the forest." I smile back at him. He has it right. For a good long time now we've had no inkling of where the forest might end or what might be beyond it. I keep the thought in mind as we continue down the trail.

8

In the course of its route across Wisconsin, particularly in the northwest section of the state, the Ice Age Trail passes through rugged terrain, where forests are deep and broad and chances of encountering black bears and at least hearing timber wolves are not unlikely and backpacking is the only way to get from one trailhead to another. In those sections it's possible to truly feel as if you're walking the wilderness. At times on the Lapham Peak and Scuppernong trail segments I had a similar feeling of immersion, of being intimately connected to the landscape, as if I were only one more of its standard elements. It's a feeling I prize, as if for a little while I have surrendered connection to the inorganic, man-ufactured world and merged my essence with the organic, natural world. It's a very temporary, ephemeral feeling. I welcome it when it comes and I'm sorry but not surprised how quickly it passes.

But I have no illusions about the wildness or naturalness of the Waukesha portions of the Ice Age Trail. The very trail itself is a constructed thing, and as local members of the Ice Age Trail Alliance, Sue and I have been on volunteer work crews rerouting and maintaining portions of the trail we've trod on as hikers. In the state natural areas and the state forest, long-term projects have focused on clearing away invasive plants, restoring native growth, conducting controlled burns, and building boardwalks and bridges. Almost anywhere we're likely to see prairies and wetlands and oak savannas that resemble those of presettlement years, we're seeing restoration successes at the hands of dedicated volunteers who have removed the impact of almost two centuries of cultivation and development to bring those places back to what they were. And, though the Ice Age Trail often avoids them, historical reminders of the uses to which the land has been put remain sprinkled nearby throughout the Kettle Moraine— remnants of the marl plant, rail bed, trout hatchery, and hotel at Scuppernong Springs, remnants of the spring house, bottling plant, turbine dam, trout pond, and hotel at Paradise Springs, at least three log cabins and one homestead site—and all those contemporary recreational areas—campgrounds, hiking, biking, and skiing trails, horse and snowmobile trails, a winter sports center, dog trial grounds, three Ice Age Trail backpacking shelters. There are times when you can imagine what the country was like when it was a string of farms, when it was dotted with commercial enterprises, when what we pass through now wasn't here.

In the natural order of things, terrain changes all the time, often in infinitesimal transformations invisible at the moments they occur and perhaps over unimaginable stretches of time; or sometimes in tumultuous alterations—the bursting of an ice dam, the gushing of floodwaters, inundation at one time, depletion and draining at another. Although human beings for centuries had an impact on the Wisconsin landscape through prairie fires and agriculture and burial and effigy mounds and the wearing of paths into the earth, after the influx of European American settlers in the mid-nineteenth century, change more often was radical, extreme, and myopic, impelled by short-term goals that had long-term consequences for the land.

Everywhere we walk along the Ice Age Trail in Waukesha

County we are walking through terrain that human beings have changed, sometimes in dire and damaging ways, sometimes in restorative healing ways, sometimes in ways that valued personal goals over an appreciation of land as a part of a biotic community, as something more than a commodity. The gulf between community and commodity is likely unbridgeable.

Still, among all those homeowners who have built with an eye to a vista, all those walkers and joggers who make paths from their own backyards onto the trails in parks and forests, all those who choose to locate their neighborhoods near woods and wetlands and rivers, many must be people who feel connected to their home ground, who value it, who don't want it to change.

Muir, Leopold, and Derleth each dealt with change in their home ground—they had to deal with it by virtue of feeling a part of it. As tempting as it is for someone like me to desire a pristine, thoroughly natural setting for the Ice Age Trail, the very act of maintaining it the way we do assures that it can't be pristine and natural. And it may be that in all the places the landforms of ten thousand years ago share space with the constructed elements of the nineteenth, twentieth, and twenty-first centuries, we have the opportunity to recognize how transient our constructions are, especially when measured against the endurance of the country we're passing through.

9

By the end of June, we're in the midst of a drought and the mosquitoes that usually plague summer hiking haven't been around. We leave the northern trailhead of the Eagle segment on a balmy day bright with unobstructed sunshine. When we enter the trees, I recall walking through them a few years before, impressed by their height and breadth, immediately entranced by Wisconsin oaks. I point out certain trees to Sue. Some of the oaks here are more than a century old. Often the undergrowth is thick, but in places leaf fall keeps the forest floor open. At the moment the ground is dry, yet the long winding stretches of recently installed puncheons tell us the trail is usually muddy in the woods and in the low wetlands beyond.

The trail breaks out of the trees to cross a portion of the Kettle Moraine Low Prairie State Natural Area, filled with wet meadow plants like blue-joint grass, shrubby cinquefoil, valerian, grass of Parnassus, and Ohio goldenrod. We spot two bluebirds, a common yellowthroat, a chipping sparrow, some Henslow's sparrows, a yellow warbler, and a bobolink. The trail takes us across a gravel road that leads to a dirt parking lot where we'd rendezvoused with a dozen other members of our chapter two months before for an IAT workday. That morning we rerouted a portion of the trail away from an imminent subdivision, established the tread on the new trail, pulled invasive plants like garlic mustard, and replaced blazes. Across the road we climb up a grassy knoll, arcing around a cluster of trees and high shrubs and past a side trail leading off to a Leopold bench and a scenic view north across the low prairie. At the top of the knoll another Leopold bench, more in the open, provides an even more expansive view.

From that bench the trail veers west toward the woods, dips down to cross a creek on a solid bridge, then climbs to the section of the trail we rerouted on that workday. We try to stay alert to the changes in the landscape a couple months have wrought. The trail now curves more deeply into the woods, toward glimpses of the prairie, and then crosses a midslope section leading toward the Brady's Rocks loop. Brady's Rocks were what drew me to the Eagle segment the first time I came. As far as I knew they were the southernmost outcropping of the Niagara Escarpment in Wisconsin and the last visible sign of the arc that extends all the way back to my hometown. I set out to find them on a crisp fall day, on a side trail then more remote from the main Ice Age Trail. I found some blocks of stone visible on the ground, completely coated in thick coverings of moss, and soon reached an area where I was surrounded by the rocks.

Michael and Kathleen Brady were Irish immigrants who settled in the area in 1855 to farm and at some point quarried some of the Niagara dolomite on their property. Remnants of a stone fence and the escarpment outcropping itself are now all that remain. I moved slowly around the slope where the outcropping was visible. The light-colored underlayers seemed evenly laid down while the darker capstone layers, which bear the brunt of weathering, were bumpy and weathered and uneven. Crevices and ledges and shelves revealed how much more erodible the lower layers were, how resistant the top layers. I thought of how Niagara Falls retreats upriver, the soft underside of the dolomite wearing away support for the resistant rock above, until it breaks off from its own weight and plummets into the debris at the base of the falls. The same principle is at work here, though hardly on such a dramatic scale.

In the interval since my first visit there, the main trail was re-routed to make Brady's Rocks less remote, and the path looping through the rocks was cleared to make the rocks more readily accessible. Today we walk the cool, shady loop slowly, the out-croppings often higher than our heads and surrounded by under-growth. We look closely at the greenery atop the rocks, hoping to identify three unique types of ferns found here: walking fern, fragile fern, and cliff brake. Walking fern, named for its tendency to grow a new fern where the tips of the old one touch the ground, is the fern for which Brady's Rocks are best known.

Beyond Brady's Rocks and back on the trail, the terrain levels out as we move through another stretch of the Kettle Moraine Low Prairie, this section lower, wet-mesic and dry-mesic inter-mingled. We walk in the open, in sunshine with an infrequent but welcome breeze, aware that in the past this part of the segment was agriculturally hard-used. Eventually we find ourselves back in a narrow shady corridor of trees. A boardwalk takes us across marshy wetland, where I'd once startled a smooth green snake that startled me; he surprised me again when I learned he actually is called "smooth green snake." We pass through an extensive pine plantation, the trees too regularly spaced to be a natural grove.

When we come out of the last of the woods, we can see a long way to the west, across a panorama of grassland, the most extensive we've seen so far. We're looking across the Scupper-nong River Habitat Area. Its boundaries include the Scuppernong Prairie Natural Area, as well as the Kettle Moraine Low Prairie Natural Area, but the whole of the habitat area is much larger than the sum of those parts. For over a decade and a half the State Department of Natural Resources has been attempting to restore the prairie through controlled burns and brush cutting, and the area has the chance to become, at 3,500 acres, the largest low prairie east of the Mississippi. Even if we know it's only a remnant of an area tens of thousands of acres broad, it's pretty impressive to gaze upon and walk through, and its combination of sedge meadows, low prairies, fens, and tamarack swamps reminds me of the landscape John Muir entered as a child.

We've entered the bed of Glacial Lake Scuppernong. The lake existed roughly 15,000 to 12,500 years ago, created by meltwater trapped between the terminal moraine of the Green Bay Lobe and the retreating glacier. The lakebed runs along the western edge of the Scuppernong, Eagle, and Stony Ridge IAT segments in Waukesha County, but it also once covered the whole of neighboring Jefferson County and portions of Walworth, Rock, Dane, Columbia, and Dodge counties beyond it. We'll be in the bed of Glacial Lake Scuppernong toward the end of the final segment of the Ice Age Trail in Waukesha County, and once I know that, I am continually aware of it.

We walk under a clear sky across open prairie. A sandhill crane takes wing from deep in the grasses, and along the way a plenitude of bobolinks post themselves prominently to sing, all highly visible and occasionally fairly approachable. Kingbirds, a Baltimore oriole, a yellow warbler, a bluebird, and some kind of flycatcher distract us from time to time. I try not to let my attention on my immediate surroundings be diverted by reflections about Brady's Rocks and Lake Scuppernong, but I can't help feeling that together they help conjure that white ghost of a glacier for me.

That the Green Bay and Lake Michigan Lobes separated and in their joint advance and final retreat left us the Kettle Moraine and all the glacial features around us is due in part to the presence of the Niagara Escarpment evidenced by Brady's Rocks. Glacial Lake Scuppernong rested above the land west of the southern Kettle Moraine for thousands of years, until the Green Bay Lobe retreated past Lake Winnebago, far off to the northeast. And here, as we walk the Eagle segment of the Ice Age Trail, the rocks and the lakebed remind us of everything that came before. For the time we're on the trail with them, at least, their presence is impossible to ignore.

At the southern end of the Eagle segment we look across the highway at the start of the Stony Ridge segment. We'd walked it at the end of April, out of sequence, at first through private property and across and along a couple county roads and then into a pine plantation. The pines were very straight and tall and generally thick; at the start of the section huge lengths of pine logs were piled up in rigidly uniform lengths. Through the bushes along the trail we saw signs of considerable logging as well as considerable slash, the residue of limbs and treetops scattered along the forest floor—a great deal of random tinder. For a while the pines soared above us but among the younger pines, more slender and not yet so tall, a solitary bur oak spread its limbs, reminding us that this was likely oak savanna before the pine plantation was installed.

We crossed railroad tracks at an intersection of trails. Two women on horseback moseyed distractedly up a horse trail, each active on her cell phone, neither noticing our approach on the footpath. Beyond a wide field thick with sand we ascended an esker, narrower than moraines and ridges we'd been on, with abundant young oaks on either side of the trail and rocky, undistributed till underfoot. Through the trees and underbrush on the steep slopes we saw water-filled kettles on either side. Off the esker the trail became a series of ups and downs, mostly kettle-free, past a nature trail loop originating in the Kettle Moraine Visitor's Center and a side trail to an IAT backpacking shelter. Topping a rise we descended onto open prairie, back onto the bed of Glacial Lake Scuppernong. Ahead of us was spacious rolling grassland and a mown trail heading for distant tall shrubs and sporadic forest and wetlands marked by a placid stream and a still pond. We reached the southern trailhead of the Stony Ridge segment at the Waukesha/Jefferson county line, near the parking lot for the Emma Carlin Trail. We knew where we were and knew what lay beyond, and felt that mixture of accomplishment and loss that comes with achieving a goal.

10

Our trail guide tells us that, once we've completed our walk through the county, we've hiked 40 trail miles and 5.8 connecting route miles; by walking a segment one way and then retracing our steps to the trailhead we started from, we've nearly doubled the in-county miles. At the Stony Ridge southern trailhead we were 273.2 miles from the eastern terminus of the Ice Age Trail, 821.1 miles from the western, and we were pretty pleased to have gotten there, but for a few days I was uncertain what we accomplished other than boots-on-the-ground mileage.

Sue has said more than once that she's come to love the Wisconsin landscape through hiking the Ice Age Trail—that she feels as strongly attached to it as she did to the Colorado landscape while we were there. It was good for both of us to be on the trail together, as we'd so often been in the west, both of us thinking about where we were and planning for the next place we'd be going. I certainly felt a greater comfort with the terrain, a greater sense of connection, than I'd felt before we started the project. But I still wasn't sure what to make it of it until one day, exercising on an elliptical machine in our local fitness center, I tried to zone out and conjure as many images of the entire trail we'd walked as I could, a kind of memory video, in order from north to south.

I found that I could visualize the Monches trailhead, the Carl Schurz Forest, the boardwalk across the Oconomowoc River, the wetlands along the river, the railroad underpass, the Merton trailhead, the walk through the woods, the trail alongside the rail bed, the walk in the open to Dorn Road, the stretch along the floodplain of the Bark River and the geese in the sunlight, the connecting route to the Hartland trailhead, the walk along the Bark River through Hartland, the streets of the downtown district, Nixon Park, the John Wesley Powell wayside, the Aldo Leopold Overlook across Hartland Marsh, the John Muir Overlook and the trail around the marsh, the Foxwood section and the subdivision behind it, the trail behind the church and along the golf course to the intersection with the Lake Country Recreation Trail, the Delafield trailhead, the bike path into and through Delafield and the marsh along the way, the Lapham Peak trailhead, the walk through prairie and savanna, the boardwalk over the marshes, the wooded section of Lapham Peak, the approach to the tower and the descent away from it, the ups and downs of the trail, the end of the flood channel, the Glacial Drumlin Trail leading to the Waukesha Field Station, the Waterville trailhead, the connecting route on Waterville Road, the woods and the dolomite and the open fields and the memory of seeing the cranes, and the connecting route on county roads between the Waterville segment and the Scuppernong trailhead, the path through the farmland to the rise into the woods, the Pinewoods campground and crossing wider trails, the dips and rises through the segment, the pine plantations, the path across and along Highway 67, the Eagle trailhead, the oak stands, the open prairie, the rise behind Kettle Moraine Low Prairie, Brady's Rocks, the views of the bed of Glacial Lake Scuppernong, the bobolinks, the cranes, the Stony Ridge trailhead, the winding trail atop the esker, the winding trail across more of Glacial Lake Scuppernong, the arrival at County Road Z and the sight of the next trailhead in the next county and having reached the end of the Waukesha segments. All of it—I could see—I can still see—all of it.

Re-walking the 45 miles in my mind wasn't simply a test of memory; it was also a test of connection, measuring the degree to which I knew where I had been. In my mind the trail isn't divided

into nine separate segments but flows continuously from one
county line to the next. The various trailheads mark the start and
stop of those units on a map or in a guidebook chapter, a more
convenient, less daunting way to view the trail, just as subdivid-
ing the Ice Age Trail Alliance into county chapters establishes
limits for maintenance and volunteer responsibility. But just as
thousand-milers tend to talk about the trail as a whole, so I have
difficulty isolating one unit from another in memory. Oh, I know
which is which and in which ones to find more specific sites, but
when I repeat the county portion of the trail in memory, as I have
now more than once, I walk without a break from beginning to
end, can even stop at favorite locales and look around. Revisiting
certain sites and remembering earlier visits there fixed them more
firmly in my consciousness, but surprisingly, revisiting previously
unknown stretches in memory along with the ones I already knew
established an unbroken chain of familiarity, so that, at least in ret-
rospect, I felt at home throughout the trail. Segments of the trail
I had never hiked before were now as a familiar and comfortable
as the ones I'd returned to.

Having walked with John Muir, Aldo Leopold, and August
Derleth, not only in their writing but also on their home ground,
further enhanced my sense of connection with the Ice Age Trail.
Perhaps the commemorative sites for Muir and Leopold helped
surface associations but, even without them, I would remember
moments at Fountain Lake, at the shack, along the Wisconsin
River and in the outskirts of Sac Prairie as I encountered the
wetlands, forests, restored prairies, pine plantations, and varied
communities along the trail. The cumulative experience of Muir
as a farm boy, Leopold as a scientist, and Derleth as an observant
resident in some sense foreshadows the experience of any of us
in Wisconsin who hope to pay attention to the world that came
before us as well as the world around us.

Hiking the trail changed the way I saw it all. In the months and years to come, because of who and where we are, we'll likely hike all of it again and again. When we do, we'll no longer be discovering where we are but rather be taking comfort from familiar terrain, companionably at ease with the white ghost of a glacier, repeatedly restored by walking what has become home ground.

Interlude

SATURDAY, JANUARY 1, 2011. The big tree just before the entrance to the woods is poised on the edge of the floodplain; beyond it, thick grasses spread out toward the Fox River. Most of the year the tree is hidden behind smaller trees and bushes, but today it stands exposed and open. I step near, press myself against it, and spread my arms, unabashedly tree hugging, and can reach less than halfway around. Its bark is rough and so deeply furrowed that I can slide two fingers and a portion of my palm into a rough groove. On the side of the trunk facing the path, the bark has been riven its length from high up to the base, but the tree still grows. Its gnarled limbs sprawl in every direction, reaching toward every compass point and under no compulsion to grow straight up. One limb begins at the trunk ten feet above me and stretches toward the path until its tips touch the ground.

Someone has nailed short boards, supports for climbing, at least fifteen feet up the trunk. The higher up the perch, the better the view into the wetlands and toward the river, and there is evidence of a deliberate perch on one particularly stout limb. On this clear, crisp winter day, bright against the cloudless blue sky, flights of Canada geese follow the river and head off to distant fields.

If I've read my *Trees of Wisconsin Field Guide* right, this is a white oak. I check off its features: single straight trunk, broad crown, gnarled branches reaching toward the ground. The picture of the deeply furrowed light gray bark, broken into reddish

scales, matches my tree. White oaks grow fifty to seventy feet
high, and this one, with its solid if battered girth of trunk and its
long reach in every direction, has a magisterial presence. No other
large trees stand anywhere around it. My guide says it has a lobed
four- to eight-inch-long leaf and an edible acorn; I'll check for
the leaf when the snow is gone, for the acorn in summer, and for
the reddish-brown color of the leaves in autumn. The white oak
is a native species found throughout southern Wisconsin, and it
lives 150 to 200 years. By its girth and sprawl, I'd guess this one
has been around a long time.

Pleased with myself for identifying the white oak, I join my
wife on the path and we walk briskly through the woods, hoping
to build up some body heat. We emerge into the open on the
southern end and wind our way up the grassy slope, glancing
toward the woods above us and the broad meadow below. In the
distance, beyond the road, a newer subdivision sprawls across
a nearly treeless plain. Just at the top of the slope a dozen or so
snow buntings rush around the curve, pass us between the path
and the woods, and dip and rise and arc across the drive into the
lower fields. They are so white they become invisible once they
light on the snow. Arctic birds, they winter along the Canada-US
border, which other birds abandon for warmer terrain. Perhaps
snow buntings think that, compared to the Arctic, this is warmer
terrain.

Once we circle the picnic area near the farthest borders of
the park, we decide to veer off the paved path and head deeper
into the woods on a snow-packed trail. We notice a large hawk
at the top of a tree, and he seems to notice us. He flies off, circles above us, and settles on another tree on the opposite side of
the road. We have no binoculars, and the distance and lighting
work against easy identification, but from the whiteness of his
breast and what we can see of his dark head and back, he's pretty

certainly a red-tailed hawk. I keep glancing back at him until we're so deep in the woods the trees close off my view.

When we leave the woods, we pass the white oak again. I slow our pace in order to gaze at it as we pass, inordinately pleased with myself for knowing what it is. I've too often walked along the river and through the woods in a state of bland and oblivious appreciation. Each time I'm able to name what I see, I feel more connected to where I am.

The Land Itself:
Walking Home Ground

1

BEFORE MY WIFE AND I moved to Wisconsin in the fall of 2008, I had given the state little thought. A decade or more earlier, I'd driven around the southeastern corner, researching the life of Ruth Douglass, a woman whose 1848 diary I'd edited. One afternoon I walked the terrain where Ruth's father-in-law had been the first to plow the prairie. Walworth County, where he had established a farm and an inn, was on the Illinois border, and Ruth recorded climbing a hill that was "the dividing rige [*sic*] between the waters of the Fox and Rock Rivers." I dutifully climbed that same hill. It took me a long time after we settled in Waukesha to finally remember that I'd heard of this Fox River before, had even crossed it traveling to and from Walworth County. The memory helped me decide to start giving the place we'd chosen to live more attention, in the spirit of fellow author Barry Lopez, who once said, "For me to know a man, I must have him walk me out into his land and tell me the stories of that place he has chosen to live."

I'd already been acclimating myself to where we'd landed through my reading—including Leopold's *A Sand County Almanac* and Laurie Lawlor's *This Tender Place: The Story of a Wetland Year*, set on Pickerel Fen in Walworth County. Leopold's and Lawlor's seasonal approaches inspired me. As our first New Year's Eve in our new home approached, I decided to keep a separate Wisconsin journal devoted solely to our local outings. I expected to write one journal entry each week and thoroughly record our first full Wisconsin year.

I started 2009 well, with five entries in January and one a week through February, but it was a cold, snowy winter and we followed the same plowed path nearby whenever we went out, and soon I was writing more about Leopold and Lawlor than about my own walks. And then came bouts of illness and excursions out of state, and by year's end I'd written thirty-seven entries instead of fifty-two. I abandoned the weekly entry idea. The journal meant to cover one year ended up covering two, and the next year's intermittent entries recorded not only some far-flung excursions around the state, but also my evolving plan to somehow write about the Wisconsin landscape. By the end of the second full year I'd resolved to read and research and walk the home ground

of Muir, Leopold, and Derleth, to see what would come of all
that, and also to explore my own home ground more attentively.

I hear an eager optimism in my remarks in the December 22,
2010, entry: "I thought I could try to walk in our woods and wetlands in Fox River Park once a week all year long, each week trying
to learn something new, like the identification of trees, plants,
birds, animals, life in the forest, life in the wetlands." In the next
entry I was wondering whether a bad winter cold would keep me
housebound the first week of 2011, but I showed signs of having
paid some attention when I claimed, "I think I want to start with
one of the sprawling oaks before you enter the forest." I thought
it promising that I knew a sprawling oak was there.

Life tends to intervene in the most ardent plans. Muir's observations of the landscape of his boyhood and youth recollected
in tranquility at the end of a long, eventful life, Leopold's observations of the landscape of his weekend shack over a dozen
years while he was a very active university professor, Derleth's
observations of the landscape of his home ground over decades
during which he wrote and edited and published voluminously—
these all can lead us, when we have only a single book in front of
us, to feel as if the author was unblinking in his attention to his
local terrain and not to recognize the way all this scrutiny and
knowledge accumulated over time. As Rachel Carson wrote, "The
discipline of a writer is to learn to be still and listen to what his
subject has to tell him."

Part of the challenge is finding the will to be still and the opportunity to listen, especially if you're also writing other books,
teaching in other states or countries, speaking at distant confer-
ences and university programs, hanging out with your children
and your grandchildren in Florida and California and Wisconsin.
Time and again we would return to Wisconsin from some distant
place and find that the seasons had changed in our absence; or we
would realize that, despite our earnest outings along the Niagara

Escarpment and the Ice Age Trail, we hadn't walked in the woods behind our home for weeks.

And so, after months of wandering Muir's farm, Leopold's shack, Derleth's prairie, and the county section of the Ice Age Trail, I found myself trying to write about the Fox River, just a few steps away from where I live, with less understanding of it than I had of all those other places. Increase Lapham referred to it early on as the *Pishtaka*, or the Fox River of the Illinois—*pishtaka* is the Potawatomi word for "buffalo," as *waukesha* is the Ojibwe word for "little fox"—and I'd been thinking of it as the Pishtaka lately because the word was unfamiliar to me, as if I'd been living in this place for so long without realizing where I was. After three and a half years of journal entries that record little about this place, I was long overdue to truly inhabit my home ground.

2

Wisconsin Journal—Sunday, January 4, 2009
"Each year, after the midwinter blizzards, there comes a night of thaw when the tinkle of dripping water is heard in the land. It brings strange stirrings, not only to creatures abed for the night, but to some who have been asleep for the winter." Thus Aldo Leopold opens the January entry in *A Sand County Almanac*, following the tracks of a hibernating skunk awakened by the thaw and prowling in the night. "His track marks one of the earliest datable events in that cycle of beginnings and ceasings which we call a year."

This winter season, here far to the southeast of Leopold's shack, has already been long. December brought more than forty inches of snow; huge ridges of snow piled high by plows and shovels and snow blowers lined the streets and walks and driveways. In the middle of the night we hear work crews scraping away the drifts in front of our garage, shoveling and sprinkling deicing pellets across the walk to our front door, clearing the driveways. The sure sign of winter here has been the beeping of their short, squat machines as they back up, and the *whoosh* and *whomp* of the city plows hurtling first down and then up the street beyond them.

Behind our condo complex the Fox River wetlands separate our neighborhood from the nearest suburb to the west. Canada geese are our commonest sighting. In the four and a half months we've lived here, almost daily I hear their honking and see wedges of them, sometimes small bands, sometimes near multitudes, sailing across the sky. Sometimes I hear them in the middle of the night. We don't know where they rest overnight and only occasionally encounter throngs of them in outlying fields.

I'd like to take them for granted. I've never been one to hide my feelings about dancing through goose poop on walks through public parks in midwestern towns. At times every riverfront park we stroll in seems to be infested with geese, hanging out and discomforting human idlers like a defiantly lounging motorcycle gang. Once, when Sue and I had been birding in Point Pelee National Park, off the Ontario shore of Lake Erie, we stopped by the Jack Miner Bird Sanctuary, where thousands of migrating Canada geese stop every year. I remember my impatience staring at the geese waddling around behind the fence, my relief that we didn't have to walk on their side of it, my eagerness to move on.

But here, along the wetlands of the Fox River, I feel as if I've settled onto the fringes of their home ground. Soon I began to rise and peer whenever they flew past my window. The sight of a dozen or so Canada geese winging out of the fog above my neighbors' homes and gliding easily toward my window, then banking toward the retaining pond just north of our complex or with a few easy strokes lifting above my roofline, has an almost mystical quality to it. For the few seconds they dominate my vision, I am unaware of the condos across the street or the slats of the window blinds, conscious only of the near precision of the geese's movements, the invisible current that flows among them and makes them a part of the air and the fog, of the morning itself. Something in their flight lifts my spirits.

Who would have predicted I'd feel that way about Canada geese?

3

Wherever most of us go in the landscape we live in, we accept without question whatever is on it now. These roads, streets, lanes, courts, parkways, boulevards, these houses, churches, schools, businesses, parking lots, these traffic signals, signs, utility poles and wires, fences, mailboxes, water towers, these lawns, gardens, trees, sidewalks, bike paths, culverts, bridges—all familiar, all taken for granted, even as we traverse terrain we've never crossed before. We seldom envision that landscape as having been any different than it now appears.

When Sue and I came to Waukesha, the bike path to the north of us traversed a stretch between a wetlands preserve with a rickety boardwalk running through it and, beyond a border of trees, a vast, open, empty field; now, at last, the rebuilt boardwalk is sturdy and solid and invites a stroll through the center of the wetlands, but now, alas, the field is filled with a shopping plaza—a couple of discount department stores, a supermarket, and the same assortment of food and merchandise franchises replicated abundantly elsewhere—that promises to double in size as quickly as possible. When we ride that stretch of bike path now, we seldom remember how open the land was when we first saw it. As Marlin Johnson trenchantly observes, "When land is used for homes and lawns, it often becomes little more than space to live on. . . . Urban and suburban life too easily loses its sense of roots with the land itself."

I call up my town on a satellite map and find, at a certain magnification, the major streets, the parks, and the golf courses all labeled, the green spaces all handily colored green. When I switch to a satellite view—What an age! We can see ourselves from space! Anyone anywhere who magnifies the view enough can see the building I live in!—distinctions blur, and gray lines and boxy shapes scatter across a background in various shades of green. I click the little arrows and center my neighborhood on the screen. Our subdivision and the subdivisions around us and all of our streets are neatly labeled, and our houses line up along the streets like legs on a centipede. I put the Fox River at the center of the screen and see two parks identified with tree symbols above their names, one to the west, one to the south. The light green of the floodplain and the dark green of the Fox River Park forest stand out; from above, our condo buildings look like conferencing gray sow bugs. I click myself closer to the river and the woods, and the age in which I live slides out of the frame. On the ground, walking the river and the woods, it's impossible to lose my awareness of the age in which I live, but by satellite and computer I can pretend for a moment that it's absent. Once, only the land and the river and the woods were here; whatever else the maps identify did not exist. I struggle to lift the scrim of modernity, and sometimes, after I've been to a restored prairie or savanna or passed through a long patch of forest, my imagination almost lets me.

I ground myself in glacial geology. Waukesha lies east of the Kettle Moraine and the ground beneath us rests upon the till, meltwater stream sediment, and offshore sediment deposited by the Lake Michigan Lobe of the Wisconsin Glaciation. All around us are drumlins that reveal the southwestward flow of the ice sheet before it melted away, leaving what geologist Lee Clayton terms "nondescript undulating topography," "moraine ridges," "flat outwash plains," and "hummocky areas of supraglacial stream sediment." It took immense amounts of time to form the highlands and lowlands of the landscape hinted at in a relief map of the county. I search that map to locate roads I drive on where I'm impressed by the steepness of a descent or ascent, the changes in elevation in a short stretch of highway, and remind myself it's always glacial outwash terrain those roads are crossing.

My portion of the county experienced glacial retreat and re-advance during the Wisconsin Glaciation 25,000 to 14,000 years ago. A glacial lake formed, drained, re-formed, and drained again. Glacial Lake Vernon once occupied the area that over time became the floodplain of the Fox River and, further south of Waukesha, the broad Vernon Marsh. It was the Fox River that finally drained Lake Vernon.

The glaciers wasted back slowly, and plant and animal life, as well as humans, continually moved into the opened terrain. Mammoths, mastodons, caribou, elk, moose, and bison were plentiful, and people arrived at least twelve thousand years ago. The flora and fauna changed over time, notably in the mass extinction of mammoths and mastodons and the increased population of elk, bison, deer, and aquatic life. By 5000 BCE, say Robert Birmingham and Leslie Eisenberg in *Indian Mounds of Wisconsin*, "the essentially modern distribution of plants and animals had been established in Wisconsin, although climatic fluctuations would affect the distribution even into recent times." In his thorough and informative article, "Natural Features and Land Use," Marlin Johnson identifies Waukesha County's presettlement vegetation as "primarily maple forests in the eastern and northwestern parts of the county and oak forests, oak openings and prairies in the central and southwestern portions. Large wetlands existed in the southcentral and western areas." The area of the county where

I live was covered by prairie, oak openings, and bur oak open forest, and the prairies across the county ranged from dry prairie on hilltops and south-facing slopes, mesic prairies on moister soils, "tallgrass prairies where big bluestem could grow eight feet high," and lowland or wet prairies "on soils saturated with water for part of the year, as along the Scuppernong River." Thanks to some of my wandering around the state and along the Ice Age Trail, I have moments when I can almost visualize fragments of that landscape.

In hopes of connecting more concretely to the unmapped terrain, I look up the oldest maps I can find online. The 1836 Government Land Office survey maps were created after settlement, part of a national effort to uniformly measure parcels of land across the country. The surveyors would walk straight lines north-south and east-west, each line six miles long, establishing blocks of space measured from an initial point where a baseline and a principal meridian met. For Wisconsin the initial point was at the intersection of the baseline established by the Illinois-Wisconsin border and the Fourth Principal Meridian ten miles east of the Mississippi River; the east-west lines parallel to the baseline were termed township lines, and those north-south parallel to the meridian were termed range lines. Each six-mile-by-six-mile square formed a congressional or survey township, identified by its relationship to the baseline and the principal meridian. My survey township, Waukesha, is Town 6 North, Range 19 East, Fourth Principal Meridian, or T. 6 N R. 19 E.

In March and April of 1836, a deputy surveyor named John Brink and his crew established the boundaries of the Waukesha township, surveying its exterior lines—the township and range lines—and its interior lines, the ones that divided the township into thirty-six one-mile square sections. The surveyors' primary concern was the potential a township had for timbering or mining or agriculture, and their field notes dutifully recorded the kinds of trees and other features they encountered on the terrain. As they walked their straight lines, they counted out their hundred links of chain, each chain 66 feet long, 80 chains in a mile (from which we get 5,280 feet in a mile). For each township, surveyors included a general description at the end of their field notes and a sketch map that would later be used to create a more precise plat map. In his general description of T. 6 N R. 19 E., Brink wrote:

> This Township may be considerd first & second Rate Land the East Side of Fox River is thick and Heavy timber with Whit Black & Bur Oak Lynn Sugar Ash Elm Ironwood White & Black Walnut and Cherry & a thick growth of Hazel Oak thorn Plum Prickly Ash Aspen & vines (Except Prairie & Marsh) West Side of River thinly timberd with White Bur and Black Oak (Except Prairie & Marsh) the Prairie is dry and Rolling Soil of Lome and Sand Snow and is generally So through-out the Township.

I've encountered white oak, black (now red) oak, bur oak, sugar maple, ash, ironwood, black walnut, cherry, aspen, hawthorn, perhaps linden (lynn), prickly ash, and witch hazel, but after 177 years, even if I were to walk Brink's survey lines, I doubt that many of the trees I'd see would be the very ones he saw.

Brink's sketch map is more helpful. The township is neatly divided by section lines into thirty-six uniform squares. The sections are numbered from the northeast corner of the township, the top row reading from left to right 6, 5, 4, 3, 2, 1, the second row reversing direction, 7, 8, 9, 10, 11, 12, the third row switching again, and so on, ending at Section 36 in the southeast corner. The map chiefly records the waterways and the marshlands and also some occasional highlands. The Fox River enters the county at the northern junction of Sections 2 and 3 and leaves it in the southwestern corner of the map, Section 31. Two walking trails

intersect in Section 10, one meandering easterly, the other heading southwest. Sections 3, 9, and 10 show evidence of human occupation, rectangles indicating cultivated fields in the latter two,
and buildings in Section 3.

When I turn to the more detailed plat map I see symbols
for buildings, the words "Prairie Village," and an indication of a
spring in the part of Section 3 that will develop into downtown
Waukesha. Two more buildings sit on either side of the Fox River
at the southern boundary of Section 9. Nowhere else on the map
is there evidence of human habitation. I check the sketch maps
and original plat maps for the other fifteen townships in what
has since become Waukesha County; no other township displays
signs of occupation other than a trail running through a portion
of it. Only one of the sketch maps is without any gridlines; the
other sketch maps and all the plat maps are rife with town lines
and range lines. Except for the occasional river or creek or lake
or marsh, or the "high hills" prominent on the map for Town 5
North Range 17 East, where my wife and I have walked in the
Kettle Moraine, the maps merely hint at topography and offer no
way to pinpoint any location that would be familiar to me nearly
two centuries later.

I live in Section 21 of T. 6 N R. 19 E., across the Fox River from
Section 20 to the west. I view these sections on the plat map close
up and recognize the wetlands along the river and the hills beyond it. I try to strip away the gridlines on the survey maps, erase
the constructed portions of the landscape on the satellite view;
I try to superimpose on the terrain the images I've collected on
the Ice Age Trail, extend the forest in Fox River Park all along the
highlands east of me where Brink found thick and heavy timber,
transfer the restored prairie and the oak savanna of Glacial Lake
Scuppernong to the land west and north of me, where the Fox
River and Pebble Creek wetlands still hint at what once was there,
the landscape that made Prairie Village so aptly named. I close my

eyes and concentrate and see the grasslands roll away and the bur oaks stand out against the horizon and the blue sky and watch the river flow through the wetlands nearby. It doesn't last long, but for an instant or two I sense myself in the presence of the land itself.

4

Wisconsin Journal—Monday, January 24, 2011
Yesterday Sue and I made a chilly circuit of the Fox River Park. We've had a lot of snowy days, often light flurries, and not too many sunny ones in the past few weeks. The cold spell has persisted, with nights below zero and days in the single digits or teens. It's been colder further north, temperatures reaching double digits below zero anywhere within reach of Lake Superior or bordering Canada, but the wind everywhere over Wisconsin can be insistent and strong, and wicked wind chills discourage walking—or at least discourage us. The dog walkers and joggers are still out there daily, though perhaps a little more glum or a little more stoic than usual. We took our walk while the wind was light, knowing the forest would shield us some once we were in it.

We were the only ones in the woods. I'd wandered through the park a couple times the week before, while Sue was gone, and I pointed out the trees I'd managed to identify. We started at the white oak and moved on to a short evergreen with two trunks located on the river side of the path just past the entrance, the only eastern white cedar I've seen anywhere in the woods. Though it grows throughout Wisconsin, its solitary presence here was a surprise.

On the other side of the path near the north entrance was a stand of red pines, easy to identify by their single straight trunks, absence of lower branches, and broad round crowns. We both know white pine well, a favorite tree when we lived in Michigan and notable for its five-needle clusters, and I eagerly showed her how the brittle two-needle clusters of red pines break cleanly, to demonstrate how well I could distinguish between them.

Near the river overlook we stopped by a shagbark hickory, a tree easy to identify by its, well, shaggy bark, all those gray strips curling at the end, and hard to confuse with anything else. I knew that northern red oak and bur oak could also be found in the woods—I'd found the distinctive red oak leaf with its deep lobes and sharply pointed tips—and I was eager for spring, when I'd get deeper into the woods and gain a deeper understanding of what we've been walking through.

The wind was beginning to pick up, increasing the cold. We didn't linger long on the observation deck. Snow had fallen enough in the past few weeks to coat the ground without covering the hummocks of marsh grass along the river. Ice was creeping out from the bank on the inside of the bend, but the river still flowed quietly, its surface dark and gleaming, like smoked glass, reflecting barren trees and gray skies and, in the distance, just a hint of sunshine. If it hadn't been for some ripples on the water, we might have thought the river had stopped moving.

We turned back. From different locations we could hear wood-peckers in the woods, hammering away. Despite the cold, the sound of life around us was cheering, as was our sense that we've furthered our acquaintance with where we live. As we passed them again on our way home, silently I named the trees I knew.

5

One traveler who came to Prairieville from Milwaukee in 1836 reported passing through dense forest all the way until he crossed Poplar Creek, an eastern tributary of the Fox River, and "came into the oak opening. I thought it the most lovely sight I had ever beheld. The country looked more like a modern park than anything else." His enthusiasm reminds me of an N. C. Wyeth illustration for an edition of *The Deerslayer,* where Hurry Harry March breaks out of the forest into a clearing, flings his arms into the air, and exults, "Here is room to breathe in!" The Wisconsin traveler might well have re-enacted that moment at Poplar Creek.

However, the terrain that traveler saw was not unpopulated, and I remind myself not to imagine postglacial Wisconsin as an empty wilderness. Paleo-Indians traveled through the landscape as long as twelve thousand years ago, making the most of what was then a very northern habitat: spruce and fir forests, tundra, a cold climate. Archaeologists divide the precontact history of Native Americans in Wisconsin into several overlapping but varied periods: the Paleo-Indian beginning around 10,000 BCE, the Archaic roughly from 8500 to 1000 BCE, the Woodland from 1000 BCE to 1100 CE, and the Mississippian, 900 to 1600 CE. Distinctive technology and customs—projectile points, tools, pottery, ornaments, burial processes—mark each period. By the time Wisconsin began to be "settled," descendants of thousands of years of North American residents already occupied the territory, and European Americans had been encountering—and displacing—Native Americans for more than three hundred years. On the site that would become first Prairieville and then Waukesha, specifically on the hill where Carroll College would soon be established, Potawatomi had established a village estimated to have a thousand occupants. It was a site long familiar to Native Americans.

The Woodland period was marked by the development of clay pottery and a movement away from an earlier hunter-gatherer lifestyle into a more permanently settled tradition. By the beginning of the Woodland period, Native Americans had already begun to construct burial mounds, as early as 5600 BCE in Labrador, and 4000 BCE in areas along the Gulf of Mexico. When Europeans began exploring the Northwest Territory, between 15,000 and 20,000 Indian mounds were scattered across Wisconsin. "More Indian mounds were built in the territory now called Wisconsin than in any other equivalent area of land in midwestern North America," Birmingham and Eisenberg say, at more than 3,000 locations. Dane County, two counties west of Waukesha, had more than 1,500 mounds, and Grant County, on the Mississippi across from what is now Effigy Mounds National Monument, had more than 1,000. Sauk County, home to both August Derleth's Sac Prairie and Aldo Leopold's shack, had more than 900 mounds—one new resident claimed to have been "rather irked by the large number of Indian mounds we had to plow down," more than 25 on his land alone. In Marquette County John Muir played on a mound on Fountain Lake Farm. Waukesha County had as many as 500.

The significance of this information to someone striving to envision a landscape before pioneer settlement is simply this: the land had been occupied, by one Native American group or another, for centuries. It is a fact sometimes ignored in early histories of the county. For example, Theron W. Haight, in his introduction to *Memoirs of Waukesha County* written in 1907, hurries to recount the appearance of the first white settlers, Morris and Alonzo Cutler of LaPorte, Indiana, who "chose their place of settlement within hearing of the rippling waters of the Pishtaka river (later known as the Fox) where the descent from what is now the mill pond at Waukesha to the flats a mile below gave promise of a future development of waterpower." Note how quickly Haight celebrates development. He pictures the area as essentially untouched, extolling "the most luxuriant flora to be seen in these latitudes," "magnificent oak openings," "marshes covered with heavy grasses and flowering plants," and "a few patches of prairie ... with their rank grasses swaying in the summer winds like the waters of the sea, and annually involved in the great fires which swept over the whole of the country." He admits that the "evidences of conflagrations were also evidences, of course, that other human beings had preceded the white settlers in the occupancy of the land"—namely the Potawatomi, who were "still using the waters of the lakes and rivers here for fishing, while their squaws attended to a primitive gardening of maize and beans." But their presence has no significance for him, since they "hardly wrought any change in the general appearance of the country," which he thought resembled "the Sleeping Beauty of Tennyson's poem and of the older legend, who lay year after year through the centuries, slumbering with all else within the castle, until the right prince arrived to waken her." The analogy of the land to Sleeping Beauty and the European American settlers to Prince Charming is not one that leaps immediately to my mind, but it reveals how little the Indians counted in Haight's starry-eyed history of the county. He attributes the mounds to "another population . . . before the advent of the modern Indian tribes" and, rather than speculate about them, prefers to let them "repose in their primeval mystery." History in Waukesha County, according to Haight, begins with the arrival of the Cutler brothers.

Luckily, Increase Lapham, a less myopic observer, was exploring the area in 1836, a couple of years after the Cutlers arrived. In *Wisconsin: Its Geography and Topography, History, Geology, and Mineralogy,* Lapham described Prairieville as "situated on the Pishtaka (or Fox) river, on the site of an old Indian village, sixteen miles west from Milwaukee. It is at the head of a beautiful prairie, occupying the valley of the river, which here has a descent of ten feet in the distance of half a mile." In *The Antiquities of Wisconsin as Surveyed and Described,* his later book on Indian mounds, he tells us:

Much of the ground around Waukesha was, in 1836, covered with "Indian corn-hills," or remains of their recent culture

of maize. In this locality, as at numerous others, the mounds
occupy the highest ground and the points of hills and other
places, whence the most extensive view, both above and
below, can be obtained. The town of Waukesha stands on
a slightly undulating plain, surrounded by hills, forming a
fine amphitheatre, which, in ancient times, was doubtless
crowded, as it is now, with numerous population.

I strain my imagination to envision that beautiful prairie in the
valley of the river, that slightly undulating plain surrounded by
hills, but I try not to leave out, as Lapham did not, that numerous
population with mounds abounding.

When I view Plate XVIII in *Antiquities,* "Ancient Works at
and Near Waukesha, Surveyed in 1836 & 1850 by I. A. Lapham," I
orient myself by the presence of the Pishtaka River and the location of Carroll College. The string of mounds off village streets
near the river are the ones whose remnants still exist, three small
conical mounds near the library, in Cutler Park, where Morris
Cutler first lived. The flat prairie is evident in the plate, as well as
surrounding elevations, including that near the college, and the
location of fields of Indian corn are clearly marked. In Plate XIX
Lapham shows two turtle-shaped mounds, one from the college
grounds and the other close to what would become the center of
the village. When he surveyed them in 1836, "the log-house near
these mounds was the only evidence of civilization in the place;
and the works were uninjured by the white man, except that the
large mound was made use of for a root-house, or potato-hole."
It also had a recent grave marked by pickets, and a trail from the
river to the Indian village ran across the top.

The mound impressed Lapham. "This turtle was then a very
fine specimen of the ancient art of mound-building, with its
graceful curves, the feet projecting back and forward, and the tail,
with its gradual slope, so acutely pointed that it was impossible

to ascertain precisely where it terminated." He and his associate William Culley measured the mound, finding the body to be fifty-six feet long, the tail to be two hundred and fifty feet long, and the height to be six feet. When Lapham returned to examine the site in 1850, he found it "covered with buildings. A dwelling-house stands upon the body of the turtle, and a Catholic church is built upon the tail."

Just as, almost from the moment he arrived in Wisconsin, Lapham had urged conservation of forest trees, so he was the earliest to encourage preservation of Indian mounds. Plate XXI recorded a "very fine group" of mounds surveyed in 1850, which, he wrote, "is upon the grounds of Carroll College; and we may, therefore, hope it will be for ever preserved as a record of the past." The turtle there measured thirty feet in the body and one hundred thirty feet in the tail. It and the other mounds have since been obliterated. Another group on a high hill east of town, consisting of "two round, four oblong, one turtle, and one bird-shaped mound," was partly on cultivated land then and since has disappeared entirely. The three paltry conical mounds near the library alone inadequately represent what once could be found in Waukesha.

It's in the chapter about Waukesha, "Ancient Works Near the Pishtaka River," that Lapham gives one of the earliest assessments of the connection between the mound builders and the recent Indian populations of Wisconsin. It's an assessment that Haight, fifty years later, ignores in favor of "mystery." Haight wasn't alone; theories about the mound builders ranged widely and imaginatively, from the Aztecs—the Aztalan site in Jefferson County was so named because of that association, though the more accurate connection is with Cahokia, a Middle Mississippian site in southern Illinois—to an unidentifiable "Lost Race" or to one of "the lost tribes of Israel." Such theories imply inferiority on the part of the "savages" the white culture displaced, which helped justify that displacement. But with his keen curiosity and analytical mind, Lapham, as Birmingham and Eisenberg point out, "saw links between the mound builders and the modern Native Americans in the types of artifacts recovered from the mounds," particularly in his investigation of a mound in what is now downtown Waukesha. Lapham's findings led him to declare that the "mound builders were none other than the ancestors of the present tribes of Indians." With qualifications, his theory has since been generally accepted. Given the relentless destruction of Indian mounds in the past two centuries, where out of 15,000 to 20,000 original mounds only around 4,000 remain, the meticulous, prescient work of Increase Lapham is now the earliest primary evidence of what has been lost.

In his wanderings to survey mounds, Lapham also witnessed one of those "great fires" Haight mentions sweeping across swaying "rank grasses." Near Pewaukee, just north of Waukesha, Lapham encountered a prairie fire "raging through the woods about us, consuming the dry leaves and brush, and filling the air with smoke. . . . The peculiar noise made by the fire as it entered the marsh, caused by the bursting of the hollow stems of coarse grass and weeds, was very great." It was the kind of fire that had kept the oak openings and the prairies open in the past, and would be yet another element of Wisconsin life that white settlement would eliminate.

Settlement eliminated a great deal of Wisconsin life. Marlin Johnson notes that, prior to settlement beginning in the 1830s, the mixture of forests, prairies, oak openings, swamps, wet meadows, marshes, lakes, and streams harbored a wide variety of wildlife. Hunting, trapping, and loss of habitat swiftly reduced their numbers. The last bison in the state was killed in 1832; the last elk was seen in 1846; otter, beaver, prairie chicken, grouse, quail, wild turkeys, black bear, cougars, wolves, bobcats, lynxes—all were eliminated from the state; the passenger pigeon, which once thronged in the millions over Vernon Marsh, south on the Fox

River, was slaughtered into extinction. As Johnson writes, "Most of this presettlement vegetation has now been replaced by agricultural and urban uses of the land." It's as if, to recall Theron Haight's fairy tale allusion, Sleeping Beauty was awakened not by Prince Charming but by entrepreneurial hordes intent on ravaging and exploiting her.

It didn't take long to alter what Lapham and the surveyor John Brink and that early traveler from Milwaukee saw when they reached Prairieville in 1836. In his 1846 history of Wisconsin, Lapham reported that, due to the "descent of ten feet in the distance of half a mile," the Pishtaka River was being "used to propel one of the largest flouring mills in the Territory." He estimated the population to be around several hundred and noted "many new and handsome dwelling-houses . . . three hotels, five churches, an academy, a saw-mill, several stores, and a weekly newspaper," as well as the newly established Carroll College. He also gave the numbers of barrels of flour and pork and pounds of hides exported in 1841, "valued in all at thirty-eight thousand eight hundred and fifty dollars." Prairieville was well on its way to becoming the city of Waukesha.

Having gleaned some sense of what the landscape once was, I should make certain, as I wander contemporary Waukesha, that I remember historic Prairieville and what was here before it. I will also need a better understanding of what came after it. A great deal of obliteration has occurred in the nearly two centuries since.

6

The point at which the Fox River descended ten feet over half a mile attracted early settlers because it promised water power for a mill around which a community could grow. Certainly Increase Lapham appreciated the location's potential. Though he had the

foresight to recommend preservation of Indian mounds and conservation of forests, he was a man of his era who came to Wisconsin because of his engineering skills. In his early travels around the
territory, surveying potential routes for the Milwaukee and Rock
River Canal, he also considered the possibility of an east-west
canal connecting the Menomonee and Pishtaka (Fox) Rivers. Of
the Pishtaka he wrote of a proposal "to improve the navigation
of this river, by means of dams and locks, so as to create a slack
water from its mouth, where it is connected with the Illinois and
Michigan canal, as far as the rapids at Prairieville." Lapham saw
"no practical difficulty in the way of accomplishing this important
work." Between Prairieville and Elgin, Illinois, he noted, the river
made "a descent of ninety-six feet, or nearly one foot per mile,
on an average," and thus "would require twelve dams, of eight
feet each, and the average length of each pond would be about
seven or eight miles." His remarks sound judicious, practical and
objective.

Today the Fox River of the Illinois, as it's generally termed,
has a total of eighteen dams, three in Wisconsin, at Waukesha,
Waterford, and Rochester, and fifteen in Illinois. According to the
environmental group Friends of the Fox River, thirteen dams in
Illinois impede the river's flow, and most of the dams no longer
serve a purpose, as they did when they powered mills. The dam
in Waukesha principally makes Frame Park more scenic and that
stretch of river more navigable for canoes and paddleboats; it also
helps to flood the riverbanks most springs.

Waukesha County can be divided into four watershed areas.
A narrow portion in the northeast feeds the Menomonee River,
which empties into the Milwaukee River and Lake Michigan;
an even narrower portion in the southeast feeds the Root River,
which empties into Lake Michigan in Racine (the French
word for "root"). They are east of a subcontinental divide running through the county. West of that divide, in the county's

westernmost townships, the watershed belongs to the Rock River, which joins the Mississippi at Rock Island, Illinois—two of its tributaries are the Oconomowoc and Bark Rivers. The central portion of the county, the part of the county where I live, is drained by the Fox River and its tributaries. The Fox begins just over the northern county line in Washington County, runs 84 miles across Waukesha, Racine, and Kenosha Counties to the Illinois line, and flows another 118 miles to the Illinois River and then on to the Mississippi.

Most communities in Waukesha County originally sprang up around water-powered mills, usually sawmills that eventually became flour mills. In time these communities and the growth of nearby farms diverted enough water from local rivers and streams that by 1880, less than fifty years after settlement began, longtime residents noted a major decrease in the flow of streams and, in some cases, the complete loss of fish populations.

Settlement had a far-reaching impact on every aspect of the natural landscape of Waukesha County, as it did throughout Wisconsin. Marlin Johnson notes the county's "dynamic vegetation pattern of uncommon richness—maple and oak forests, prairies, oak openings and marshlands." But, with the influx of white settlers in the 1830s and 1840s, Johnson observes, "Land was judged mainly on its capacity to become cropland. . . . Probably no single acre in Waukesha County has remained unaltered by the agrarian society that dominated the landscape for more than one hundred years." Agriculture and fire prevention "all but eliminated natural oak openings and prairies from the county," Johnson says. A sizable portion of farmland has since been further altered by suburban development; much of the terrain, like that seen from Observatory Hill in Marquette County by John Warfield Simpson, is the result of the abandonment of the land the first settlers so thoroughly altered from what they found when they arrived.

In the less than two centuries since settlers arrived at

Prairieville, the Fox River has gone through its share of transformations. The mills built near the rapids, where the Frame Park dam still stands, are gone and the millrace has been filled in, but the shape of the river has been altered by commerce, particularly during what is referred to as the Springs Era, roughly 1868–1918. This was, according to the authors of *Spring City's Past,* "by far the most fascinating period of Waukesha's history." All history since then they label the Post-Springs Industrial Era.

One solid reminder of the Springs Era is the octagonal concrete structure housing Silurian Spring. In 1874, during a period when springs proliferated throughout the city and Waukesha was touted as "the Saratoga of the West," the Prairieville postmaster found a naturally flowing spring on his property and built a park around it. Spacious, sprawling, and well landscaped, the park had a bathhouse, a pond, a roller coaster, a bandstand, and a bottling plant, and the Casino Theater offered plays in the summer in a building behind the spring.

Today, it's hard to imagine where all the buildings and gardens and pond might have been. The park, now Waukesha Springs Park, is small, mostly lawn, with a playground, a baseball backstop, and a few picnic tables. Houses line the park on two sides, as well as the parking lots for the YMCA and the post office, and railroad tracks run up the west side, eventually passing Frame Park and paralleling the Fox River north. The splendid pavilion that once stood here is now gone, though it's been replicated on a smaller scale in the center of the city, overlooking the river and surrounded by a huge parking lot and a bank, where it serves as an attractive but anomalous artifact.

During the Springs Era, according to Marlin Johnson, "Waukesha boasted twenty-two hostelries, five hotels and sixteen springhouses. . . . Three railroads served the city with twenty-five daily trains coming from Chicago alone." One extravagant hotel, the Fountain Spring House, "could hold 800 guests in 475 fully carpeted rooms and seat 500 people at tables at one time. A full orchestra, bowling alley, a stable, and separate billiard rooms for men and women provided entertainment." Other accounts refer not only to the glories of Bethesda Spring Park, where the river had been deepened and widened for pleasure boating, but also to the boats that would take tourists upriver a little north of the dam—the river deepened and widened there as well—to visit the park, springhouse pavilion, and entertainment at White Rock Spring. In the period 1868–1918, most of the spring water that made Wisconsin first in production "of mineral waters sold as table water, medicinal water or carbonated drinks (ginger ale)" came from Waukesha. At one point more than twenty local breweries also used spring water.

Of the sixty-five springs that once operated in Waukesha, thirteen are still active—that is, they are not defunct, although they are also not in use. Several are on private property and most have been sealed or enclosed, like Silurian Spring and Bethesda Spring. Minniska Spring is still open on a tiny plot between huge housing units in a sprawling subdivision. Most accessible is the exposed and unimpressive Hobo Spring in Frame Park, which gives no indication that a lucrative and popular tourist destination might have developed out of mineral water springs.

The springs initially lured visitors thanks to claims of their miraculous curative powers. Colonel Richard Dunbar named his spring site Bethesda in reference to a healing pool in the Gospel of John. "I drank of the modern Bethesda," Dunbar declared; "I was healed of an incurable disease, one that baffled the skill of the most scientific men, here and abroad." White Rock Spring's early proprietor, Hiram Colver, advertised that he "was a hopeless invalid for three years; and, by the use of *Waukesha Mineral Waters,* an enlarged and hardened liver was brought to its natural size, and enabled to perform its healthful functions." Even after the Springs Era, as a tourist industry ended, some of the bottling plants continued to market and ship Waukesha mineral water across the country.

The irony that underlies all this is that, one hundred years after the end of the Springs Era, the city of Waukesha has depleted its readily available water supply to such a degree that ever deeper wells have been drilled into less healthful, radium-laced waters. Residential and commercial development reduced the opportunity for natural springs to replenish themselves, the proliferation of private wells competed for groundwater, and contamination flowed in from industrial and agricultural runoff. The present water supply comes mainly from wells drilled two thousand feet deep into a sandstone aquifer where water levels have dropped more than five hundred feet in the past century. For the time Sue and I have lived here, the city has been trying to strike up deals to pipe in water from Lake Michigan. In the Post Pure Spring Water Depletion Era that defines the contemporary period, relatively few people seem to be looking back at a golden age of healthful water and wondering whether we might learn something from our profligacy then, something that might benefit us in the future. The Waukesha Water Facility, though it's been pumping contaminated water for eighty years, has fought the Environmental Protection Agency in court to keep using wells with ever-higher radium levels. It lost but still will use contaminated water until 2018.

While it lasted, the prosperity of the Springs Era not only brought changes in the river but also inspired future changes. In 1891, an editorial in the *Waukesha Freeman*, apparently reacting to the dredging and widening of the channel through Bethesda Springs Park, called for "dredging and ornamenting the upper part of the stream, a thing that is so commendable and would contribute so much to the prosperity of the town." The editorial argued that, with railroads passing close to the river, "annually thousands of travelers would be impressed with the added attractiveness" and vacationers might enjoy a "magnificent drive that might be formed along the shore, and facilities for boating."

Thirty-five years later the banker Andrew J. Frame donated fifty thousand dollars to purchase land along both sides of the river above the dam and to dredge the channel, and Frame Park was created. In 1974 a Downtown Development Task Force recommended riverfront development through creation of a bike path, a pedestrian path, foot bridges, water jets in the river, and an outdoor theater, but it wasn't until 1990 that any concerted effort to achieve these things was set in motion—almost a hundred years after the idea was first raised. In a 1998 promotional publication, *The Fox River Corridor Plan, Waukesha, Wisconsin,* the introduction blandly mentions that, after the "famous 'Spring Era'" "the river banks were the home of foundries, machine shops, breweries, and other industries which prospered in Waukesha"; it doesn't mention the pollution that all those industries and businesses poured into the river, but it does see the city's role as tied to "regional efforts to clean up the watershed and provide a recreational corridor for the entire region."

The self-congratulatory note that runs through a document like this plan or the articles in the local newspaper that celebrate the success of the plan tend not to discuss the ways in which development still threatens the health of the river. Pebble Creek, one of its tributaries, is likely to fall victim to a plan for a multilane traffic bypass connecting the interstate highway to the north with the Les Paul Parkway that runs past my neighborhood; lands for residential or commercial sale encroach on the borders of the Fox River wetlands; the shopping plaza near the Fox River Sanctuary has just doubled in size.

7

Unlike August Derleth, who often passed through Sauk City to get to his river, I have easy access to mine, visible to me whenever

I turn the corner of my row of buildings. My river, however, has to pass through Waukesha to get to me, and what it passes through is not only the existing city but also the city's history. I knew about the bike route along the river between our neighborhood and Frame Park, in the center of the city; but, after steeping myself in history through my reading, I needed a slower, more attentive approach to the river if I hoped to know it as it is now. I took a few bright, brisk October afternoons to walk as much of it as I could.

To its credit the City of Waukesha maintains more than a thousand acres of public parks. Granted, much of this parkland serves multiple purposes, combining neighborhood recreation with historic or environmental preservation, but the local parks department sets aside almost half of its acreage for "significant natural resources, remnant landscapes, open spaces, and visual aesthetic/buffering." Walking from Frame Park to the county park behind me, I passed through parks with all those purposes.

If I want to connect to the origin of Prairieville-Waukesha, I have to walk the loop around Frame Park. Two parallel pathways now circle the park on either side of the river, one for walkers, one for bikers, merging only at the north and south boundaries of the park where bridges take street and sidewalk traffic across the Fox. We usually walk north up the east side, cross over and return south on the west side, and I like to stop midway both in the hike and on the north bridge, between concrete statues of foxes, to gaze back at the river flowing through the middle of Frame Park. I have once or twice dashed across the street to see where the Fox River comes from. The riverbanks north of the bridge are thickly wooded up to the bend where the river arches out of sight. From here north, the Fox is hemmed in by highway to the west and railroad tracks to the east, with one long stretch beyond highway and railroad scoured by quarrying operations that have dug deeply into the Niagara dolomite that underlies this part of the county. Eventually the woods thicken again and the river meanders through them. I've squinted into the distance, wondering how far upriver a man in a canoe might travel, well aware there would be no walking in that direction.

The west side of Frame Park is the narrower side, the footpath running close to the river, the bike path a little further inland. A long stretch of trees camouflages the chain-link fence that closes the park off from the businesses lining St. Paul Avenue. Sometimes it's hard to ignore the proximity of industry just behind the trees; I try to concentrate on what might be along the river: a flotilla of geese heading upstream, a squadron of gulls sailing in for a landing, a cluster of mallards asleep on the shore, a large willow whose twin I passed at the same point on the opposite bank. Near the end of the walk, close to a large state office building in a quiet plaza, a bronze map of the city is imbedded in the stone underfoot. My neighborhood is too recent to appear on it, but I often look for its absence as we go by.

The east side of the park is more sprawling, more inviting. It offers a well-maintained baseball field, a grassy amphitheater, a floral garden, a picnic shelter, and a large playground. At some distance from the river, off to one side near a parking area and within earshot of the freight trains that rumble past across the road, is Hobo Spring, a nearly dry stone circle indentation in the lawn at the bottom of a slight slope. The Rotary Club Building, a low brick edifice, sits midway along the bank, and in summer a small building in front of it offers snacks and rents boats, bikes, and pedal-powered surreys that often crowd the bike path. Two docks extend off the riverbank, seasonally lined with rental boats, some shaped like a flamingo or a swan or a dragon, others more traditional paddleboats, canoes, and kayaks. The river is wide throughout Frame Park and the current doesn't challenge novice boaters. Powerboats only appear on some summer evenings when a ramp anchored midriver is the center of a lively water-skiing show and people on blankets and lawn chairs line the riverbank to watch.

Near the south end two midriver fountains spray forcefully into the air. The park narrows here, hemmed in by multistory apartments, parking lots, and a recreation center. The river pours over the dam where the mill once stood, a broad, steady water-fall into a pool that spreads out from its base. Semicircular stone steps lead to the water's edge, and off to the side, out of the main channel of the river, the statue of a dragonfly on a water lily rises from the pool. I check the statue each time I'm here, measuring the water level by the dryness or wetness of the dragonfly; in high water I've seen it nearly submerged. In good weather fishermen often sit on the steps and idlers lounge on benches nearby.

Frame Park ends at the Barstow Street Bridge, where the river narrows and becomes swifter and shallower. The riverbed is rocky and lower than it was above the dam. Two levels of walks run on either side of it. The street-level walks are high above the river, passing through the Riverfront Plaza alley behind Main Street businesses on one side and a vast parking area with large, defunct antique shops on the other. Pedestrian bridges cross from one side to the other, convenient for the farmers' market on Saturday mornings. The lower walks, closer to the river and sometimes submerged in high water, have plenty of places to sit, where people often snack and lunch and chat on cell phones. At one point on the north bank are statues of a mother bear and two cubs that children often clamber upon. Near the Broadway Bridge, the lower walks end and force walkers up to street level, on one side near an elaborate replica of the open-air Silurian Springhouse pavilion. A tall commemorative clock tower stands across the bridge.

Beyond the tower, the river runs barely visible below high concrete walls and behind parking lots on either side; it continues under the four-lane Wisconsin Avenue Bridge, out of Historic

Downtown Waukesha. From Moreland Boulevard to Broadway, a mile-long stretch, the riverbanks are often bustling, an amiable retreat from downtown; from Broadway to Wisconsin Avenue the river runs largely unheralded and almost invisible. Once it leaves the commercial district, its presence becomes less marked, less explicit, less a part of the community.

Just past the Wisconsin Avenue Bridge the river's eastern bank is closed off by a concrete wall below an antiques building and a residential parking lot and then becomes briefly accessible only to owners of some large backyards. On the western bank, Grede Park is open to the water's edge, but the combined pedestrian-bike path winds through a wide strip of green lawn and sporadic trees on the far side of a block-long street that provides passage through the park to a sizable cluster of apartments. The park is small, little more than three acres, with only a couple of picnic tables; it ends where the apartment complex begins. The day I walked the narrow strip of lawn close to the riverbank, the only other person I saw was a woman at an unshaded table, eating her lunch and reading, comfortably sleeveless on a sunny and warm afternoon. The river widens again here, and in the shallows near the opposite bank several ducks appeared to be miraculously standing right on top of the water.

The path turns at the end of Grede Park to cross the street and climb onto a metal footbridge leading into Bethesda Park. Beyond Grede Park the riverbank is lined with trees and bushes and, even as they block the view of the apartments from Bethesda Park, they must block the view of the river from the balconies attached to every apartment. I followed Riverwalk Drive to its end at North Prairie Avenue, where the shrubbery thickens and the river turns south. A small hawk burst out of the bushes, crossed in front of me, and sailed into a thick low spruce nearby, prompting small birds to dart out of the spruce—unexpected confirmation of the natural world going about its business in the middle of the city.

Here the land rises to meet a railroad bed, where the river passes below a trestle, turns southwest again, and flows under the Prairie Avenue Bridge into the Fox River Sanctuary. That afternoon I looped back across the river on the railroad trestle. Below me on the riverbank, two teenage boys talked as they shared a large bag of tortilla chips. They ignored me when I slid carefully down the stony slope into Bethesda Park. It's a broad, open space, nearly two-thirds the size of Frame Park but quieter. A woman in a T-shirt and shorts did paperwork at a picnic table close to the river; further on, two men sat in camp chairs near propped fishing poles. Trees scattered across the lawn were mostly bare and stark but tall and some seemed very old. A covered picnic area and a playground stand near the street. Nearby is a red octagonal concrete block structure with no windows, securing Bethesda Spring, the one that started Waukesha's Springs Era.

In 1868, while visiting in Waukesha, Richard Dunbar drank from this spring and rested under a nearby oak. He suffered from diabetes and by his own account had expected to die soon, but the spring water had a restorative effect. He wrote that, after drinking six tumblerfuls, he "immediately sought rest under the shade of a wide-spreading oak which then stood and now stands overlooking the spring, like a guardian angel watching it." He developed Bethesda Springs, with advertising featuring an angel hovering over the spring, which he claimed offered a miraculous cure "for all kidney diseases, Bright's disease, diabetes, torpid liver, dyspepsia," and so on. In time the park had a magnificent pavilion, a pond, a formal garden, a bathhouse with separate wings for men and women, and a widened and deepened riverbed for boating.

The tree that Dunbar rested under was celebrated for more than a century as the Dunbar Oak, and it stood long after the Springs Era ended and all the development in the park was gone. When a 1994 storm blew the tree over, it was found to be three hundred years old. Past the concrete housing for the spring, a historical marker near a small oak tree identifies it as a clone of the Dunbar Oak. Beyond the oak and the sealed springhouse are only restrooms and a bike rack and the open lawn of the park, nothing else to suggest this was once a bustling and popular place. As at Waukesha Springs Park, only the present is here.

The character of the river changes again when it enters the Fox River Sanctuary, home to an interpretive center and a parking lot used as the trailhead for the Fox River Trail, which cuts south into my neighborhood, and the Glacial Drumlin Trail, which heads west toward Madison. The sanctuary sprawls across a broad and open lawn dotted with trees and occasional thickets. From the Prairie Avenue Bridge, I followed the riverbank past platforms for canoes and a launch site and colorful birdhouses on the trees. Several openings along the shore offered access to the river. The trees on the opposite bank mostly hid the traffic and industry beyond them, though a constant drone and whine and occasional *whomp* made it impossible to hear the river. At one point downstream a fallen tree blocked two-thirds of the channel, though a canoe could still get around it.

Near the end of the open space, considerable dead tree debris has piled up against an abandoned wooden trestle, impeding canoe passage underneath. Beyond the lawn, woods and underbrush have taken over. Of the Fox River Sanctuary's ninety-five acres, eighty-one are reserved for natural resources, and not all of them are accessible on foot. I clambered up on the trestle, where a wide, intact walkway runs beside the tracks. The tracks arch around up the opposite riverbank toward all the industry and begin to parallel active tracks. Downstream from the trestle I saw riders bike across the river on a footbridge taking them to the trailhead for the Glacial Drumlin Trail. I realized if I followed the defunct tracks back to the bike path and circled around a densely

overgrown area, I could reach that footbridge. Just before it, paths
veer off either side of the trail, leading to hidden campsites, with
canoe rests and openings leading down to the river.

When I reached the bike trail, I climbed onto the footbridge
and gazed upstream and down, enjoying for a moment the decep-
tive seclusion and the river's quiet flow and trying not to let graffiti
marring the base of the bridge distract me. From the footpath
heading south, I could see across the river to the railroad tracks
through the trees, and I recalled that when we biked the Glacial
Drumlin Trail we were beyond the tracks and beyond an often
waterlogged wooded ditch, with no sense of the river once we
had crossed it.

Along the eastern bank the footpath winds through the woods
close to the shore and for a while it feels isolated, but at Camp-
site 7 it begins to loop around near a fenced border with a municipal waste treatment facility and a recycling center. The high
steel fence extends into the river, blocking my progress. Behind
the municipal property, the river twists and turns in four large
U-shaped bends, creating at least two islands in high water. It's
hard to tell if canoes can navigate that stretch.

On the west side of the river the Glacial Drumlin Trail and
the railroad bed it parallels soon veer away from the stream, and
on the east side the Fox River Trail keeps its distance as well,
running between the municipal facilities and the street until it
turns west, passes the last of the city buildings, and curves around
a long stretch of thick woods in view of the backs of shopping
center businesses. Occasionally, barely discernible side trails lead
off the pavement into the bushes and trees. On my walk I found
a path that took me into the woods to an area with seven new
canoe rests. Two narrower paths led away from them, one toward
uncrossable marshland, the other twisting and winding through
underbrush in no particular direction.

South of the woods a wide marsh opens up, with a couple of

cattail-ringed ponds where I've seen great blue herons and sand-hill cranes in the past. A new boardwalk offers a long exposed walk at geometric angles, most of the way through open marsh and sometimes near a throng of large sprawling trees and thickets. In most seasons of the year it's difficult to realize that the Fox River runs down the west side of the marsh, but past the end of the boardwalk, near Sunset Drive, a worn footpath close to the street leads across a bridge toward a wooden sign announcing the southern end of the Fox River Sanctuary. Looking north, neither the point where the river might veer away from the marsh or where the northern limits of the marsh might be is readily visible.

From Sunset Drive south to the city limits, the Fox River flows through open wetlands in the midst of what the parks department calls "greenways." Here, where the Fox River Trail follows, little development intrudes. Sweeping views of the river and the wide wetlands on either side often are visible from the trail. Just past a canoe access, the trail slopes down to the riverbank and runs beneath Les Paul Parkway. Several times a year that part of the trail is closed because of flooding that leaves inches of silt drying on it for days after the water level has gone down.

Beyond the bridge the trail turns sharply east and heads back to Fox River Parkway again, a winding street now even farther from the river than it was on the north side of the bridge. It will parallel the street south past the restrooms and playground, picnic shelter and playing field, and a few retaining ponds until just before it reaches my complex, where it turns toward the wetlands again and arches around to enter the woods of Fox River County Park. But just at that first turn away from the bridge, a grassy footpath leads off behind a row of trees along the riverbank. The day I took that path I noticed a few places where I might have access to the river, though the bank was narrow and usually obstructed. Soon the foliage thickened and the path moved farther from the trees. I emerged onto an open field, with a grassy wide track between the trees and the wild flora that dominated the field. Farther on my view of the river opened up somewhat, and I startled a half dozen mallards who flew off squawking. A long stretch of sedge meadow stood between me and the river, and I chose to follow a circuit around the field, near a substantial stretch of young woods. I hadn't realized how much land there was between the parkway and the river here or how little of the land in the greenway was tended as recreational park. On my way back home on the Fox River Trail, I kept gazing off at the woods and thickets beyond the open fields, newly aware of what lay behind them.

Beyond the county park where I walk the woods and the trail along the wetlands, the river enters a final park, Rivers Crossing, named for an expanding subdivision nearby, and leaves it midway through. If you could travel a straight line from the north side of Frame Park to the south end of Rivers Crossing, you'd walk around seven miles, the first two in downtown Waukesha, in the midst of high-rise apartments and commerce and industry, then a mile or so in the Fox River Sanctuary and its municipal plants, and then three miles or so with the river and its wetlands dominating your sense of location. You would also have traveled from where the development of the city and the exploitation of the river began to a place where you would feel as if you were seeing the Fox River in something like its more natural state. You would almost be able to feel you had traveled back in time.

8

Walking the length of the Fox River in Waukesha makes me appreciate the section behind my home, the open floodplain, the enclosing woods, the Deep Marsh and Fox River overlooks, everything that makes me pay attention to the natural world there and gives me a sense of seclusion and something like tranquility. Given the uses to which the river in the heart of the city has been put in the past, it's to Waukesha's credit that so much of the river has been cleaned up and made easily accessible, especially considering the county's growth as a Milwaukee suburb. My hometown in western New York bought into the myth of urban renewal in the 1960s and decimated its downtown, encouraging the growth of outlying malls and plazas, which have themselves been decimated in their turn. Waukesha touts its "historic downtown"—it almost seems a state law for cities and towns in Wisconsin to do so. Enough of the old buildings are left, a solid core of late nineteenth- and early twentieth-century structures, to give downtown an air of authentic longevity, if not bustling prosperity. The Riverwalk corridor adds to the ambience of the downtown, gives it a place for ready retreat, and lets the rest of the frantic world go about its business somewhere else. With a population of more than seventy thousand, ten times that of Derleth's Sac Prairie, there's little sense of a single community here. As in any city of its size, niche communities bump shoulders from time to time but don't seem to share much of a common core.

With only a few exceptions the much vaunted and long defunct Springs Era is invisible in what is still nicknamed Spring City. In the few months since I walked along the river downtown, an immense (and, to my mind, defiantly styleless) "lofts" building has risen on the riverbank where a grassy area and a parking lot had been, closing the Fox River Trail there temporarily and, for the foreseeable future, casting the trail and the river itself into permanent shadow. Not far away, one side of a building above the river just beyond the Wisconsin Avenue Bridge now sports a mural proclaiming, "Welcome to Guitartown," and more murals and large decorated guitar sculptures have been mounted all over town, including the interior of the public library, all trying to repackage Waukesha as a city-wide memorial to musical pioneer Les Paul, who was born in Waukesha and is buried in the Prairie Home Cemetery here. As much as I admire Paul, it's unlikely that the Guitartown Era the city is trying to launch will rival the Spring City era in the imagination. It seems simply to be a costume change, a new layer of veneer. Not since we were called Prairieville has our identity been connected to the land itself, to linking who we are to where we are.

In such an overpopulated area, the preservation of parklands along the river, no matter what the scale, at least acknowledges certain minority values. Granted, as when the first settlers founded Prairieville, the renovation of the Fox River corridor was motivated more by commercial high hopes than by aesthetics or ecology, but aesthetic and ecological benefits have resulted. Majority values need not determine everything a community does with its resources; there are other places to pursue those. Most of what I pass through here every day has the familiarity of everything I passed through everywhere else I've lived, in four other states and half a dozen other cities and towns. For the most part, except for variations in weather, anywhere you go in the United States you find yourself where you've already been. It can take some effort to search beneath the familiar for the land itself. It's harder to locate along the river corridor but it's still possible to find it.

In the places I've lived, it's been the waterways that most distinguished the communities—at least they were what made me feel most connected there: the Erie Canal in Lockport, the Iowa River in Iowa City, the Chippewa River and the Pine River in Michigan (both of which I've canoed), Boulder Creek and Coal Creek and Cherry Creek and the Platte River in Colorado (which I mostly walked or biked along), and now the Fox River in Waukesha. Everywhere I've felt most at home, a river—or creek or canal—runs through it. All these waterways were at the center of the communities that grew up around them and eventually grew away from them; but despite neglect and abuse and exploitation, it's those bodies of water that remain at the center of the landscape, if not always at the center of the society. Muir's Fox River and Fountain Lake, Leopold's Wisconsin River, Derleth's Wisconsin River, the Oconomowoc and Bark and Fox Rivers of Waukesha County: if I take a close look at where I've been, I can't avoid thinking about the waterways.

At times as I've been walking the Fox River, I've been a solitary hiker, and the people I've encountered, be they strollers or joggers, bikers or sunbathers, fishermen or idlers, have all had their own relationships with the river. Beyond the riverbanks and the pathways the energy it takes to be part of the hustling, rushing mainstream shuts down our sense of where we are. In our frequent trips between Waukesha and Wauwatosa, where our daughter's family lives, Sue and I are continually aware of the intensity and pace of traffic, the thumping and bellowing of the car stereos in the next lane, the concentration on cell phone conversations or arguments in the cars ahead of or behind us, the frenzy of the tailgaters and lane changers. To drive amidst all that takes concentration and some degree of resignation. When my wife drives I try to gaze out the window at the passing landscape, looking forward to the lowland marshes on one road, the dips and rises of another, the occasional wooded stretches—anywhere the land reminds me of its presence despite what squats and clusters upon and around it. As when I walk through the woods and stroll along the river, I can often feel that I don't simply dwell upon this terrain but truly inhabit it. I have no way to connect with the urgencies and anxieties of the travelers beside us on the highways, but even as we flow among them I can feel connected to the land itself, can remember that I'm passing over home ground.

9

Wisconsin Journal—Wednesday, December 12, 2012

Though the sky is a clear bright blue and the sun bright and high, the air has no warmth and a persistent breeze lowers the temperature more. I'm alone on the bike path at midday and hear only the clomp of my winter boots, donned in case of wet as well as in case of cold. My pace is brisk, in hopes of generating enough body heat to sustain me as I explore.

Beyond the deck overlooking the river, the path swerves away from the shore and arcs toward the forest. To the east the forest is at first level with the path and then, beyond a parallel footpath in the woods, rises toward a high ridge. To the west the forest changes character and drops away below the level of the path, the trees more often cottonwood or alder than oak. In spring's floods the floor of this floodplain forest is usually underwater, even the trees near the path standing in water up to their ankles. When the water at last recedes, it takes a long time for the forest to drain and dry. Throughout spring and summer the shrubs and grasses flourish and the thickness of the canopy shades the forest floor. I've never stepped off the path in that direction.

But today I'm intent on wandering through the floodplain forest out to the bank of the river. I've wanted to do this since coming down the kame in Glacier Cone Park a month ago and realizing that, by living near the river where it flows out of town, I live in the lowest local section of the watershed. A couple days of rain deterred me earlier this week, but I've found my rubber winter boots and wool socks, so I'm undeterred by possible puddles and pools.

At a point on the path where the floodplain forest gives the longest, least obstructed view, I step into the leaf litter and brush past leafless branches and limbs, aiming for a large patch of grass.

Almost at once I am reminded of the way fallen leaves and collapsed grasses can camouflage debris beneath them and offer no solid footing. I step carefully on leaf-covered branches and feel the spongy give of the grasses once I reach them. I stoop and weave to get past the smaller trees and lower branches and emerge into the open, feeling my way across long, thick layers of grass that catch my feet if I don't raise them high enough and give me no idea what lies below them. And then I'm on the riverbank.

The opposite shore is a little lower than the one here, and the grassy space between the water and the woods is wider. The grasses drape over the riverbank, so it's hard to tell exactly where solid ground ends. A southerly wind ripples the water against the current, so that the river's broad blue surface seems to be flowing upstream. At certain angles I can forget about the houses beyond the woods. I'm now in the middle of a stretch of river I've only seen and photographed from the observation deck to the north.

I have to backtrack into the woods and make my way farther south before I can get out to the riverbank again. I'm getting close to the place where the river bends sharply to the east, flows up to the canoe access site in Fox River Park, and turns south again. Here, my side of the river is more open, the grasses a spacious expanse, the woods farther back from the water. I cross the open space to the river with careful steps, feeling my weight compress the dry spongy surface under my feet, looking for anything that resembles a trail that deer or foxes might have made. I can see the observation deck upstream. I cut back through the floodplain forest, noting signs of high water on some trunks, and circle around to the riverbank one more time, upstream from the canoe launch, to give myself a view of the distant woods I've just left.

From the canoe launch looking south, the riverbank on this side is less accessible, more overgrown, though the western bank is broad and open. I know the river continues under a highway bridge and flows at some distance from a paved path leading to

a newer subdivision, on its way to Vernon Marsh. But I have no
need to follow it further. Satisfied with my sojourn in the floodplain forest and along the riverbank, I head back up the bike path.
At the observation deck I stop to gaze upstream and down, reminding myself how often in the past I've let this be the closest I
got to the river. When I glance across the widest part of the floodplain, I realize that, if I were able to tromp through the floodplain
forest, I could likely reach the riverbank here as well. I circle the
deck and launch myself out across the grass, heading toward the
long bend that comes closest to the path. Once I'm standing on
the outside of the curve I appreciate how much higher the banks
are here than across the river, where the meander is forming an
island and where I've seen sandhill cranes standing still and Canada geese busying themselves.

    The grasses, those infinite papery tan strands, rustle in the
wind, shake themselves, and settle and rise to shake themselves
again. I watch them for a long time before I lift my gaze and notice

a street with rows of houses on either side climbing a slope beyond the floodplain. I look through the viewfinder of my camera and see four distinct stripes: the pale blue of the sky, a horizontal row of multicolored houses and deep green lawns, the thick sepia plain of the wetlands, the deep rumpled blue of the river. The neighborhood is the thinnest stripe, almost insignificant in the midst of river, earth, and sky. I lock the image in my memory before I turn away.

When I return to the path, I'm still warm and my boots are still dry. I realize I've been smiling since I left the riverbank. I've reached some level of contentment here, some level of connection, and it keeps me smiling all the way out of the woods.

Epilogue

LATE SEPTEMBER. UNDER A cloudless sky and in a persistent wind I walk the woods slowly, checking the maps from time to time to make sure I take paths I don't usually walk. The trails are leaf-strewn now after a few nights of temperatures in the thirties and the leaves that still wave in the wind are losing their green. At midday, with the sun high and the wind lively, the trees shake their shadows across the ground. I take my time on the trail, occasionally angle off from it in the high stretches to gauge the angle of the slopes and the depths of their depressions. Except for a squirrel and a downy woodpecker, I haven't seen any wildlife, but I'm staying alert in hopes of spotting a fox, as others have reported seeing. The wind in the trees drowns out any sounds from the surrounding roads and only once does a jet airliner intrude overhead.

I've come armed with tree guides but haven't much used them, except to confirm a suspected ironwood. I spot the white oak just before the entrance, the red pines just inside, the solitary cedar and every shagbark hickory I pass. I pause to admire the largest oaks and identify the maples, elms, and black cherrys. I like the variety but mostly I like the abundance, so many trees, so high the canopy, so shaded the ground and camouflaged the sky.

I climb one leg of an unfamiliar loop, one I usually cut off to shorten my walk, and descend the other leg, rejoining the trail that will take me to the marsh. Once I'm on the observation deck, the grasses are too high for me to see if the pond at the center of the marsh has any water after this year's drought. For a few minutes the marsh is silent, but then I hear a chuffing sound and see a deer bounding away along the distant margin of the grasses, heading for deeper woods. I was unaware of him until his cough and flight alerted me, but he may have been too aware of me.

On my walk today I've only encountered an older man trudging one way and a younger woman power walking the other way, and I've liked feeling mostly alone in the woods. But now I hear voices, a few women airing their affairs and opinions as they walk together. I think this kind of companionship doesn't always honor serenity in a setting like this. I leave the observation area and increase my pace to get some distance from their voices, but their conversation seems to stall once they walk onto the deck. I circle up the trail on familiar terrain, temporarily join the bike path, and look for yet another path new to me, one that will take me back to the river through the woods. From the high point of the woods I make a slow descent to a point where I retrace a long stretch to get back on a familiar trail heading farther down toward the river and the western arm of the bike path.

I'm pretty pleased with the afternoon, the long stretches of quiet, the soundtrack of wind and rustling leaves, the flitting shadows that are sometimes leaves and sometimes birds, the sense of the woods and the winding trails as my home ground.

~

Mid-December. Time. Terrain. Transition. These words were on my mind when I woke up today. When I think about my efforts to connect with my home ground, these are the words that come to mind. Terrain of course, for that's what I wander through and upon. And time as well, for every effort to understand what's here now raises questions about why it's here in the form it is, what was here before, and how and to what degree it changed. And that's transition—or do I mean, transformation? Or are these the same thing? I seem to be someone for whom walking any sort of terrain is virtually a form of time travel, and if you travel through time you can't avoid awareness of transition.

I am now (I was surprised to be thinking as I lay in bed in the darkness before the dawn) older by roughly a decade than Aldo Leopold and August Derleth when they died and not yet so old as John Muir at his death, though firmly in his age group. This puts me at a disadvantage in this stumbling after a sense of home ground. I'm discovering mine at an age when Muir was reminiscing about his discovery of his, those dozen years of his adolescence when nature streamed into him and he labored, with some regret, to transform it. Muir's sense of loss over what he couldn't preserve stayed with him throughout his life; my experience of where I am is more immediate and limited than his, more vicarious than visceral, and yet Muir's experience transmits to me an alertness to what was here before.

Whenever I tend to write in our house, whether upstairs in my study before the windows above my desk, or downstairs at the dining table across from our windowed front door, I gaze out at condominiums across the street that mirror those of my neighbors and me. Beyond them are family homes on residential streets climbing the slope away from the river plain. Most of the houses are only a few decades old. I almost never walk through those neighborhoods and have no sense of the lives of the people who live there. I will never have the sense of place that August Derleth had, living six decades in the town where he was born, walking through familiar neighborhoods, passing houses whose occupants he knew by name and by sight, steeped in their conversations. I am closer to the Derleth of his interludes, the one whose walks took him into the woods and over the river and off to the places where he knew the morels would be found in season. Closer to him but not so intimate with my landscape as he was with his. He was profoundly aware of loss and failure in the human community; but by his final book about his own Walden, he had grown elegiac about loss and transformation in the natural world as well. His sense of time's effect on terrain reverberates in me, perhaps all the more deeply for my closeness to my landscape and my distance from the society that occupies it.

It's fair to say that Aldo Leopold's spirit hovers above all those who work to restore and conserve natural areas. Certainly those of us who serve as volunteers for the Ice Age Trail Alliance have the hope that opening up the forests and grassland and bringing back native plants and removing invasive and exotic ones will bring anyone who walks any portion of the trail closer to the land, not simply as a site for recreation but also as an opportunity for communion. The spirit is there in the park workers nearby who have been clearing land to bring back the prairie that early settlers once saw (and quickly plowed under), even if it's in a narrowly circumscribed setting.

Enough time has passed since the publication of Leopold's great book—and his death—that the wisdom of his philosophy has been confirmed by widespread practice. I'm grateful for every instance of accomplishment I see in the ecological community. "When we see land as a community to which we belong, we may begin to use it with love and respect," Leopold wrote in his foreword to *A Sand County Almanac*. He also wrote, in "The Land Ethic," "A thing is right if it tends to preserve the integrity, stability, and beauty of the biotic community. It is wrong if it tends otherwise." Those who agree with him have done a great deal of the right thing with the biotic communities that matter to them.

Unfortunately, those who see land as a community to which they belong are a minority, and those who don't see land at all are the overwhelming majority. Little in our culture invites us to do more than to interact with our culture. "The world is too much with us," Wordsworth observed more than two hundred years ago; "late and soon, / Getting and spending, we lay waste our powers: / Little we see in Nature that is ours." We do a lot more getting and spending now than we did then, and the odds are in favor of our doing more rather than less in the future.

It's our great devotion to getting and spending that leaves us largely impotent, willingly aloof, in regard to the climate change we're living through. Our cluelessness won't impact the climate, except to accelerate change. There will be a transition over time, as anyone who considers the ecological history of Wisconsin can confirm, and the only question is whether we will be able to do what's right for our biotic community—and how much we are willing to do what's right—during our short time within it. Only time will tell, and someone else will have to write that book.

So perhaps this book is merely an invitation to walk home ground, to understand what the terrain is now and what it has been across time, and how the transition that created what it is now came about. Perhaps too it's a time capsule, a message in a bottle from someone given to looking over his shoulder even as he tries to examine the ground beneath his feet, something that one day might interest another such seeker, someone looking over her shoulder while she attentively walks her own home ground.

Sources and Captions

Epigraphs

Carson, Rachel. Rachel Carson to Ruth Nanda Anshen, January 7, 1956. In *The House of Life: Rachel Carson at Work,* by Paul Brooks, 2. Boston: Houghton-Mifflin, 1972.

Macfarlane, Robert. *The Old Ways: A Journey on Foot.* New York: Viking, 2012:198.

Prologue

Bremer, Frederika. *The Homes of the New World: Impressions of America.* Translated by Mary Howitt. 2 vols. 1853. Reprint, New York: Johnson Reprint Corp., 1968.

Lawlor, Laurie. *This Tender Place: The Story of a Wetland Year.* Madison, WI: Terrace Books, 2005.

Moor, Robert. *On Trails: An Exploration.* New York: Simon & Schuster, 2016.

Perry, Michael. *Population 485: Meeting Your Neighbors One Siren at a Time.* New York: HarperCollins, 2002.

Thwaites, Reuben Gold. *Down Historic Waterways: Six Hundred Miles of Canoeing Upon Illinois and Wisconsin Rivers.* Chicago: A. C. McClurg & Co., 1910.

Nature Streaming into Us

Allman, Laurie. *Far from Tame: Reflections from the Heart of a Continent.* Minneapolis, MN: University of Minnesota Press, 1996.

Audubon, John James. "Passenger Pigeon." In *Audubon Reader: The Best Writings of John James Audubon,* edited by Scott Russell Sanders, 116–123. Bloomington: Indiana University Press, 1986.

Benyus, Janine. T*he Field Guide to Wildlife Habitats in the Eastern United States.* New York: Touchstone, 1989.

Brynildson, Eric. "Restoring the Fountain of John Muir's Youth," *Wisconsin Academy Review* (December 1988). Revised 1996 for the Sierra Club John Muir Exhibit, http://www.sierraclub.org/john_muir_exhibit/geography/wisconsin/ftn_of_youth_brynildson.aspx.

Eggers, Steve D., and Donald M. Reed. *Wetland Plants and Plant Communities of Minnesota and Wisconsin.* 2nd ed. St. Paul, MN: US Army Corp of Engineers, 1997.

Greening, John. "A Mazomanie Pioneer of 1847." *Wisconsin Magazine of History* 26, no. 2 (December 1942): 208–218.

Lawlor, Laurie. *This Tender Place: The Story of a Wetland Year.* Madison, WI: Terrace Books, 2005.

Leopold, Aldo. Aldo Leopold to Mr. Ernest Swift, April 14, 1948. Quoted in *Yearning for the Land: A Search for the Importance of Place,* by John Warfield Simpson, 99. New York: Pantheon, 2002.

Lopez, Barry, ed. *Home Ground: Language for an American Landscape.* San Antonio: Trinity University Press, 2006.

Muir, John. *The Story of My Boyhood and Youth.* Boston: Houghton-Mifflin, 1913.

———. Address to the Sierra Club, November 23, 1895. Quoted in *The Heart of John Muir's World: Wisconsin, Family, and Wilderness Discovery,* by Millie Stanley, 116. Madison: Prairie Oak Press, 1995.

Teale, Edwin Way. Introduction to *The Wilderness World of John Muir,* xix. Boston: Houghton-Mifflin, 1954.

Wilson, Alexander. *American Ornithology; or, The Natural History of the Birds of the United States: Illustrated with Plates Engraved and Colored from Original Drawings Taken from Nature.* Edinburgh: Constable, 1831; Philadelphia: Bradford and Inskeep, 1808–1825.

Wisconsin Department of Natural Resources. *Wisconsin, Naturally: A Guide to 150 Great State Natural Areas.* Madison: Wisconsin Department of Natural Resources, 2003.

Interlude
Leopold, Aldo. "Marshland Elegy." In *A Sand County Almanac and Sketches Here and There,* 96. New York: Oxford University Press, 1949.

The Taste for Country
Bradley, Nina Leopold. Afterword to *A Sand County Almanac Illustrated,* by Aldo Leopold and Tom Algire, 149–151. Madison: Tamarack Press, 1977.

Callicott, J. Baird, ed. *Companion to A Sand County Almanac: Interpretive and Critical Essays.* Madison: University of Wisconsin Press, 1987.

Flader, Susan. "The Person and the Place." In *The Sand Country of Aldo Leopold,* by Susan Flader and Charles Steinhacker, 7–49. San Francisco: Sierra Club, 1979.

———. "Aldo Leopold's Sand County." In *Companion to A Sand County Al-*

manac: Interpretive and Critical Essays, edited by J. Baird Callicott, 40–62. Madison: University of Wisconsin Press, 1987.

Knopp, Lisa. "Visiting Frederic." In *Interior Places,* 245–262. Lincoln: University of Nebraska Press, 2008.

Lawlor, Laurie. *This Tender Place: The Story of a Wetland Year.* Madison: Terrace Books, 2005.

Leopold, Aldo. *A Sand County Almanac and Sketches Here and There.* New York: Oxford University Press, 1949.

———. "Country." In *A Sand County Almanac with Essays on Conservation from Round River,* 177–180. New York: Sierra Club/Ballantine Books, 1970.

———. *Round River: From the Journals of Aldo Leopold.* Edited by Luna B. Leopold. New York: Oxford University Press, 1953.

Meine, Curt. *Aldo Leopold: His Life and Work.* Madison: University of Wisconsin Press, 2010.

Ross, John, and Beth Ross. *Prairie Time: The Leopold Reserve Revisited.* Madison: University of Wisconsin Press, 1998.

Tallmadge, John. "Anatomy of a Classic." In *Companion to a Sand County Almanac: Interpretive and Critical Essays,* edited by J. Baird Callicott, 110–128. Madison: University of Wisconsin Press, 1987.

The Pattern of the Seasons

Blei, Norbert. "Hills, Trees, Ponds, People, Birds, Animals, Sun, Moon, Stars: The *Walden* Books." In *Return to Derleth,* edited by James P. Roberts, 11–19. Madison, WI: White Hawk Press, 1993.

Boyer, Dennis, and Justin Isherwood, eds. *A Place to Which We Belong: Wisconsin Writers on Wisconsin Landscapes.* Madison, WI: 1000 Friends of Wisconsin Land Use Institute, 1998.

Derleth, August. *And You, Thoreau.* Norfolk, CT: New Directions, 1944.

———. *Atmosphere of Houses.* Muscatine, IA: Prairie Press, 1939.

———. *Concord Rebel: A Life of Henry D. Thoreau.* Philadelphia: Chilton Company, 1960.

———. *Countryman's Journal.* New York: Duell, Sloan and Pearce, 1963.

———. *Rendezvous in a Landscape.* New York: Fine Editions Press, 1952.

———. *Return to Walden West.* New York: Candlelight Press, 1970.

———. *The Wisconsin: River of a Thousand Isles.* 1942. Reprint, Madison: University of Wisconsin Press, 1985.

———. *Village Daybook: A Sac Prairie Journal.* Chicago: Pellegrini & Cudahy, 1947.

———. *Village Year: A Sac Prairie Journal.* New York: Coward-McCann, 1941.

————. *Walden Pond: An Homage to Thoreau.* Iowa City: Prairie Press, 1968.

————. *Walden West.* New York: Duell, Sloan and Pearce, 1961.

————. *Wisconsin Country: A Sac Prairie Journal.* New York: Candlelight Press, 1965.

————. Review of *A Sand County Almanac,* by Aldo Leopold. "Minority Report," *The Capital Times,* November 5, 1949.

Derleth, August William, Papers. Wisconsin Historical Society Archives. Wis Mss WO Correspondence, box 23, folder 6, Walter Harding.

Derleth, August William, Papers. Wisconsin Historical Society Archives. Wis Mss WO Correspondence, box 31, folder 9, Letters to Aldo Leopold.

Litersky, Dorothy M. Grobe. *Derleth: Hawk . . . and Dove.* Aurora, CO: National Writers Press, 1997.

Seeley, Ron. "Derleth Was Wisconsin's Thoreau." *Wisconsin State Journal,* October 9, 1983, 40.

Teale, Edwin Way. *The Wilderness World of John Muir.* Boston: Houghton-Mifflin, 1954.

Turner, Frederick. *Rediscovering America: John Muir in His Time and Ours.* New York: Viking, 1985. Reprint, San Francisco: Sierra Club Books, 1987.

The White Ghost of a Glacier

Allman, Laurie. *Far from Tame: Reflections from the Heart of a Continent.* Minneapolis, MN: University of Minnesota Press, 1996.

Andrews, Candice Gaukel. *Beyond the Trees: Stories of Wisconsin Forests.* Madison: Wisconsin Historical Society Press, 2011.

Bates, Milton J. *The Bark River Chronicles: Stories from a Wisconsin Watershed.* Madison: Wisconsin Historical Society Press, 2012.

Bergland, Martha, and Paul G. Hayes. *Studying Wisconsin: The Life of Increase Lapham.* Madison: Wisconsin Historical Society Press, 2014.

Clayton, Lee. *Pleistocene Geology of Waukesha County.* Wisconsin Geological and Natural History Survey, Bulletin 99. Madison: University of Wisconsin–Extension, 2001.

Ice Age Trail Alliance. *Ice Age Trail Companion Guide.* Cross Plains, WI: Ice Age Trail Alliance, 2011.

Lapham, I. A. *The Antiquities of Wisconsin, as Surveyed and Described.* Washington, DC: Smithsonian Institution, 1855. Reprint, Madison: University of Wisconsin Press, 2001.

————. *Wisconsin: Its Geography and Topography, History, Geology, and Mineralogy.* 2nd ed. Milwaukee: I. A. Hopkins, 1846.

Lapham, I. A., J. G. Knapp, and H. Crocker. *Report on the Disastrous Effects of the Destruction of Forest Trees, Now Going On So Rapidly in the State of Wisconsin.* Madison: Atwood & Rublee, State Printers, 1867.

Leopold, Aldo. "Marshland Elegy." In *A Sand County Almanac and Sketches Here and There,* 95. New York: Oxford University Press, 1949.

Lopez, Barry, ed. *Home Ground: Language for an American Landscape.* San Antonio: Trinity University Press, 2006.

Mickelson, David M., Louis J. Maher Jr., and Susan L. Simpson. *Geology of the Ice Age National Scenic Trail.* Madison: University of Wisconsin Press, 2011.

Nurre, Robert P. *Introduction to The Antiquities of Wisconsin, as Surveyed and Described by I. A. Lapham.* Madison: University of Wisconsin Press, 2001: xia-xxva.

Reuss, Henry S. *On the Trail of the Ice Age: A Hiker's and Biker's Guide to Wisconsin's Ice Age Scientific Reserve and Trail.* Milwaukee: Ice Age Park and Trail Foundation, 1976.

Thwaites, Reuben Gold. *Down Historic Waterways: Six Hundred Miles of Canoeing upon Illinois and Wisconsin Rivers.* 3rd ed. Chicago: A. C. Mc-Clurg, 1910: 256–257.

Interlude

Tekiela, Stan. *Trees of Wisconsin Field Guide.* Cambridge, MN: Adventure Publications, 2002.

The Land Itself

Behm, Don. "Waukesha, Once Swimming in Water Resources, Now Struggles," *Journal Sentinel,* April 19, 2010.

Birmingham, Robert A., and Leslie E. Eisenberg. *Indian Mounds of Wisconsin.* Madison: University of Wisconsin Press, 2000.

Carson, Rachel. Rachel Carson to Ruth Nanda Anshen, January 7, 1956. In *The House of Life: Rachel Carson at Work,* by Paul Brooks, 2. Boston: Houghton-Mifflin, 1972.

Clayton, Lee. *Pleistocene Geology of Waukesha County.* Wisconsin Geological and Natural History Survey, Bulletin 99. Madison: University of Wisconsin–Extension, 2001.

Cooper, James Fenimore. *The Deerslayer.* Pictures by N. C. Wyeth. New York: Charles Scribner's Sons, 1925.

Haight, Theron W. *Memoirs of Waukesha County.* Madison, WI: Western Historical Association, 1907.

Johnson, Marlin. "Natural Features and Land Use." In *From Farmland to Freeways: A History of Waukesha County, Wisconsin,* edited by Ellen D.

Langill and Jean Penn Loerke, 1–43. Waukesha, WI: Waukesha County Historical Society, 1984.

Lapham, I. A. *The Antiquities of Wisconsin, as Surveyed and Described.* Washington, DC: Smithsonian Institution, 1855. Reprint, Madison: University of Wisconsin Press, 2001.

———. *Wisconsin: Its Geography and Topography, History, Geology, and Mineralogy.* 2nd ed. Milwaukee: I. A. Hopkins, 1846.

Lopez, Barry. Quoted in "Almost Paradise," by Kim Barnes. *In Landscapes with Figures: The Nonfiction of Place,* edited by Robert Root, 30. Lincoln: University of Nebraska Press, 2007.

Schoenknecht, John M. "Fox River Improvements." *Landmark* 40, no. 1 (Spring 1997): 30–32.

———. *The Great Waukesha Springs Era, 1868–1918.* Waukesha, WI: J. Schoenknecht, 2003.

Spring City's Past: A Thematic History of Waukesha. Rev. ed. Waukesha, WI: City of Waukesha Landmarks Commission, 2002.

The Fox River Corridor Plan, Waukesha, Wisconsin. Madison, WI: Hitchcock Design Group, 1990.

The History of Waukesha County, Wisconsin. Rev. ed. Waukesha, WI: Waukesha County Historical Society, 1976. First published 1880 by Western Historical Society.

Image Captions

p. 6, Ennis Lake, Muir Park State Natural Area
p. 38, Inlet stream, Muir Park State Natural Area
p. 45, The shack, Aldo Leopold Legacy Center
p. 72, Leopold benches, Aldo Leopold Legacy Center
p. 82, View of Wisconsin River from Ferry Bluff
p. 120, Wisconsin River Trestle Bridge, Sauk City, Wisconsin
p. 136, Lapham Peak, Kettle Moraine State Forest
p. 175, Brady's Rocks, Kettle Moraine State Forest
p. 186, Fox River in winter, Waukesha, Wisconsin
p. 226, Cranes in the mist, Fox River, Waukesha, Wisconsin

Index

Note: Locations are in Wisconsin unless otherwise noted. Page numbers in *italic* refer to photographs. **Nature observed** in entries refers to people, terrain, vegetation, and wildlife that Root encountered on his walking tours.

About the Author

ROBERT ROOT has long been immersed in the nonfiction of place. He is the editor of *Landscapes with Figures: The Nonfiction of Place* and *The Island Within Us: Isle Royale Artists-in-Residence 1991–1998,* and the author of *Recovering Ruth: A Biographer's Tale,* named a Michigan Notable Book in 2004, *Following Isabella: Travels in Colorado Then and Now,* and *Postscripts: Retrospections on Time and Place.* His writing for radio includes the collection *Limited Sight Distance: Essays from Airwaves* and contributions to *Wisconsin Life.* Other books include the memoir *Happenstance,* and the craft studies *E. B. White: The Emergence of an Essayist* and *The Nonfictionist's Guide: On Reading and Writing Creative Nonfiction.*

Root teaches nonfiction in Ashland University's MFA Program in Creative Writing and for the Loft Literary Center in Minneapolis. He and his wife live in Waukesha, Wisconsin. This is his twentieth book.